ISBN 978-1-330-00788-4
PIBN 10002518

Similar Books Are Available from
www.forgottenbooks.com

A-B-C of Golf
by John Duncan Dunn

On Safari
Big Game Hunting in British East Africa, With Studies in Bird-Life, by Abel Chapman

Ourdoor Sports and Games
by Claude Harris Miller

Practical Golf
by Walter J. Travis

The Sport of Rajahs
by Baden-Powell Of Gilwell

Sports in War
by Baden-Powell Of Gilwell

Hunting in British East Africa
by Percy C. Madeira

The Complete Hockey Player
by Eustace E. White

Wild Sports of Burma and Assam
by Colonel Pollok

Athletics and Football
by Montague Shearman

Golf for Women
by Genevieve Hecker

The Young Folk's Cyclopedia of Games and Sports
by John D. Champlin

Football, the Rugby Game
by Harry Vassall

The Book of Athletics
by Paul Withington

Cricket
by A. G. Steel

Hockey As a Game for Women
by Edith Thompson

Lacrosse
The National Game of Canada, by W. George Beers

The Boys Book of Sports
by Grantland Rice

Tennis
by John Moyer Heathcote

Riding and Hunting
by Matthew Horace Hayes

THE COMPLETE HOCKEY PLAYER

BY

EUSTACE E. WHITE

WITH CONTRIBUTIONS BY PHILIP COLLINS
AND L. M. AND J. Y. ROBINSON

WITH THIRTY-TWO ILLUSTRATIONS, INCLUDING MANY SPECIAL
ACTION-PHOTOGRAPHS, AND A PLAN

THIRD EDITION

METHUEN & CO. LTD.
36 ESSEX STREET W.C.
LONDON

GVI
H7W-

First Published . . . . March 25th 1909
Second Edition . . . . December 1910
Third Edition . . . . November 1922

PRINTED IN GREAT BRITAIN

PREFATORY NOTE

I WISH to record my indebtedness to the following for kind help rendered in connection with the compilation of this work:—W. M. Johnstone, Eric Green, S. H. Shoveller, Philip Collins, L. M. Robinson, J. Y. Robinson, P. M. Egan, the Rev. A. E. Bevan, H. F. Beaumont, E. F. Edge Partington, and H. E. Robinson, and also to *Fry's Magazine* for kind permission to use a photograph.

E. E. W.

CONTENTS

LIST OF ILLUSTRATIONS

The action photographs have been specially taken for the book by
Mr. S. J. BECKETT, Baker Street, London. W.

THE COMPLETE HOCKEY PLAYER

CHAPTER I

ORIGIN, PROGRESS, AND POPULARITY OF HOCKEY

MODERN hockey is a glorified form of that game, played at different times and in different countries under such varied names as hurley, shinty, bandy, hoquet, and caman. The game's Irish designation was hurley, its Scottish shinty, while bandy was its title in Wales. Hoquet was its French name, and the French love to aver that "Hoquet" is a name of hoarier antiquity than any of the others by which the game has been called, thereby claiming for France the honour of hockey's nativity. Much delving into the past reveals to the historian nothing which enables him definitely either to confirm or to negative this French claim.

The little that research does discover seems to point all one way, in the direction of Ireland, as being the native land of hockey.

In Ireland the game seems to have been played under two names—hurley and caman. One Irish authority describes hurley as it was played in the middle of the nineteenth century as "a modified form of the ancient game of 'caman.'" But the evidence of written history shows that hurley itself was played in Ireland as far back as the second century.   So it is reasonable to suppose that hurley was not a copy but an original.   The source of its earliest record is the will of the Irish Cathair Mor, first king of Ireland, who died A.D. 148.   This record, as translated by O'Flaherty in *Ogygia*, runs as follows : " Cathair gave Crimthaun fifty hurling balls made of brass, with an equal number of brazen hurlets."   Evidently hurley, as played by the ancients, was a game for individual rather than collective skill, as we read of players matched single-handed against fifty and thrice fifty opponents.   And hurley, under this its old name, is still played in the less civilised parts of Ireland, a survival of the long centuries which have rolled away since Cathair's gift to Crimthaun.

The tenacity of the Scotch, and the loyalty with which they cleave to old friends, old traditions, old customs, has remarkable emphasis in the case of shinty, Scotland's contribution to the past of hockey.   Every boxing day, and high up on Wimbledon Common hard by the old windmill, foregather a motley crew, armed with an equally motley set of weapons—sticks, staves, crooks—all more or less twisted to some semblance of the primitive hockey stick. It is a truly heterogeneous gathering this, with, nowadays, sadly little of the Scottish flavour about it.   Occasional colour is lent to the scene by a kilted figure, and realism by an occasional Glengarry cap.   But for the most part there is little romantic about the appearance of the gathering and little to remind one that its purpose is essentially Scotch—the celebration of the ancient game of shinty. Time was when this annual gathering partook of no little importance and dignity.   Now, apart from the interest and dignity always attaching to the maintenance of an old custom, the gathering is meagre and touched with pathos. A few white-haired Scotsmen, there to honour the old game and the old custom, and for the rest a rabble of youths and small boys.   And of the game played little need be said save that it is as irregular as the players.

Makeshift goal-posts are pitched on the rough common, and these form the only definite landmark of the game.

To start the game, a ball, a soft ball, is thrown into the air, and struck at by the players the moment it comes within reach of their sticks, extended above their heads. The subsequent play is simply a wild scrambling after the ball. According to legend, shinty dates back to the twelfth century. Alexander the First of Scotland is said to have taken a great interest in the game, and as he was named the Fierce, it is likely that shinty was a very rough game in his day.

There is no evidence to show what antiquity may be claimed for bandy, the Welsh form of hockey, but there is evidence to show that it was vigorously played by the Welsh at the beginning of the nineteenth century. In a small work entitled *The Kalendar of Amusements* occurs the following account of bandy, played by the peasantry of Wales, and written in 1830. After remarking on the proneness of the Welsh towards all sports, and their manner of devoting their evenings to rural dissipations, the writer goes on to say, " But the most popular of all the rural diversions of the Vale of Glamorgan is the important game of bandy. It consists in a contention between two sets of players which of them shall succeed in striking a ball with bent sticks along the ground to opposite goals. Even the loftiest pride of a parish is its repute at this game ; and a rivalship about it between two neighbouring parishes will occasion such heartburnings and bickerings as may not very readily be conceived." The account then proceeds to a graphic and humorous description of a match played between two rival parishes—Llantwyt and Llancarvan. The contest was decided on the seashore, " upon a field of hard sand," and was eagerly watched by the assembled inhabitants of the vale. Hard hitting was the vogue and " under-cutting," players sending the ball with " blows of their bandies whizzing aloft through the air." After a while excitement ran so high that the spectators could no

longer control themselves and "closed down with a roar"
upon the play and players, and the ball got lost among the
throng, concealed deliberately by a female partisan.   Either
team had one special champion—Llantwyt, a converted
Methodist; and Llancarvan, one called Shanko.   The final
scene is a mighty race between these two for the ball, the
verdict resting with the Methodist, who, " stretching out his
foot, by a trip of the heel sends his rival ploughing the
sands before him with a headlong fall as the spray is dashed
before the vessel."   And victory is with the men of Llantwyt, the plaudits of their partisans " pealing from one tall
cliff to another."

The bibliography of hockey is limited, and furnishes
little information about the exact antiquity of the game in
England.   In one of the few histories on hockey, written
by H. F. Battersby, the author says, " Its trail may be
found here and there across the story of social England
from quite early days."   And in his famous essay on John
Bunyan, one of the masterpieces of English prose, Lord
Macaulay says, " Bell-ringing and playing at hockey on
Sundays seem to have been the worst vices of this depraved
tinker."   The love of hockey was one of Bunyan's darling
sins which he "could not let go."   Possibly the extreme
sinfulness of hockey in his eyes lay, not in the game itself,
but in its indulgence on a Sunday.   Or perhaps it was
Bunyan's idolatrous love of hockey that he regarded as
a sin and a snare, and not any intrinsic sinfulness in the
game.   Whatever may have been his real attitude towards
the game, it is certain that hockey was played on the
village green in the seventeenth century, and with
enthusiasm.

Of visual evidence of the antiquity of hockey none
is so unique or interesting as an ancient relic in the
Copenhagen National Museum.   This is an altar pot,
made about the year 1330, on which are depicted two
hockey players armed with genuine hockey sticks and
engaged in an orthodox "bully," quite after the modern

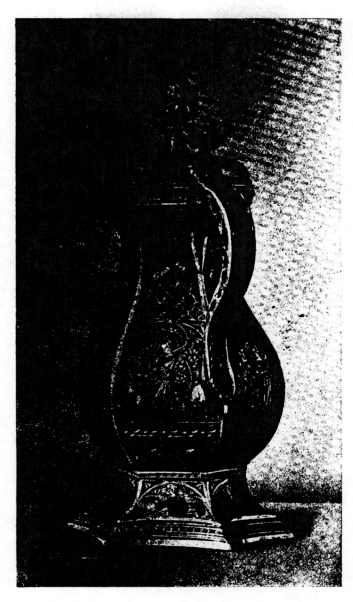

FOURTEENTH CENTURY ALTAR-POT IN COPENHAGEN
NATIONAL MUSEUM, SHOWING HOCKEY PLAYERS
ENGAGED IN A "BULLY"

fashion. So authentic is this evidence thought to be in Denmark, that an engraving of this altar pot appears in the year-book of the Danish Hockey Association.

It is impossible to trace at all closely the history and progress of the game down to about the middle of the nineteenth century. Then it begins to assume a more definite form. The implements of the game were primitive enough —a large cork bung, a piece of rubber fashioned to the appearance of an oblong ball, or an indiarubber bottle cut close to the neck, formed the "object of contention"; while the sticks used were of oak, crab, holly, or ash, and cut from tree or hedge.

At one time, it is amusing to note, the game was called " shinney " in the North of England, from the custom which prevailed of striking the shins of a player who had the ball between his feet. The objective of the players was just what it is to-day, namely, to hit the ball into a goal at either end of the ground. But the means to that end were very different. The game gradually gained in favour, and in the sixties was played in many parts of England.

In his reminiscences, which cast a lurid light on the hockey of those days, and which he wrote specially for this chapter, the Rev. A. E. Bevan, one of the hoary veterans of English hockey, says: " Hockey was played twenty a side with an indiarubber ball about the size of a cricket ball, but cut in angles all round, so that it should not bounce equally. Our weapons were light oak sticks, often weighted with lead to give greater driving power, as a goal might be scored anywhere in the field, a half-circle not being in existence. There was no limit, to the best of my recollection, to the field of play, except so far as the goal-line was concerned. Should any player come in on the wrong side (*i.e.* the left side) as you were dribbling down, you were at liberty to hit him across the shins; and if one of your own side was following up closely, instead of shouldering off the ball, he could apply kindly but hurtful attentions in the same way." This was on Wimbledon Common, and many a hard-fought battle did Mr. Bevan and his contemporaries fight on a stretch of turf no great way from the scene of the shinty festival described earlier in this chapter.

A decade before these "hard-fought battles" of Wimbledon Common the Blackheath Hockey Club was formed, and played under rules of its own, which, being altered from time to time, were in their final state very similar in several instances to the modern rules of the game. It is an honourable fact for the Blackheath Club, that it was not only the parent of the Union game—that is, the game as authorised by the National Hockey Union, a predecessor of the present Hockey Association — but also of the renowned Blackheath Football Club.

The size of a team and the disposition of the players were very different then from what they are in modern hockey. For matches each side consisted of fifteen players—a goalkeeper, two backs, two three-quarter backs, three half-backs, and seven forwards. The half-backs were sometimes called flag-men, and the centre man was chosen usually for his hitting powers and accurate eye, and was often one of the chief goal-scorers of the team. The game suffered extraordinary fluctuations in its rules. At one time kicking would be allowed, then it would not. One year the use of the hands in stopping the ball would be permissible, the next year it would not. Even dribbling was at one time illegal. Left-hand hitting is one of the few things which has always been illegal. "Shinning" was the penalty a player paid for breaking the rules, and yet shin-guards were unknown, so that our forebears were evidently a hardy race.

In addition to the Blackheath Club, there was a flourishing club at Bristol, and the Metropolitan and the West of England Club played an annual match for nearly twenty years, the initial match taking place in 1875. Six wins each and four drawn games were the record.

During the seventies, clubs began to form round London, and there is extant the record of a match between Surbiton and Richmond, played in 1875. This record tells of many disputes throughout the game, and urges the formation of a Hockey Union for the making of definite rules and the furtherance of the game. Accordingly an Association was established, and the rules revised.

Under these rules, the size of the ground was left almost entirely to the fancy of the players, and was anything from 100 to 150 yards long and 50 to 80 yards wide. The goals, too, were on the same generous scale as the ground, being 6 yards wide and 7 feet high. No goal could be scored if the ball was hit from a distance of more than 15 yards from the nearest goal-post. The half-circle was not yet, but it is evident from the 15 yards' restriction that its necessity was bound to force itself upon the game. It is not easy to guess 15 yards, and it could not be long before players would realise the need of a definite mark.

The next landmark in the progress of the game was the birth of the famous Wimbledon Club. This occurred in 1883. Wimbledon owed very much to past members of the defunct Surbiton and East Surrey Clubs, who had been responsible for the introduction of the cricket ball and the rule preventing a goal being scored at a greater distance than 15 yards from the goal. The following comment on this subject occurs in *Hockey* of the " Isthmian Library " series : " The great significance of these two principles was fully appreciated by the men of Wimbledon, who fashioned their game accordingly, giving up the string ball (one of the many variants used), and surrendering at the same time the light ash sticks of an earlier generation." The main difficulty with which Wimbledon was faced, and the one that retarded their more rapid advance in the game, was the absence of clubs against whom they might test their skill. Their first match was against a Stock Exchange team captained by E. Brookes, a past member of the extinct Surbiton Club, and the result a draw. The ground was a selected pitch on Wimbledon Common, in the neighbourhood of the golf club. In view of the dearth of opponents, members engaged chiefly in club practices. The Wimbledon Club grew apace, and became a mighty power in the game, and the strength of the team which they could put into the field in 1896 was such that six of its members were deemed good enough that year for places in the English team.

In 1884 the Molesey Club was formed. The object of this club's formation seems to have been simply the playing of friendly club games—members against members. It is doubtful, indeed, whether the founders of the club knew of the existence of other hockey clubs. It was a strange game, that game played by the Molesey Club's members in 1884. They used ordinary ash sticks, and a worsted ball covered with netted string. There was no disposition of the players, who simply followed the ball. But once the existence of other clubs was known and Molesey quickly changed their ways. Some idea of the rapid progress of the game during the next ten years may be gauged from one simple comparison. In the season of 1885–86 Molesey played five matches. Ten years later their season's programme had swelled to twenty-three encounters.

Clubs began to multiply, Ealing, Westgate, and South-gate being among new clubs of the next year or two, while Teddington and Surbiton were revived.

And the game was spreading, spreading beyond the limits of the London area, to the Midlands and the North. It was already established in the West. In 1885 the Solihull Club was started in the Midlands, the next year Edgbaston. A year later the North followed suit with a club at Timperley in Cheshire. This was the beginning of the great wave of hockey enthusiasm which, mounting higher and higher, eventually swept every corner of England, Ireland, Scotland, and Wales almost.

But the real birthday of modern hockey was January 18, 1886, the date of the formation of the Hockey Association, a full and particular account of which is the subject of the succeeding chapter, and of the ordination of the striking circle. Commenting on the introduction of the striking circle, H. F. Battersby says "it was that line of white about the goals which converted hockey from a dangerous scrimmage into an affair of skill, and its first authorised appearance must constitute the game's Hegira."

The red-letter years in the hockey calendar since 1886, which mark advances in the game, are: 1887, the year of the first inter-county match ; 1890, the year of the first inter-divisional match, in which the North played the South ; and 1895, the year which inaugurated International encounters.

It will form a pleasant diversion to turn aside for a moment and view the progress and growing popularity of the game in Ireland, and to view it through the medium of a player who has been associated with the palmiest days of Irish hockey and is himself its leading exponent.   So let us listen to the story of Irish hockey unfolded by W. M. Johnstone: " The modern game of hockey was introduced into Ireland, I believe, in the winter of 1892.   Hockey had been played at the High School and the King's Hospital School in Dublin, and at some of the other schools throughout the country, for many years before.   An old graduate of Dublin University has told me that he has played many a game of hockey nearly fifty years ago in the College Park.   There is no doubt that we Irish inherit a natural ability to play the game.   Hockey was played with bent sticks, the majority of which were cut by the players themselves in the hedges and woods.   The rules allowed considerable licence, as, for example, when a player pushed the ball to the right of an opponent so that the opponent was on his left or in his way, he was at liberty to whack him across the shins if he did not at once make himself scarce.

" In the winter of 1892–93 some old hurley players and others banded themselves into a hockey team under the name of Palmerston, and played matches against the High School, the King's Hospital School, and the Dublin Banks. In the following year great progress was made.   The two schools mentioned definitely adopted the game ; a club was formed in the University ; the team which had played under the name of Palmerston procured a ground and founded a club, destined to fame in the annals of Irish hockey; and the Three Rock Rovers, Corinthians, Dundrum, Donnybrook, and Monkstown clubs were formed. The game quickly spread from Leinster to the other provinces, and became in a few years one of the most popular winter pastimes in Ireland. The Irish Hockey Union was founded with the Rev. Canon Gibson, then headmaster of King's Hospital School, as its first president, a post he held for many years. Since his resignation the Presidential Chair has been occupied by Mr. W. T. Graham (Ulster), and Irish hockey owes much of its success to these two gentlemen, who have given so much time and energy to help on the 'game that grows.' At the close of the year 1908 the clubs affiliated to the Irish Union numbered over 100, and the numbers increase steadily each year.

"Since the Union was formed there have been many changes in the game. When I started playing at Dublin University in 1896, hockey was a far from popular game with undergraduates. It was despised by football, cricket, and rowing men, and in those days men were eager to conceal rather than to display their hockey sticks. An article appeared in the *T.C.D.*, the University weekly magazine, which contained the following sarcastic allusion to hockey: 'Cricket we know, and football we know, but what is hocquet?' Despite this, and many another, attempt to ridicule it, hockey continued to gain in popularity. It is an interesting and significant fact, and one worth noting, that the author of the sarcastic sentence just quoted subsequently became an enthusiastic disciple of the despised 'hocquet.' It was the same all over Ireland—the game steadily and surely increased in popularity and in the number of its recruits. The Press noticed the game more and more, and matches came to be reported with all the graphic and enthusiastic phraseology devoted to football.

"And great changes came in the style of play. Combined play gradually usurped the entirely individual play of the early days. When I first commenced hockey, the forward line consisted of two right-wing forwards and two left-wing forwards who hunted in couples, while the centre forward was merely the hinge keeping the line connected. At that time the opposing wing half-backs took up their position between·the opposing wing forwards, endeavouring by this means to break up wing combination. That old order of things is long since changed, and the wing half now stays with the outside man, and the chief combination lies between the three inside forwards, the wing men getting few chances to distinguish themselves as in former years.

"Great changes too were wrought upon hockey by legislation, and for the most part these were to the benefit of the game."

Then the grounds improved, by slow degrees perhaps, and good grounds are one of the very best mediums to the progress and popularity of the game.

The extraordinary progress and popularity of hockey is written clearly for all to read in the number of clubs affiliated to the various Unions and Associations of the British Isles. Approximately the number of affiliated clubs is 900. Of these 700 are English and affiliated to the Hockey Association through their respective counties, which number 33. The Irish contribution to this total is 100, the Welsh 56, and the Scottish about 40. Beyond these there are several hundreds of unaffiliated clubs, small and unimportant for the most part but still clubs, and subscribers to the game's popularity.

So popular is the game round London, that many of the leading clubs have no fewer than four teams in the field every Saturday afternoon. Any time between one and two o'clock of a Saturday afternoon the great London termini will present a spectacle of hockey activity almost unbelievable to those who are far from London and its business, social, and athletic stir.

And what a change has been wrought in the attitude of the public towards the game! They come in their thousands now to see an International match where formerly they came in their fifties and hundreds. And inter-divisional matches are little less popular. In view of the almost miraculous skill of the leading exponents of the game, this public enthusiasm for hockey is not a cause for surprise. Owing to the smallness of the ball, the quickness of the game, and the consequent difficulty of following it with an appreciative eye, hockey is rated lower as a spectacle than football or cricket. But there is no gainsaying that it has considerable spectacular merit, which may quite conceivably be enhanced in the years to come.

The progress of the game in Wales, its rise in Scotland, and its ever-increasing adoption by the schools and colleges of England, there is the will but not the space to detail.

On every hand the manifestation of the game's popularity is overwhelming, and a convincing proof that hockey is a game, no matter what its origin, of great intrinsic worth. Otherwise, would the game appeal so strongly to English, Irish, Scottish, and Welsh athletes, and to athletes in almost every country in the world? And, answering in concert, these hockey-playing athletes of many climes shout an emphatic "No!"

But there is another potent reason besides its intrinsic worth for the phenomenal spread and popularity of hockey. It is a game of amateur purity, without the smallest taint of professionalism or the dread of its in-creeping. For this amateurs love it, and many Association football players, wearying of the pungent commercial flavour of "soccer," turn to hockey with great delight and hopeful hearts. Nor are they disappointed. In hockey they find a game which is played for its own sake, and not for any material rewards, because cups and shields and trophies are unknown in hockey—that is, in English hockey.

And this amateur attitude has been nobly and ardently fostered by the Hockey Association, which has always set its face like flint against anything tending, however slightly, towards professionalism.

CHAPTER II

HISTORY OF THE HOCKEY ASSOCIATOIN

By Philip Collins

THE Hockey Association was founded at a meeting held in London on January 18, 1886. at which the following clubs were represented: Wimbledon, Molesey, Teddington, Surbiton, Ealing, Trinity College, Cambridge, Blackheath, and Eliot Park School, Blackheath.

The chair was taken by Mr. E. L. Agar of Wimbledon, who immediately passed a resolution that "a Hockey Association be formed."

The first president of the Hockey Association was H.R.H. King Edward, then Prince Edward of Wales; while the vice-presidents were Messrs. Agar and Pope, with F. G. Howell of the Molesey Hockey Club as hon. secretary and treasurer.

It is not possible to go into details of all the many council and general meetings that have since been held, but this chapter will include a few interesting extracts from the minute books of the Association. The "ball" question seems to have early caused considerable discussion, and at the first council meeting a proposal to play with a white solid indiarubber ball was discussed and negatived. Shortly after this the following note appears at the foot of the minutes of one meeting: "A hockey stick with a piece of wood glued on to the bend, and a cricket ball left white in the manufacture, were shown to the meeting." It is not quite clear what is meant by " a piece of wood glued to the bend," but possibly it was a forerunner of the "bulger" type of stick which came into fashion over fifteen years later.

In April 1887 there is the first note of a County match being played; this was Surrey *v.* Middlesex, and some discussion took place as to what County qualification should be adopted. This discussion led to a special resolution that actual residence should be the sole qualification. In December 1889 a council meeting was called to consider an application from the then recently formed Northern Counties Hockey Association for the recognition of its right to control the game in the North of England. After somewhat lengthy discussion, it was decided to agree to this request, and to allow the new association five representatives on the council, hitherto composed of eight representatives elected at each general meeting. This number was now increased to twelve, exclusive of the N.C.H.A. representatives.

By 1890 the Hockey Association had got well started, having twenty-six southern clubs affiliated to it, and in addition the N.C.H.A.

At the fifth general meeting, Mr. Agar, who had presided at the first meeting, resigned the post of vice-president, and was succeeded by Mr. Yerburgh. It was in this year that the first divisional match was played, the North meeting the South in January 1890 at Queen's Club, London, when the South won by 6 goals to *nil*.

The South team consisted of two backs, three half-backs, and six forwards—two "extremes," two "centres," and a "right" and a "left."

The North adopted a slightly different arrangement of their team, namely, a goal-keeper, a back, three half-backs, and six forwards.

The reason advanced for the playing of six forwards was that "with two good backs, the extra forward, being in play the whole time, would be of more advantage to the side than a goal-keeper, who possibly might have little to do that could not be easily performed by one of the backs."

The year 1891 was an important one, in that it saw the foundation of the Surrey and Middlesex County Hockey Associations and the spread of the game to Wales, as is shown by a dispute as to the control of the game in the Principality, which was eventually compromised by the Hockey Association taking the southern half and the N.C.H.A. taking the other half. Very shortly after this date the question of " cup ties " appears for the first time on the minutes, and an application from the Northamptonshire Hockey Association for affiliation was only granted on the express understanding that they abolished all cups or prize competitions—evil ways to which they seem to have become addicted, and to which, as will be seen later, they eventually returned.

In 1894 there were sufficient clubs in the Midlands to warrant the formation of a separate Divisional Association to take control of them, subject to their recognising the suzerain authority of the parent body. It was, too, at the commencement of this season that a challenge was received from Ireland, which was promptly accepted, and the first International hockey match accordingly took place at Richmond in March 1895, resulting in a win for England by 5 goals to *nil*. It may be remarked that at the outset the precedent was established of asking all affiliated clubs to scratch their fixtures on the date of this match. It will also be of interest to note that the first English International team was constituted as follows: W. B. Barchard, goal; F. Terras, B. S. Smith, backs; E. L. Clapham, W. W. Fletcher, F. J. Seddon, half-backs; H. W. Tindall, J. F. Arnold, F. G. Buchanan, E. R. Hardman, S. Christopherson, forwards.

About this time the West started an Association of its own, and the first of its series of matches with the Midlands was played, though it was not until several years later that the other divisions gave the West fixtures.

At the commencement of 1897 there was trouble in Northamptonshire, which resulted in all their clubs retiring from the Hockey Association and starting a cup-tie competition amongst themselves.

It says a great deal for the governing body, and the spirit in which the game has always been played, that there were no other seceders.

The clubs in question very soon found out that they had done the wrong thing, the practical result of their action being that after one, possibly exciting, season the game gradually died out in Northamptonshire. It was not revived until some time later, when a new County Association was formed on proper lines and affiliated to the Hockey Association.

This season also saw the foundation of a Welsh Hockey Association, and an International match, England *v.* Wales, which was played at Manchester in the spring of 1898, and won by England by 7 goals to *nil.*

At the end of the season 1898–99, Mr. Stanley Christopherson, who had for some six years done yeoman service as honorary secretary and treasurer of the Association, found it necessary to retire, and was succeeded by Mr. Frampton, who was destined to make a most worthy successor. It is impossible to overestimate Mr. Stanley Christopherson's services to the game of hockey. In addition to most ably filling the posts of honorary secretary and treasurer, he had captained the English team and been chairman of the English Selection Committee. It is only necessary to glance through the pages and pages of minutes of meetings carried through under his guidance, to see the immense amount of time and work that he devoted to the interests of the game.

Early in 1900 the first traces of an International Rules Board are to be found in a long discussion as to " the advisability of having an International Committee to frame and amend the rules of the game." This question was raised by Mr. Frampton, but no definite steps were taken until after that season, when a special general meeting decided that such a board should be formed, and that the governing bodies of Ireland and Wales be each asked to send two representatives to meet three from the Hockey Association and revise the rules of the game.

It is evident that by 1900 the game was making considerable headway in every direction, and a letter was received from the authorities of the Paris Exhibition, held that year, asking that an English team might be sent over to play a French one in the Exhibition grounds. For some reason or other, however, the invitation was not accepted.

Up to this time the Hockey Association had, in addition to being the governing body of the game, also looked after the interests of the game in the South; but in 1901 it was felt that the time had come for a separate Southern Counties Hockey Association to be formed, and this was accordingly done. Half the accumulated funds were handed over to the new body, and from that date the Hockey Association ceased to have any direct interest in divisional hockey, and confined itself to the administration of the game from an International point of view only, each division being entirely self-governing, with a right of appeal in every case to the Council of the Hockey Association as to the final tribunal.

The records of this same year also contain the first reference to a player who has since come to be acknowledged the finest centre-forward, if not player, the game has ever produced, namely, Stanley Shoveller. He played for Middlesex against Surrey, and so astonished the Surrey defence that they made careful inquiries, which resulted in the discovery that he had no qualification for Middlesex, but was, as a matter of fact, qualified for the county against which he had been playing! He was therefore invited to play for them in the return match with Middlesex, but the latter county (who required his services) objected, since they maintained that a player could not represent two counties in one season. Their objection came before a special meeting of the H.A. Council, who upheld it, and effectually decided the matter by passing the following resolution, which had the result of "suspending" the future English captain for the rest of the season, so far as county hockey was concerned: " Mr. S. H. Shoveller, having played for Middlesex during the current season, is debarred from playing for any other county during the same season; and as he has no qualification to play for Middlesex, he, of course, is not eligible to play for that county." Very hard this on Shoveller!

The year 1902 saw Scotland taking up the game, and the newly formed Scottish Hockey Association was invited to send two representatives to the International Rules Board meetings. It was about this time, too, that the constitution of the council was altered so as to allow the divisional associations to elect their own representatives instead of the whole council being elected in a somewhat haphazard way at each general meeting

It says much for the spirit in which the game has always been played, that only in very isolated instances have applications to "suspend" players been made to the Hockey Association. One occurred in 1904, when the minutes record that a stormy dispute in a certain club match ended in a forward hitting the opposing goal-keeper over the head with his stick, after which the game came to an untimely end owing to " the unseemly behaviour of the spectators." A lengthy inquiry took place, which resulted in two suspensions and wholesale reprimands!

In 1904, Mr. Frampton, who had with untiring zeal fulfilled the duties of honorary secretary and treasurer for five years, and had been instrumental in carrying through a most careful revision of the whole rules of the game, retired from office, and was succeeded by Mr. Tennent. The latter continued the work of revision rendered necessary by the great growth of the game and initiated by his predecessors, and revised the rules governing the Hockey Association in such a way as to "decentralise" as much as possible, and to make every club affiliate to its county, each county to its division, and each division to the Hockey Association.   He had just completed his task, when, in 1907, he too found that he had not sufficient time for the work, and retired, the writer of this chapter being elected to succeed him.   Since that date two more important changes in the constitution have become necessary by the formation of an Eastern Counties Hockey Association and an Army Hockey Association.   It only remains for some enthusiast to start a Navy Hockey Association, and for the North and East to follow the example of the other divisions and start their own Independent Umpires Associations, and then everything will be complete, so far, at any rate, as can now be foreseen.

There is one other branch of the work of the Hockey Association which has not possibly received sufficient notice, namely, that which it undertakes as the parent body of the game in all the world.   In the countries of France and Germany, Belgium, Holland, Denmark, Austria, and in our colonies of New South Wales, West Australia, New Zealand, and South Africa, in our Empire of India, and in the Dominion of Canada, it is recognised as the ruling body of the game.   Wherever the game is started, there the players follow its rules, and apply to it for advice and for decisions on all disputed points.

CHAPTER III

THE ELEMENTS OF HOCKEY

FEW games, perhaps, are so easy to learn as hockey. The beginner embarking on his hockey career is not faced by the prospect of a long and hard novitiate, constant and assiduous striving, and possible fulfilment in some far distant future. His experience will not be that of the lawn tennis player, who must battle through ten years of tournament play—so it is authoritatively asserted—before he can achieve first-class form. No, the hockey tyro's is no such alarming outlook. At the most it will be but four or five years before he is at his best. In his very first season he will attain to a measure of proficiency possible in the case of few other games.

The fact is that hockey is a natural game, one of the games which come readily to any one with ordinary physique, a good eye, and average intelligence. It is as easily learnt as football, and more easily played. The cricketer's transition from the summer game to hockey is without violence. The one game is full of strokes which occur in the other. And the Association football player passes to hockey almost as readily, so akin are the general outlines of the two games.

But simple as hockey is to learn and to play, the beginner will serve a pleasanter novitiate and the more quickly and surely overtake the skill of his desires, by starting aright, by being grounded in the rudiments of the game, and by early acquiring a knowledge of the strokes used in hockey, and the best manner of making them.

Years of practice—daily practice—and a close study of the game and its theory form the basis, the foundation, of this chapter. So the reader may approach the perusal of it in a spirit of confidence, assured that it contains no heresies.

First-class hockey players are, curiously enough, not much given to theorising or making a study of each individual stroke of the game. Asked to illustrate in cold blood a stroke which he frequently makes, and with effect, in the heat of play, the first-class player will in many cases plead his inability to illustrate it, saying that he makes the stroke in play, but knows not how. Habit has become second nature, and the strokes cost him as little thought or effort as the laying of an egg costs a hen. But then perchance these players are geniuses, and a genius is one of those fortunates in whom gifts take the place of effort. Anyhow, it is folly for the beginner to imagine that he will come by the strokes of the game without patient endeavour and attention to detail. So at the very threshhold of his career let him resolve to seek perseveringly and intelligently a mastery of each individual stroke one by one, and to eschew that lazy expectation which many players indulge, that the strokes will come along in due course.

What is wanted at hockey is more diligent practice of the strokes and movements required in the game. There is probably no game in which so little preparation is deemed necessary for match play. When Saturday comes round, players go straight from their office on to the field without having touched a hockey stick since the previous Saturday. In many cases, of course, mid-week practice is impossible, but large numbers of players have leisure time on their hands and odd hours of freedom from business which they could, with profit to their health and their game, devote to a little definite practice. Another player eager to improve his game and a couple of balls, and the best practice in the world is possible. Nor is it necessary to make the ofttimes long journey to the club ground. Practice, and profitable practice, may be obtained nearer home, on the lawn or in the paddock. Many a player has earned familiarity with the elements of hockey, a more dexterous and confident handling of his stick, and a greater resourcefulness in some such circumscribed space.

The strokes at hockey are neither so numerous nor so varied as in golf, lawn tennis, or cricket. But it is certainly not the one-stroke game of untutored fancy. The strokes include: the drive, mow, reverse, left-hand lunge, left-hand cut or thrust (to coin a name) right-hand cut, job, scoop, push, volley, behind the back, between the feet, right-hand thrust, and other variants of these prompted by the exigencies of the moment.

Possibly a sense of dismay will steal over the beginner at this long array of strokes with their technical names, and at the knowledge that he must perfect himself in many of them if he would make good progress in the game. Let him disabuse his mind of alarms. True, hockey cannot be learned in a day, but it will soon yield to patient practice, and the strokes which seem so fearsome will be found to be so only in the imagination. Some players appear to prosper well enough on a minimum of strokes, but from this it should not be inferred that they would not achieve greater prosperity if their repertory were a longer one. Resourcefulness is largely dependent upon a full armoury of strokes. On the other hand, it is quite possible for a player with every stroke at his command to be so impressed with the fact that he is ever hot to be experimenting therewith. He indulges in clever and fancy strokes when he should be hitting the ball in plain and unromantic fashion. This is the abuse of what is otherwise a source of strength.

The advisability, if not the necessity, of acquiring a mastery over the strokes enumerated above, is to be found in this fact—that occasions arise, no matter how infrequently, when each one of these strokes should be used, and when no others will prove either so timely or so effective.

Surely it is a superfluity to say that only one side of a hockey stick, the flat side, may be used. But as there is an Alpha as well as an Omega to hockey, it would be letting in incompleteness to omit mention of it. The next step, a very elementary one, in building up a would-be player's game, is the manner of holding a hockey stick. It is held like a cricket bat, the right hand beneath the left, although players will now and again be met with who reverse the order and hold the left hand underneath the right. Such players, it will be found, are generally left-handed. Such a heterodox and cramped grip is, of course, to be heartily condemned. And here it should be said that left-handed players, forbidden by the rules to play in the way natural to them, are greatly handicapped at hockey, except in certain strokes which favour their peculiarity.

Now the beginner gripping the handle of his stick firmly in the manner described, with his hands pressed close together, may set himself to learn what is the paramount stroke of the game—

THE "DRIVE"

Emphasis must be laid upon the importance of having the hands packed close together on the handle of the stick. The cause of most bad hitting is the habit, contracted at the beginning of a player's career, of holding the hands wide apart on the stick. The inevitable result is that the right hand does practically all the work, and the stroke which accrues is more of a push than a hit. There are occasions when this manner of holding the stick is right. That will be dealt with later. The nearer the hands are together the greater the power, because the greater the leverage. The overlapping grip of the golfer is out of place at hockey, just as it would be at cricket.

After the hands, the feet; these should be at right angles to the ball's intended line of flight and about half a yard apart subject, of course, to the height of the player.

The ball should be nearer the left than the right foot, so that chopping may be avoided, a method which causes the ball to kick in dangerous fashion. The body should be in the same line with the feet, and the eye kept rigidly fixed on the ball. It is impossible to overestimate the importance of keeping the eye on the ball. After looking once to the destination for which he intends the ball, the player should concentrate his gaze on the ball and never raise his eyes from it till it has been struck.

Seeing that the stick may not be raised above the shoulder, that member will play only a subservient part in the stroke. The genuine hockey drive is made chiefly with forearms and wrists, the stick being allowed to follow through to the full extent of the arms, and not checked the moment the ball has been struck. And the follow-through, how important it is, affecting as it does the whole character of the stroke. How, say some, can the follow-through, which occurs after the ball has gone away, have a beneficial effect upon the stroke? For the simple reason that the *intention* to follow through gives the stroke a freedom which it could not possibly have were the intention to check the stick after the striking of the ball. Then the follow-through gives an accuracy, the accuracy which results from a full-blooded, confident stroke. To obviate the risk of " sticks "—that is, the elevation of the stick above the shoulder at the end of the forward swing—the hands and wrists must be turned over sharply from right to left. This motion turns the point of the stick, and presses it downwards. Players err far oftener in the matter of " sticks " in the back swing of the stick. There is a way of absolutely nullifying this tendency, but it is seldom employed, and perhaps scarcely to be commended. The right hand is held down somewhere near the splice of the stick. This prevents the stick from getting out of control in the back swing. As the stick descends, the right hand slides up to join the left at the top of the handle. When used it is generally as a natural stroke, not as an acquired

FINISH OF DRIVE—WRISTS TURNED OVER FROM RIGHT TO LEFT

one. It is mentioned here as an item of interest and curiosity, and not as a method to be cultivated.

In hockey, as in golf, correct timing and the speed at which the stick is moving at the moment of impact with the ball are responsible for the pace imparted to the latter. Some players have the valuable knack of applying a certain snap of the wrists just as the ball is struck, which brings the happiest results. This again is a native faculty which defies practice.

The alternative method of executing the "drive" is that method which results in the stroke known as the "mow." This is not a stroke loved of the author of this book. It is inelegant and dangerous, time-wasting and tending to inaccuracy. But it is an ingredient of hockey, and as such must be described. It is sometimes claimed that the stroke has greater severity than the "drive," because of the lengthened swing it allows the player. But what it gains in swing it loses in wrist play, and power comes from the wrists. Its best illustration is that of a man using a scythe. The stick in its back swing makes a half-circle round the back on the right side of the body, while the follow-through completes the circle on the left side. It is essentially a back's stroke. Its dangerous tendency is to loft the ball. This method of driving is difficult to acquire, so difficult indeed that the game is hardly worth the candle, and should be left to those to whom the "mow" is a natural stroke.

Let the beginner avoid that abomination known as undercutting. Avoidance is secured only by acquiring a correct style of hitting. Laying the blade of the stick back and drawing it across and under the ball is about as clear a verbal definition of what undercutting is as could be given. The effect is the dangerous lofting of the ball. This undercutting was at one time of very common occurrence, an habitual practice of some players. To tee the ball up for a free hit and loft it over the heads of the defence into the circle where the forwards are waiting for it

is the most extreme use to which this, now illegal, practice
has probably ever been put. This was actually done in an
International match in the twentieth century. But since
undercutting was made illegal it has been the outcome of
a naturally bad style of hitting rather than of deliberate
intention. The backs for their hard hitting and the
forwards for their shooting both employ the "drive,"
although in the case of the latter the stroke is of necessity
often shorter and sharper, and wisely so too, because a
forward must not run the risk of a disallowed goal, disallowed because of "sticks." So long as the rules forbid the
elevation of the stick above the shoulder, players should
endeavour to keep their sticks within this prescribed limit,
although it is common knowledge that umpires do not look
for literal obedience to the rule. Certainly hockey would
be a better and less dangerous game were the sticks of
players kept under stricter control.

Having learned the "drive," the beginner may go on to
a study of the other strokes.

THE REVERSE

The drive is made from right to left; the reverse, as its
name declares, the other way, from left to right, across the
body. The bend of the stick is turned outwards and the toe
of the stick inwards, pointing towards the player. The
right hand is held below the left and close to it. In the
case of left-handed players the left hand is usually moved
below the right. The stroke is not a hit, but a flick of the
wrists, the point of the stick propelling the ball. To try
and hit hard with the stick reversed is to court inaccuracy
and win it nine times out of ten. There is a difference of
opinion as to the angle of the stick when the stroke is
made. Some are of opinion that the ball should be hit
when some way in advance of the player, while others
think that the player should be well over the ball and hit
it when close to his right foot (about a foot in front) and

THE REVERSE STROKE (ERIC GREEN)

with almost perpendicular stick. A little reflection should bring conviction that the latter opinion is the sounder. Let the player hold the stick in the orthodox manner for right-side play, and then walk round the stick and face it. He will then be standing with the stick placed for the reverse stroke. Now the nearer it is for its position for this stroke to the position used for the orthodox stroke the better. Surely that is obvious. And the more upright it is held the nearer it is to that position. Then the balance of the stick is all in favour of the more upright position, as is generally the experience of those who have tried various angles. Let the player put this argument to the test, as the author has frequently done, by hitting the ball when it is, say, 2½ feet and then when it is 1 foot in front of him. The shorter distance will enhance the power and accuracy of the stroke, provided the flick of the wrists is applied at the psychological moment. But as the reverse is chiefly an emergency stroke, it will be made with the stick at whatever happens to be the most convenient angle at the moment.

It is astonishing what pace can be imparted to the ball by means of this stroke, if well timed, and especially if the ball is coming towards the striker at a few inches from the ground. When travelling at top speed, too, the player, if he take time for the shot, can get considerable pace on the ball. To left half-backs and left-wing forwards the reverse stroke is a *sine quâ non.* It will, however, only respond, in any degree of effectiveness, to constant practice.

LEFT-HAND LUNGE

This is among the most useful strokes in a player's armoury. In both defence and attack it is invaluable. It is essential to the make-up of a back or half-back, and an asset which no forward can spare. Indeed it is indispensable in the case of every player on the field. The only possible substitute for it is the right-hand thrust, and this stroke is not its equal, either in point of quickness or reach.   The stick is held in the left hand and at the end of the handle, the player lunging out in the direction of the ball much as he would if he were a left-hand player making a back-hand stroke at tennis.   A strong wrist is the only possession essential to the successful execution of this stroke.   A half-back will use it for spoiling, and a back for the same purpose, while a forward will find it the sole means of keeping control of a ball which has strayed to the right.   It adds very considerably to a player's reach, takes an opponent so by surprise, and, so far as personal safety is concerned, carries far less risk than the right-hand thrust, which exposes the full front of the body.   Those are some of the advantages of the lunge.   Only those who employ it know how greatly it strengthens a player's game.   It is a very favourite stroke with the Irish and with all left-handed and ambidextrous players.

A right-wing forward will often find it useful for spoiling purposes when his opponents roll in from touch. The stroke, to be effective, must be made deftly and with a quick swing.

RIGHT-HAND CUT

This stroke is of the same genus as the reverse.   The stick is firmly held in the right hand, several inches down the handle, with the toe of the stick pointing towards the ground.   The stroke is made from left to right, although there is very little swing about it.   It is, as its name implies, a cut rather than a hit, and of course a purely defensive stroke.   When he makes it, the player is sideways on to the ball, probably running parallel with the opponent against whom he employs it, and in such a position that only great caution will enable him to exploit the stroke without the certainty of a foul.   The stroke is used chiefly, and almost only, when a half or back finds himself on the wrong side of an attacking forward—that is, on that player's left side, the side from which it is so risky to operate.

THE LEFT-HAND LUNGE AS USED BY HALF-BACK FOR DEFENSIVE PURPOSES

Those against whom it is employed find it most irritating, which is a good reason for commending it. The player to appreciate its utility and to have recourse to it most frequently is the left half. If the stroke is to have any power in it, the stick must be gripped firmly and rather low on the handle. After the stroke has been successfully employed, the player must hasten to get away from the risk of a foul and into a position from which he can make the more orthodox strokes.

LEFT-HAND CUT OR THRUST

This stroke is used in the same circumstances as the above, and for the same purpose—the checking of a forward. The stick is held in the left hand with its toe facing the ground, the player reaching out in the direction of the ball. Many halves use it either as an alternative to its brother of the right hand, or in preference to that stroke. A great exponent of the left-hand method is L. M. Robinson, captain of the Cambridge team in 1908. A strong and supple wrist is necessary to the effective use of this stroke, which is, at the best of times, a little weakly. It requires much practice and quick transference of the stick from the right to the left hand. It has not perhaps the power—that is, the rigidity—of the right-hand cut, nor its safety so far as the person of the player is concerned. It is often used of forwards. When the ball is rather wide of the player on his left, he has only this means of restoring it to his control and so continuing his dribble. Travelling at full speed, this feat of hooking the ball from the left is as difficult as it is useful and economic. S. H. Shoveller is very adroit with his left hand, while the ambidextrous T. Pethick could dribble as comfortably with the ball on his left as his right side. But such dribbling is very apt to provoke a penalty for obstruction. And here it may be explained that obstruction is placing the body between an opponent and the ball, with the single exception of the occasion when the player with the ball on his right places himself so that his opponent is on his left. This latter is not obstruction. In truth it is strategic hockey, and counted to the player for righteousness. Outside lefts will find many occasions for the use of the left-hand stroke portrayed above. It bears no recognised name, but is none the less valuable on that account.

THE " JOB "

To thousands of hockey players the word " job " conveys no hockey meaning at all. To them, as to other people, the word stands for some allotted task. It has no other significance. If told that it was a hockey stroke which they themselves used, possibly once a match, they would be surprised, but unashamed. Unashamed, because the ignorance of hockey players as a whole is dark and rampant, both as to the rules and the details of the game, while no stigma seems to attach to the circumstance. It would be a fine thing for hockey if players were compelled to pass an examination in the theory of the game. The hockey examination is quite an institution among ladies, who are far better versed in the theory and rules of the game than men.

To return to the " job "—it would be more apposite to style it " jab "—it is employed by many players all unconsciously—all unconsciously, that is, that the stroke has a name or that its name is " job." The stroke scarcely lends itself to a clear literary definition. It can be made with either hand equally well. The arm is stretched to its fullest extent, the back of the stick blade is laid on the ground with the face uppermost and on an inclined plane. By a succession of quick stabs the ball is made to jump the stick of an opponent, or is propelled till the player has worked himself into a favourable position for disposing of it. The stroke is a child of necessity, being requisitioned when a player, crossing from the left of an

opponent, reaches the ball first. Not in a position for any more effective stroke, he essays to manœuvre himself, through the medium of this "jobbing" stroke, out of an awkward position int███e less embarrassing. For the most part it is the bac█████es the "job" and finds it useful, albeit forwards now █████then make use of it to check the drive of a back.

THE SCOOP AND PUSH

These strokes are practically similar, with this difference, that in the case of the scoop the ball is lifted from the ground, while the push keeps the ball along the ground. To all intents and purposes they are identical, and may be treated as one and the same stroke. The right hand is held low on the stick, from six inches to a foot beneath the left, the stick is slightly laid back, and without any swing, any drawing back of the stick, the ball is jerked, flicked, or scooped away. The work is done almost entirely with the right hand and wrist. The stroke can be either to the right, which is most frequent, or to the left, while it is so under control that at the last moment the player can deflect the ball according to the urgency of the moment. It forms a very large part of twentieth-century forward play. Without it the short passing game is impossible, and a forward, especially an inside forward, most miserably under-equipped. The ball being pushed and not struck, and so the stick not taken back, this stroke economises time, a vital consideration in forward play, where quickness and promptness form the keynote of efficiency. It is no inconsiderable part too of the half-back's game. All the best halves in modern hockey employ this stroke in feeding their forwards. It gives them much wider scope in passing, and enables them to dispatch a pass much sooner or much later, according to circumstances, than was possible in the case of the old-fashioned hit stroke. When attacking at close

quarters, halves and forwards will make a generous use of
this push-cum-scoop stroke, a stroke practically unknown in
the days when the Earnshaws and Stanley Christopherson
were the shining lights of hockey.

RIGHT-HAND THRUST

This is a spoiling stroke, the ordinary two-handed
stroke, made, however, with one hand.   The stick is held
firmly in the right hand and thrust out to the right to
stop the ball or check the dribble of an oncoming forward.
It is the alternative of the lunge, but nothing like so
elegant as that fencing-room stroke.   It is a stroke for
backs and for players with iron wrists.   E. V. Jones, an
International back from the Midlands, was much given to
this stroke, his stalwart right arm shooting out stiff and
sudden, to the discomfort of the advancing forward.
H. S. Freeman, too, England's captain on many occasions,
uses this means of lengthening his reach, and with telling
effect.

THE VOLLEY

The ability to play the ball when it is off the ground
and in the air, that is the volley, or rather the actual
playing of it is.   Hockey has become such a quick game
that no longer do players, as they formerly did, allow the
ball to fall to the ground before attempting to hit it.
Time was when volleying the ball at hockey was unknown,
or known only as an occasional fluke.   Now it is a recognised part of the game, noticeably the University game.
Cleverness is associated with 'Varsity hockey, and to volley
accurately is undeniably clever, because extraordinarily
difficult.   The formation of a hockey stick is such that
early attempts at volleying the ball result in the stick
missing it altogether.   The ability to volley with any
certainty will respond only to constant practice.   Occasionally, very occasionally perhaps, clever forwards will take

CENTRE HALF-BACK, L. M. ROBINSON, CHECKING INSIDE LEFT BY MEANS OF RIGHT HAND THRUST

FORWARDS PASSING BALL ON THE VOLLEY

the ball a considerable distance down the field on their sticks, the ball being transferred from one stick to the other. T. Pethick was marvellously clever at keeping the ball going in the air. He has been known to run down, tapping the ball on his stick, and loft it over the heads of the backs. This sort of thing would be possible only in club hockey. A first-class defence would speedily bring it to nought.

But is it not bad hockey for the ball ever to be in the air ? Not necessarily. The scoop stroke, for example, will lift the ball, and it is generally this stroke which initiates a volleying run, and the scoop stroke is good, not bad, hockey. On other occasions of the ball being off the ground, the cause is either the roughness of the ground or else a bad style of hitting. As a defensive stroke, or as a pass from a half to a forward, the volley is often most useful, indeed the only course a player can adopt with benefit to his side, because of the promptitude with which it enables him to act. If yielded to, the temptation to volley a ball head-high involves the player in a penalty for " sticks."

The stroke behind the back and that between the feet are seldom used, but the fact of these being used at all is sufficient reason for their inclusion and description in this chapter. It will sometimes—alas! often—happen that a forward will overrun the ball. Instead of stopping and getting at the back of the ball again, and so checking the run of his fellow-forwards, he can play the ball behind his back, provided no opponent is within striking distance of the ball. With the stick held low down in his right hand, he will hit the ball from right to left to the forward immediately on the latter side. The stroke must be executed without delay, must be used only in such an emergency as that stated, and must never, of course, be paraded for " gallery " purposes.

As to the stroke between the feet, this is another of the emergency species. It is used more often than the stroke just set forth, but only in the event of the player being

3

pressed for time.   A left half-back will often be driven to
the employment of this manner of hitting between the feet.
He will, in most cases, have his back to his opponents' goal.
This means that he can make the stroke with safety only
when none of his opponents is within striking distance of
the ball.   Now that it is scarcely possible for the player
to play the ball when facing his own goal, so strict is the
umpire's interpretation of "obstruction," he will have few
opportunities of playing the stroke between the feet.

Writers on hockey—and they have been many and
voluminous—seldom discuss the subject of fielding among
the most important of the elements of hockey.   There are
three recognised ways of fielding the ball at hockey—
with hand, foot, and stick: of these the best is the stick.
Accurate fielding with the stick is all a matter of a good
ground and watchfulness on the part of the player.   Let
the beginner learn an early reliance on his stick, especially
if he is qualifying for a forward position.   Except that the
wings should occasionally use their hands, the forwards
should always field with their sticks.   Backs and half-
backs may field with hand or foot when they have time,
but when pressed they must use the stick.   In fielding
with the hand, the left hand should be used, the right hand
retaining its hold of the stick.

Just a minor point which may be noted before it
escapes the memory.   When the player is running about
the field, and not immediately playing the ball, he should,
for greater freedom, carry the stick in one hand.   To hold
it with both hands, as many players do, is to prevent the
free swinging of the arms which is natural and necessary
to the runner.   It is different when the player is in close
touch with the game or is expecting a pass.   Then both
hands on the stick is the right attitude.

When pursuing a forward the back or half-back will
get along much more quickly if the stick is held in either
the right or left hand.

No apology is needed for stretching the title of this

chapter to cover such an important item as the equipment of the player.

The stick forms the most important part of a player's equipment. And how privileged is the player of the twentieth century in the matter of sticks! What a work of art is the modern hockey stick, and how conducive to good and accurate play! In the primitive days of the game the hockey stick was a rude weapon cut from knotty holly or oak, and roughly fashioned to a resemblance of the prevalent idea of what was deemed good enough for playing the game with. Later, sticks of seasoned holly or oak and of stouter build were tried, and held sway for many years. The club probably had its sack of twenty or thirty sticks, from which each player, as he came on to the field, took his pick. But as the game developed players became more and· more particular. They bought their own weapons. The club stock diminished until a few spare sticks, in case of breakage, were all that the club deemed it necessary to provide. The evolution of the hockey stick proceeded apace. Leather binding took the place of rough and knotty handles, thereby detracting from the sting and jar so often experienced when the stick met the ball. So far the sticks had been of nature's formation. Necessity being the mother of invention, the need of better sticks stimulated the inventive powers of manufacturers, and the steam-bent implement was introduced, and quickly ousted all use or thought of the rural hedgerow weapon. The stick grew better and better. Players designed their own to meet their special fancy and had their names branded on the design. Bulgers came in, and bulgers went out and came in again. All manner of coverings for handles was tried—waxed thread (as on cricket bats), cork, chamois leather, glazed surgical whipping, corduroy, and rubber, the majority of players favouring the last named—a rubber grip rolled on to the handle. This grip has the grave disadvantage of being absolutely unholdable when wet, unless the player is wearing cotton gloves. Then numerous inventions have been tried for giving resilience to the handle, and without doubt the insertion of rubber or some kindred substance between the strands of cane down the centre of the handle does take from the jar created by impact with the ball, while it enhances the driving power of the stick. Some such device is present in all the best sticks of to-day. Formerly the makers were solely responsible for the shape of the stick. Now nearly every stick manufactured is the outcome of ideas and suggestions supplied by leading players.

So the choice of a stick should be as simple as it is important. To choose, however, a stick which will exactly suit his individual requirements is a matter which calls for caution and deliberation on the part of the player. In his choice he must be guided by his style of play, his position in the field, and his physical qualities. He must be satisfied that in balance, weight, and length the stick coincides with his wants. Thus a player short of stature and of only moderate strength will not choose a long and heavy stick. The real safeguard against a mistake in this important choice is the advice of an experienced player. Go direct to the makers and choose your stick, is my advice to young players, to all players. If this cannot be done, then write to them, stating explicitly the requirements in respect of weight, length, thickness of handle, and shape of blade.

As to the length of his stick, the player may take the height of his hip as a fairly safe guide, while as to its weight it may be anything from 20 to 24 oz. And let players remember that age adds weight to a stick, and that a stick which was 22 oz. when new is likely to weigh a couple of ounces more in its third or fourth season.

Backs require longer sticks than half-backs, and half-backs than forwards. But there are exceptions to every rule, and many forwards, for example, use long sticks. The backs are the hard hitters of the team, and hold a long handle; the half-backs are less vigorous, and keep their hands lower on the handle; while the forwards, who, except in the circle, and often there, hold their hands much nearer to the blade, hit the ball directly beneath them, and find three inches of superfluous handle a constant menace to their ribs. And just in the same gradation is the weight of the stick, the backs generally using the heaviest and the forwards the lightest. On this subject of the weight of the stick, Eric Green—and if Eric Green does not know, who does?—says, "I would recommend, as a rule, a stick weighing 21 or 22 oz. for a forward, 22 or 23 for a half-back, and 22 to 24 for a back or goal-keeper." The same authority is unfriendly to the "bulger" pattern of stick, on the ground that it militates against accuracy and promotes undercutting.

The ideal stick is the golden mean between the "bulger" and the flat-backed stick. It is upright of build and short of toe, whippy of handle, and with the wood dispersed along the blade, not bunched all in one place at the back of it.

Bunching the wood just behind the centre of the blade certainly imparts great driving power to a stick, but encourages "topping." Then this sort of stick, with its sharp ridge at the bottom of the blade, chips and breaks up. The stick for accuracy and durability is the one which is nearly as thick at the bottom, where it touches the ground, as in the centre of the blade.

Then there is the grain to be considered. A wide grain means durability; the narrow is sweet to play with, but less durable. My advice to the player is—choose a stick with a wide grain, pass an oily rag over it twice a week, use it frequently, and in time it will play as sweetly as the narrow, while long outlasting it.

When ordering a stick by letter, the player should remember that the length is taken from the toe to the top of the handle. As regards the thickness of the handle, there are three trade sizes—"thick," "medium," "thin." The maximum weight of a hockey stick is 28 oz.

Ash and hickory are the two woods of which the modern stick is made, and the former is unquestionably the better.   The price of good reliable sticks ranges from 7s. 6d. to 12s. 6d.

Let the player avoid that abomination the rubber ring on the stick.   It upsets the balance of a stick, and seldom saves the hands.

One word about the care of a stick.   After use in the wet it should be wiped over with a dry rag, and then oiled back and front, the blade only, with *raw linseed* oil. Should the stick show signs of chipping, a whipping of adhesive plaster, such as used by surgeons, is the best of all protectives.

The player who goes on to the field with unprotected shins is nothing less than a fool.   But there is no occasion for the cumbersome pads some players affect.   A small shin-guard shorn of all its straps and buckles and slipped inside the stocking cannot be bettered.

And gloves are nearly as necessary as pads, if not two, then one on the right hand, and let it be a padded glove, as worn at cricket.   The player who braves the dangers of the hockey field without gloves must not look for sympathy when he gets his knuckles badly rattled. Irish players usually affect ordinary white kid gloves. These keep the hands warm and save them when fielding.

Light boots, with some sort of protection on the inside, should be worn.   And let the player beware the wide welt if he would escape a sprained ankle.   Studs on the heel and bars in the shape of the letter Z across the sole of the foot give the firmest foothold.

The remainder of the player's outfit is a matter for individual taste and comfort.

CHAPTER IV

THE GROUND—ITS CARE AND EQUIPMENT

A BAD ground and good hockey are an impossible alliance. A first-class team may occasionally rise superior to the roughness and uncertainty of a bad ground, and by virtue of sheer cleverness appear to be little hampered by the adverse conditions; but their confidence is bound to be disturbed and their play to be unequal. Their exchanges with the ball are given and taken on faith. If the luck is with the ball, they will get on comfortably; but if against it, and it takes to perverse kicks and jumps, then their efforts at combination will be brought to nought.

A good ground is the *sine quâ non* of scientific hockey. It is as important as a good pitch for cricket, a good lawn for croquet, and a good table for billiards. A moderately level surface answers the requirements of football, but not so in the case of hockey. The nearer the surface is brought to the perfection associated with the bowling green, the better will be the hockey played upon it.

Nothing influences play so much for good or ill as the ground. The nature of the ground upon which players are accustomed to play is clearly branded upon their game.

Is that not strikingly exemplified in the case of the Irish?

Where the grounds are bad the play is almost certain to be rough and ready, and quite certain to be destitute of the finer and more scientific touches. For illustration of this one need seek no farther than the West of England.   Good grounds in the West—good, that is, as compared with such grounds as the Richmond Athletic ground, the old Surbiton ground, Bromley, and many another ground near London—are almost unknown.   The East Gloucester Club's ground at Cheltenham is one of the best.   There has been a marked improvement in the grounds in recent years, with which the improvement in the play has fittingly kept pace—with lapses.   But much is left to be desired, and, generally speaking, hockey grounds in the West compare very ill with those in the other divisions.

This curse of bad grounds is what, more than anything else, retards the progress and refinement of the game in, especially, the country districts of the West.   Here hockey grounds are often rough meadows, worked into some semblance of order at the beginning of the season from a condition of chaos.   Hitherto they have provided grazing for horses, cattle, sheep.   Impressed into the service of the local hockey club, a ground such as these is subjugated by the application of scythe and roller.   The grass is coarse, the turf is pitted with holes and puckered with lumps, and the result is a crop of accidents each match and much execrable hockey.

But that is perhaps a somewhat extreme case, although common enough a few years ago.   The times are more enlightened, and hockey is universally recognised as a scientific game, and as such dependent on level grounds. For the encouragement of those clubs who do not enjoy the privilege of a good ground, nor the wherewithal to employ skilled labour to bring their ground to a higher state of excellence, let it here be said that a little amateur labour on the part of members will work wonders in the amelioration of an uncouth and unsatisfactory piece of turf.   And the pleasure of playing on it will be enhanced because the players themselves have ministered to its improvement.

I am a firm believer—and my faith is the product of a

lengthy experience of grounds of all sorts—in the mowing machine and the roller, and their refining influence on the coarsest of turf. If members of clubs were truly keen, and the only alternative was neglect, they should be glad to give a couple of hours a week to pulling and pushing these two implements of improvement. There was once an enthusiast —and there need be no mystery as to his identity ; he was the writer of this chapter—who, alone and unaided, cut the entire surface of a hockey ground with a 12-inch lawn mower. And the grass was of the thickest and richest description. The task occupied a couple of days, which, in view of the subsequent enjoyable hockey, were well spent. Such excessive ardour is seldom necessary, but it serves as a text from which to exhort club members to some little interest in the care and preparation of their ground.

When once the grass is close enough, nature and wintry conditions will keep it at that. Constant use of the roller, save after a deluge of rain, and a heavy roller, will now be necessary. And let the rolling be all one way up and down the field, and let the circle have an extra dose. After a match all bad holes and heel indentions should be carefully attended to, and that before the roller is put on. An excellent method of healing these scars is to raise the hole with a fork, make an incision in the turf at the side of and underneath the hole, and then insert a little loose soil to bring the hole up to the right level. Carefully trodden down and rolled and the injury will become invisible. But great care must be taken in cutting the turf.

Probably the finest ground on which hockey was ever played was the old Surbiton cricket ground. Regarding this almost flawless piece of turf, the Rev. A. E. Bevan, a well-known Southern veteran and for many years Surbiton's hardy goal-keeper, says : " It was my privilege, as well as pleasure, to look after the well-known hockey pitch on the old Surbiton cricket ground,—now, alas ! occupied by Metropolitan Water Board's filters,—and the accuracy of that ground was mainly due to the care taken after every match to have all heel marks and 'slides' attended to before the roller was put on."

In the case of amateur preparation and care of the ground there is another point worth emphasising. After heavy rain, and when the ground is soppy, it is a mistake to use a heavy roller, often a mistake to use a roller at all. A heavy roller brings the moisture to the surface, and the ground, when many feet trample upon it, becomes a quagmire. So a light hand-roller should be used. This will smooth out the more superficial roughnesses of the turf without drawing the moisture to the top. If it is undesirable to use a roller at all, that may be taken as a pretty sure sign that the ground is unfit for hockey.

If time forbids to roll the entire ground, let the available attention be given to the circle and to that part of the ground between the 25-yards line and the circle.

The ideal hockey ground is, of course, the cricket ground. Nor does hockey, as many erroneously suppose, seriously damage a cricket ground. Rugby football, with its desolating " scrums," does do irreparable harm to a cricket ground, wearing out its winter coat and giving it the appearance of a dog with the mange, but not so the lighter-footed game of hockey. Happily the committees of cricket clubs realise this more every year, and in hundreds of cases the hockey club is an off-shoot of the cricket club, and the ground a common one. Once the merits of hockey are recognised by the officials of cricket clubs, and they are certain to give the game their cheerful support and co-operation, and all the more seeing how decided a kinship there is between the two games.

Before passing on to the equipment of the ground, it will be useful to note the probable cost of levelling an ordinary meadow for the purposes of hockey. Something like £20 would be the cost if local labour were employed, but considerably more if an expert undertook the work. Draining, if deemed necessary, would be an extra. This rough estimate is a minimum, and only in the case of a

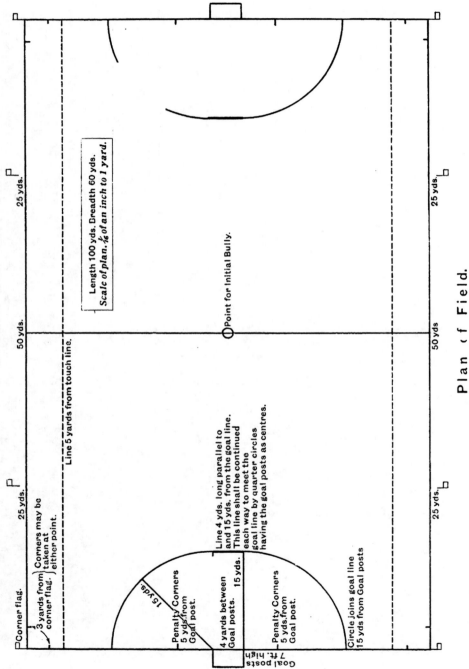

Plan of Field.

Length 100 yds. Breadth 60 yds.
Scale of plan. 1/16 of an inch to 1 yard.

Line 5 yards from touch line.

Point for Initial Bully.

25 yds.

50 yds.

25 yds.

Corner flag.

3 yards from corner flag. Corners may be taken at either point.

Penalty Corners 5 yds.from Goal post.

4 yards between Goal posts.

15 yds.

15 yds.

Line 4 yds. long parallel to and 15 yds. from the goal line. This line shall be continued each way to meet the goal line by quarter circles having the goal posts as centres.

Penalty Corners 5 yds.from Goal post.

Circle joins goal line 15 yds from Goal posts.

Goal posts 7 ft. high.

ground which required simple levelling, and none of that banking up so often necessary.   The dimensions of the levelled portion of the meadow should not be less than 110 yards by 70.   This will give a margin of 5 yards for each boundary line.   A ground laid down in the autumn of one year—the right time for the work—will be fit for play in a twelvemonth.   The importation of turf is a very costly business.   Few hockey clubs, unless allied to a cricket club, and thus partners in the expense, could afford the luxury of turf from Salisbury Plain or some other El Dorado.

The correct marking out of a ground is of the utmost importance.   The full dimensions of a hockey ground are 100 yards by 60, although some grounds are a few yards under this maximum width.   This narrowing of a ground is hostile to good open play, and is hated, especially of wing forwards, who like plenty of elbow-room.

The commonest mistake, and the easiest of commission, in measuring out a hockey ground, just as it is in marking out a tennis court, is to get the ground out of the *square*. The way to avoid this is, after fixing on the exact spot for the corner flag, to measure 3 yards along the goal-line and 4 yards along the touch-line from the corner flag, and put a peg in at each of these points.   If the measurement between these two points is 5 yards, then the lines are at right angles and the corner is on the square.   This method should be applied at each of the four corners of the ground. This will assure a properly set-out ground, so far, that is, as the outside lines are concerned.   Now for the details. Parallel to the touch-line, and 5 yards distant, must be marked a dotted line, to satisfy the roll-in rule.   This *must not* be a continuous line, but only dotted.   It would be most confusing to the players were it continuous.

The centre line, dividing the ground into two parts of 50 yards each, should be drawn boldly across the ground from touch-line to touch-line, with an asterisk at 30 yards —a mark for the centre bully.

It seems almost superfluous to say that a string line, a

lawn tennis marker, and a pail of whitening (the latter mixed to the consistency of cream), and of course a tape measure, not to mention a bundle of pegs, are essential to the process of marking out a hockey ground.

The 25-yards line used to be drawn right across the ground. That is an obsolete practice. Only the extremities of the line are marked—7 yards at each end. This obviates the confusion created by a multiplicity of lines drawn across the ground, but increases the guess-work of the umpire on such an occasion as the ball, hit from somewhere near the 25-yards line by one of the attack, striking an opponent and passing over the goal-line. Hit from outside the 25 yards, this is a bye (provided the opponent struck is also outside the 25 yards); but from inside, a corner.

A corner hit may be taken from a point, on either the goal or the touch line, 3 yards distant from the corner flag. This point should be marked as a guide to the players and the umpires, and not left to be guessed.

Assuming that the ground is of a maximum width, each goal-post must be fixed in the ground 28 yards from the corner flag—that is, 4 yards apart. At a distance of 5 yards from each post, and on the goal-line, a mark should be made to indicate the minimum distance from the goal-post at which a penalty corner may be taken.

Finally comes the all-important task of marking the circle.

Exactly opposite to that 4 yards of the goal-line which is within the goal-posts and 15 yards away must be drawn a straight line 4 yards long, and parallel to the goal-line. Two quarter-circles are now drawn which cut the goal-line at points 15 yards from each of the goal-posts. The manner of drawing these quarter-circles is simple enough. The radius of each of these quarter-circles is a line stretched from the goal-post to the extremity of the 4-yards line opposite to it. If a brush dipped in whitening is attached to the end of this line and the line held taut, a quarter-circle can be drawn in less than a minute, the goal-post, of course, being taken as its centre.

The corner flags must be placed at the exact corners of the ground; but half-way or 25-yards flags, if used, should be placed 1 yard back from the touch-line. It may be remarked here that when taking a corner hit a player is entitled to remove the corner flag.

When the nets have been attached to the goal-posts and cross-bar—and let these be so closely adjusted that no chink is left large enough for a ball to penetrate—the ground is ready for play.

Six balls are the very minimum number for a match, three for each half. Let secretaries see to it that never less than this number of clean white balls, either freshly painted or newly bought, is on the ground for a match. A white ball, as well as a round and a sound one, is essential to good and accurate hockey, and to the enjoyment of players. The spare balls should either be husbanded by the linesman, if there is one, or by the umpire, or else left behind one of the goals, accessible to the goal-keeper, who will produce one at a moment's notice.

No ground should be without its sack of sawdust. From constant trampling of his circumscribed area, the goal-keeper, in wet weather, often has very muddy ground under his feet, on which he will—not of his own volition—skate and slide and slither, unless sawdust is lavishly sprinkled in and around the goal. There is another possible use for sawdust of which few players avail themselves. It is the only possible medium of effectually absorbing moisture on a rubber handle. When the rain is descending in torrents, it is almost impossible to hold a stick whose handle is sheathed in rubber. A handful of sawdust will, provided it is renewed from time to time, make the impossible possible. Players who perspire freely at the hand will find a pinch of sawdust, which may be carried in the pocket, a counteracting influence and a splendid aid to a firm grip.

CHAPTER V

IN PLAY—THE FORWARD LINE

THE FORWARD LINE

IF it were possible to watch on two consecutive afternoons a game of hockey as played in the early nineties and as played in 1909, it would be in the play of the forwards that the spectator would notice the greatest difference. In the former he would observe that the dominant style was long passing, and not a little of the hit-and-rush method, and in the latter short passing, close dribbling, and much finessing.

Evolution is a gradual process, scarcely discernible at the time, but when after a lapse of years the present is compared with the past, then is seen how great have been the changes. And this is so with hockey in general and forward play in particular. But the magnitude of the change can be adequately appreciated only by a comparison such as that suggested above. The forward play of Stanley Christopherson's day has few points of resemblance with that played by S. H. Shoveller and his contemporaries. The styles are nearly fifteen years apart, and so different that it is hard to believe that the change has come gradually, and not as the result of some sudden and violent revolution.

In the early nineties, short passing of the type one may now see illustrated any Saturday afternoon in a hundred club matches all over the country was little known and little practised. Wings banged the ball to the centre, and the centre banged the ball back to the wings. As for passing by means of the scoop and shove (or push) stroke there was none of it.   A pass was a hit every time.   Then forwards went for their objective by means of hard, straight-ahead hockey.   Deviations were not indulged in.   In modern hockey forwards compass their end through the medium of a hundred clever wiles and sudden little by-paths.   Their methods are persuasive rather than aggressive. About their play is much of the *suaviter in modo*, while it does not want for the *fortiter in re*.   And modern forward play is the more picturesque of the two, much the more.

Hockey is not, generally speaking, rated very high as a spectacular game.   But few things are better worth seeing than a first-class line of forwards in their best and most scientific manner.   And if Shoveller is of the five, and in one of his inspired moods, he must be a dull dog indeed who cannot enthuse over such festal fare.

The hit-and-rush tactics of Christopherson's day, and the plucky aggressiveness of the players, might stir the blood of the spectator and rouse his fighting instincts, but could never satisfy his artistic sense ; therefore the superior spectacular charms of modern forward play which delights the eye of the artist while quickening the pulse of the warrior.   Modern forward play is to the forward play of earlier days much what modern scientific warfare is to the barbarous methods of war employed by our forefathers. This simile falls rather hard, perhaps, on the forward of earlier days, whose play was really less deficient in science than the foregoing discussion seems to suggest.

The forwards of the present control the ball so wonder-fully.   They keep it quite close to the stick and propel it by a succession of quick pushes, diverting it to right or left and on the instant by means of a wrist turn.   Down the field these five players sweep, passing and repassing the ball by means of their wrist strokes, handing it on from one to the other, and only giving way to hard hitting when the circle is reached, or when a final centre from the wing is necessary.

And here is another point of difference between modern

and semi-ancient forward play. Earnshaw, the premier centre forward of his day, could do what if Shoveller attempted the latter would be instantly penalised for. Those half-turns of the body, which in the case of Shoveller constitute obstruction and win prompt punishment, were not in the case of Earnshaw regarded as illegalities. The strictness of modern hockey in the matter of obstruction serves to enhance the merit of Shoveller's wonderful dribbling, while, paradoxical though it may seem to say, the former laxness with regard to obstruction in no way discounts the merit of Earnshaw's skill as a dribbler. The liberty allowed the latter was also allowed the halves and backs opposed to him, while the same strictness that governs Shoveller's movements governs also the movements of the players he must defeat. This nearly balances things.

But why this strictness enhances the merit of Shoveller's dribbling and elusive manner of attack—and Earnshaw and Shoveller stand for types as well as individuals, although the latter is in many respects a player apart—is the fact that, despite the limited scope which this strictness implies, Shoveller is yet so versatile. Necessity has compelled him to create means of attack which, while obeying the laws, shall yet defeat them. In many respects instruction which would have been eminently suited to forwards of fifteen years ago is eminently unsuitable for forwards of to-day. But one of the purposes of this book is to teach the up-to-date game. So let the past be forgotten and let concentration be upon present needs.

Combination is the first collective asset of the forwards. There is the abuse as well as the use of combination. Nowadays one often sees the abuse of it. Players fall down and worship combination. It becomes a fetish. Obsessed with the idea of combination, they sacrifice all to it—individualism, common sense, personal effort. They become hopelessly stereotyped, without individuality or points of dissimilarity. The line becomes a machine, each member of it acting in accordance with convention rather than with

the need of the moment. Where convention seems to say
" pass " and the need of the moment " go on yourself," the
former injunction is obeyed. This is the abuse of combination, although perhaps it is seldom carried to just this
extreme. True combination is a very different story. It
is the welding of individual and collective effort in such
a manner that individual skill, while ministering to the
effectiveness of the whole, is never subservient to the
collective idea. Each member of the forward line is a unit,
and must remain as such. Individuality must not be
stifled. That is the danger of combination. The gospel
of combination is so preached by some coaches and
captains, that players are frightened out of their individuality and degenerate into the slaves of a system. Even
in International matches combination is sometimes over-
done, and players will pass when they should have retained
the ball. How much oftener during a game does the
observant spectator think, " Why ever didn't he go on himself ! " than " Why ever didn't he pass ! "

Just as the apotheosis of combination killed individualism
in Rugby football, so will it kill individualism in hockey,
unless the danger is recognised and guarded against. The
Rugby football enthusiast of middle life, depressed by the
dull football of to-day, thinks with a glow of the grand old
days of Stokes, Wade, Don Wauchope, Bolton, Stoddart,
and many another giant, who, single-handed, could defy
all foes. These did not want some one at their elbow to
receive or help them with a pass. They tucked the ball
under their arm in that good old way and bent their efforts
on reaching the far-off goal-line. And unless hockey
players are careful, posterity will be sighing for the days
when Shoveller and Logan and Jordan delighted the
spectators by their brilliant individual displays. Perish the
thought that combination should receive here less than its
due measure of importance ! It is absolutely essential to
the present conditions of the game. The danger is lest its
cult should sap individual brilliance.

But individual brilliance, remember, can never atone for absence of combination. The two must go hand in hand. Five players individually brilliant, and ready to demonstrate their unaided skill when the opportunity offers, working in unselfish unison, are a source of joy to their own side, of terror to their opponents, and of delight to the spectators. True combination is this, and it is also to know exactly where one's comrades are, to be thoroughly intimate with their devices,—all those quips and feints and tricks of the stick which are the munitions of the resourceful forward,— to divine just what they are going to do and to act accordingly, to pass the ball knowing that there will be some one there to receive it, to put one's self in the right position to accept a pass, to know what course should be followed under certain circumstances, and to be confident that the responsible forward will follow that course, and not do something utterly contrary to expectation. Such is a brief digest of combination in the superlative degree. Mutual confidence among the forwards is the keynote of true combination.

Collectively forwards should model their play according to the method of which a description is now entered upon.

The width of the ground being 60 yards, each forward —to allow him one-fifth of this—will have 6 yards on either side of him which he may call his own, and in which he may operate without having an uneasy conscience, although the wing forwards are seldom right in straining their inside tether. This 12-yards allotment is quoted as a sort of theoretical guide. Hockey is not a game that one can hedge about with mathematical exactitudes, it is far too volatile for that, but the general tendency should be for the forwards to play equi-distant from one another. Neither the centre nor yet either of the wings should be isolated from his confrères. Touch-line tactics make it imperative that the two inside forwards should get out of position. But this is only temporary desertion of their centre, if indeed it is so much as this, seeing that an

THE ROLL-IN FROM TOUCH

intelligent centre forward will incline to that side of the ground on which the roll-in occurs. And as to this roll-in, what should be the tactics and what the position of the forwards ? The manner of the roll-in—the ball being rolled either back or at right angles to the touch-line, but not forward—which obtained up till the year 1905 was, with the object of making the game faster and more open, superseded by the present unrestricted roll-in. The half-back usually takes the roll-in, and he is at liberty to roll the ball anywhere. This freedom, besides giving a real advantage to the side whose roll-in it is and opening up the game, increases the likelihood of an unmarked player. A multiplicity of devices may be employed to turn the roll-in to the best account. One effective device is for the forward to hit the ball back to the half-back who rolls it in. Another way is for the half to roll the ball fast down the field and just inside and parallel to the touch-line. This is very useful in the case of a speedy wing forward. But whatever the exact nature of the roll-in, whether it be from half-back to half-back, to back, or to forward, the wing and the inside forward will hover on the 5-yards line.

If it were not for the fact of its being the same for both sides, there could not be a doubt that the present roll-in occasionally proves too beneficial to the rolling-in side. At times it is hardly less useful than a free hit, and the latter is a penalty for violation of the rules, whereas a roll-in is never the outcome of anything worse than unresourceful or in-accurate play. The present roll-in is an argument against hitting into touch. There are not wanting, however, those who would substitute a free hit for the roll-in.

In defence the manœuvres of their opponents will decide the positions of the forwards. No disquisition on forward play would be adequate to the subject unless it emphasised the fact that forwards have defensive duties, even wing forwards. The forwards have their share in the responsi-bilities of defence. A common fallacy is to regard them as an attacking force pure and simple. Many forwards shape

their play on this fallacy.   As spectators they watch their
back division in the throes of a desperate defence, and
tender them no assistance, but looks only, in their moment
of sorest need.   Such conduct is reprehensible to a degree,
and indicative either of great stupidity or gross laziness.
It is constantly the part of the three inside forwards to go
back and help their hard-pressed backs by harrying the
attack.   For the time being they assume the rôle of so
many half-backs, ward off defeat, and indirectly improve
their own game by acquainting them better with defensive
methods.   And when a forward is robbed of the ball by an
opposing half or back, he must not resign himself to this
spoliation.   Highway robbery should nettle a man into an
aggressive determination to get back his own.   So it should
be with the forward.   He should pester the opponent who
robs him until he redeems the ball, or until it is hit to a part
of the field outside his province.   This is in the nature of
defence, and is among the things so neglected by forwards.
And the foolishness of many a forward is to abandon the
worrying of a half-back, when perseverance would have
given him the ball.

There can be much greater definiteness in dealing with
the play of forwards in attack.

The cardinal sin of teaching is dulness, and if lessons
are to fulfil their purpose they must be bright.   So the
effort is here made to brighten the treatment of this part of
the subject, by quoting the possible tactics of a good forward
line between the half-way flag and their opponents' goal.
Let the line be of English make, the line that carried their
country to victory in the Olympic contest—P. M. Rees,
G. Logan, S. H. Shoveller, R. G. Pridmore, and Eric Green.
At the half-way bully Shoveller, by a strength and quickness of wrist superior to his opponent's, gets the ball, and,
to defeat the centre half, passes the ball diagonally, by
means of the push stroke, to inside right—Logan, who,
after travelling a short distance in that galloping manner
peculiar to him, sees danger ahead in the person of the

left back. As outside right is being closely shadowed by the left half, inside right refrains from passing out to him, and casts about for some alternative. One of three courses remains open to him, either to dribble round the back by hitting the ball to the right of him and running round him on the other side, or to bear to the right and so have the back on his left, the side from which it is so difficult and risky to tackle, or to pass to his centre. Those who know Logan's play would lay heavy odds on his choosing the last-named course. This he does, and passes to Shoveller, or rather a little ahead of him. Quick as thought Shoveller is on to the ball, and taking it at top speed flashes past the centre half, and slightly drawing the right back causes inside left—Pridmore—to become partially unmarked. A quick pass at right angles—at this angle so that the back may not intercept it—goes from Shoveller to Pridmore, and again from Pridmore to Eric Green, this latter pass being hit well in front of outside left, so that he may take it at top speed. Overtaking the ball and controlling it cleverly, Eric Green takes it down to a point a few yards beyond the edge of the circle, and, half turning, centres it back to the edge of the circle. The inside forwards, who are now playing closer together than when in mid-field, enter the circle just as the ball comes like a rocket across it, and—to give the story a happy ending—Pridmore, with a swinging shot, defeats the goal-keeper. Or another happy ending might be a little finessing on the part of the three inside forwards, resulting in Shoveller getting to close quarters with the goal and scoring with a diagonal shot pushed rather than hit into the net.

Although the avenues to a goal are many and devious, the foregoing, or something like it, is very familiar to the hockey field.

In mid-field the forwards will be evenly spread out, but as they approach the enemy's lines the two insides will perceptibly close in. The intelligence of readers shall not be insulted by a recital of the reason for this.

Albeit the positions of the five forwards cannot be rigidly fixed, it can be said of the centre and two wings that their positions should be nearly unalterable. The centre must keep in the middle of the ground within his 12 yards, while the wings must lie out within a few yards of the side line, and keep there throughout the game, except when its exigencies demand a dash for the circle, or the loan of a helping hand to the defence. A roaming centre works havoc with combination, while wings who drift inwards cramp play and thwart good, fast, open hockey.

One fault forwards are very prone to commit is that of overhaste in the circle, especially in the circle. The moment they enter that zone of opportunity, they blindly, and with hot-headed hurry, shoot somewhere in the direction of their opponents' goal. Their chance of scoring is infinitesimally slender. They are either ignorant or heedless of the fact that nine times out of ten the defence concentrate upon the player with the ball and leave some one unmarked. Instead of this flurried, impetuous shooting, they should essay a quiet pass to the unmarked forward. True combination in the circle is the crowning attainment of a good forward line.

Then the impossible angles at which forwards will attempt to score, and the tendency of wing forwards, when they have taken the ball to within a yard or so of the goal-line, to hit the ball parallel with the goal-line right across the goal-mouth and at express speed. The substitute for such utterly wasteful practices is a pass back to the edge of the circle or to some forward who is well placed for receiving a pass and turning it to good account.

Dalliance with the ball is as common a fault as its opposite, and even more fatal. The circle is no place for fancy play or deliberation; here instant action must reign. By hesitating and fiddling about with the ball the forwards defeat their own ends and give the defence time to surge back and round them in overwhelming numbers. The

COMB NATION IN THE CIRCLE. S. H. SHOVELLER, DEFEATING RIGHT BACK BY MEANS OF THE
PUSH STROKE FROM LEFT TO R GHT. NOTE POSITION OF H S HANDS

large majority of goals, especially in first-class hockey, are scored by quick and unchecked runs, and very few as the result of long toying with the ball in the circle. So quick is modern hockey and so good defensive play, that forwards need to be opportunists to seize their chances and turn them to swift account. The game has no use for dilettantes and potterers.

The objective of the forwards is to score goals. So the *savoir faire* of goal-scoring is a subject that must claim their earnest attention. Any remark on this subject by so prolific a goal-getter as T. Pethick, the wonder that came out of the West, is entitled to a respectful hearing. This remarkable player says: "A good eye, quick action, and judgment in knowing exactly when to strike and where to send the ball," constitute the secret of scoring goals. Yes, "where to send the ball." How few forwards really place their shots! The majority of forwards shoot as hard as they know how, straight at the goal, untroubled by any thought of placing the ball with a slower shot, if needs be, to right or left of the goal-keeper and into the corners of the net.

In watching Shoveller on one of his field days—and he has a good many in the year—one is impressed by these facts: that he seldom shoots from the edge of the circle, that he sacrifices pace in shooting to placing, and that a large percentage of his goals are pushed into the net from almost under the goal-keeper's nose. Shoveller knows by experience that shots from the edge of the circle seldom score, and knowing this tries a better way. What so embarrasses the goal-keeper is, not the long shooting, but that quick, short game which brings the attack to close quarters and keeps him in a frenzy of doubt as to the time, direction, and agent of the shot.

Players like Shoveller, Pethick, and Jordan, who have a genius, all their own, for scoring goals, sometimes appear to be superior to and independent of the need for combination in the circle, but the general rule is that combination in the circle is the *sine qua non* of effective forward play, and its complement.

Now that the penalty corner is the punishment for all infringements by the defenders in the circle, except those that merit the harsher penalty of the penalty bully, it is important that a right treatment of corners should be understood and practised. The utterly slovenly and unthinking manner in which corners are sometimes negotiated is a disgrace. When the corner is an ordinary one, from the right wing say, pace on the ball is the essence of the contract. If the ball goes to inside right he will either stop it with his stick and instantly shoot, or else he will field it with his hand and quickly get out of the way for the centre forward, who is at his elbow, to make the shot. This latter method is simpler and more effective when it is a left-wing corner. In this case the centre forward will field the ball with his right hand, thereby enabling inside left to take the shot with the least possible delay. The method is mightily effective in the case of penalty corners. An old way, which one seldom sees nowadays, was for the centre forward to stop the ball with the sole of his left foot. This had the merit of quickness. Another method, possible only to a player with a cast-iron wrist, and suspiciously like an illegality, was for a forward to field the ball with his left hand in such a manner that he could get the ball on the half-volley with a one-handed hit. This method was formerly employed, and to some purpose, by forwards here and there, chiefly in Ireland. It was quicker than the other methods, but it has died out. Few wrists were strong enough for the one-handed stroke, while more often than not it was a case of " hand-ball."

As to the definite qualities of mind and body necessary to the forwards, they must be fast and quick, quick to think and quick to act, clever with their sticks, not afraid of hard knocks, and eminently unselfish.

RIGHT TREATMENT OF A CORNER FROM THE LEFT, CENTRE FORWARD
FIELDING THE BALL FOR INSIDE LEFT TO SHOOT.   THIS METHOD IS
SPECIALLY EFFECTIVE IN THE CASE OF A PENALTY CORNER

The Centre Forward

He must be endowed with certain very definite mental gifts, a player of special parts and characteristics. Much the same mental equipment which distinguishes great military leaders informs the model centre forward. This player fills a position of such strategic scope. Had he been a hockey player, what a grand centre forward the Duke of Wellington would have made—if it is not sacrilege to compare great things with small. And Napoleon too, although his genius would, perhaps, have controlled the game better from centre half.

To fill successfully the post of centre forward a player needs to have a brain, and a cunning, creative brain, and much decision of character. The Corinthian football player, G. O. Smith, is always quoted as the perfect type of a centre forward at Association football. He was a player of wonderful foresight and constructive ability. He seemed to look into the future, to see several moves ahead, and was a wonder-worker in the matter of manufacturing, out of the most unpromising material, openings for his confrères. Had he given his best years and his enthusiasm to hockey, he would surely have been to the vanguard of England's hockey team what he was to the vanguard of England's football team. The genius of G. O. Smith's type is as rare in hockey as it is in other games. Decided mental qualities are far less common than physical. There is no lack of centre forwards who can run fast and dribble cleverly, but how few who can control, and guide, and fashion the attack. The centre forward must have plastic powers and great force of character. He and the centre half must be, if no other players on the field are, strong personalities. Let clubs remember this when picking their teams. And incidentally let it be here remarked, that the authorities who pick the players and appoint them to the several positions in the field are seldom influenced in the latter respect by the temperament and character of the

players.   In deciding what position a player shall fill, the
captain, or responsible authority, should take into consideration not only the player's physical, but also his mental,
attributes.   Fancy putting a flabby-minded player at centre
half, or an irresponsible, hair-brained boy at centre forward,
no matter what their physical qualifications for these positions.   And the captain will need to watch for subtle distinctions.   Many players of a sensitive nature will be so
depressed and miserable at being moved from their regular
position to some other in the field, that they will be quite
unable to do themselves justice.   Their indifferent play is
noticed by the captain, but not its cause.   The sympathetic
captain who studies the temperaments of the players under
him will refrain from outraging their sensibilities.

But to return from digression.   The centre forward, then,
must be a player of intellect and much force of character.
He must have the alert eye of a Sherlock Holmes, early
detecting the weak spots in his opponents' armour, and
must quickly seize, as well as quickly see, an opening.   So
much of the game necessarily comes his way that he is in
danger of becoming selfish, especially in the matter of
shooting.   He must eschew the vice of selfishness and
court the opposite virtue.   The temptations to self-parade
will often assail the centre forward.   He must withstand
them, sinking personal ends for the good of his side.   He
must be an apostle of *esprit de corps*.   And yet his individualism is to be allowed proper play.   The striking of
the golden mean is the hall-mark of a great player.

Besides being quick and fast, the centre forward needs
to be a past master in the art of dribbling and a sure
shot.

Seeing that the forward line as it advances up the
ground is of a crescent shape, the centre will be slightly in
the rear of his confrères.   Thus three advantages will
accrue to him : (*a*) he will see clearly what his forward line
is doing; (*b*) he will never be off-side; (*c*) he will be able
to take his passes at top speed, and flash past the opposing

COMBINATION BETWEEN CENTRE FORWARD AND INSIDE RIGHT. THE FORMER ELUDING CENTRE HALF BY PUSH-STROKE FROM LEFT TO RIGHT

backs. The reverse of all this is true of the centre who keeps in front of the other forwards. Quibblers will be found to quarrel with this crescent-shaped forward line. To disarm their arguments it is sufficient to say that to the best of rules there are exceptions, that at times the forward line will take on very different shapes, and that the centre forward will often find it good policy to play in front of his insides. The least that can be said for the crescent-shaped line is that it is a good hold-by for the forwards in mid-field and the foundation of an orderly attack.

Opening up the game is the centre forward's great work. And what is this process which one hears so frequently spoken of and so glibly rolled on the tongue? The disposition of the players at the commencement of a hockey match gives the game a congested appearance. The centre forward is one of the parties to the dissipation of this appearance. This is the first step in the process to compel attack and defence to spread out. When the centre forward has effected so much, he will endeavour to draw back on to himself some member of the defence, who thus drawn leaves unmarked the forward he is responsible for. And choosing just the right moment the centre forward will pass to his unmarked comrade. That is a glimpse of a process of many variants.

It is usually bad policy for the centre forward to miss out the inside forward and pass direct to the wing. But when such a course is necessary he should hit very hard and in a diagonal direction, so that the wing player may take the ball on his stick. Except on these occasions, he should reserve what hard hitting may be necessary for him for the circle.

Shut in as he is in the middle of the ground, and the victim of a certain amount of jostling, the centre forward needs to be supremely resourceful in eluding and slipping past the defence. In this respect, and in most others too, S. H. Shoveller is *facile princeps* among centre forwards. Much may be learnt from a study of his devices, although in many of them he must remain inimitable.   Deception, or illusion, or whatever you like to call it, plays a big part in Shoveller's elusive running, dodging, and dribbling.   He swerves and he feints, and darts this way and that, and all with bewildering suddenness.   Then he has such a wonderful knack of getting his opponents on their wrong leg. This is a knack which the disciples of England's famous centre forward may essay to acquire with some hope of success.

A back likes nothing so little as being to the right of an approaching forward ; so placed he cannot properly tackle him.   The centre forward must give the opposing defence as much as possible of this undesirable position.   No one is so clever at this as Shoveller, who revels in presenting his left shoulder to his opponents.   Slack umpiring, of course, knocks on the head the efficacy of this practice.

These devices, and any others which the centre forward may essay, are vain unless the ball is kept near the stick and under control.   This is the basis of good dribbling. If the ball gets too far in front of him on the right, the centre forward can reach it best by means of the left-hand lunge stroke,—old Rossallians are very quick and clever with this stroke,—if on the left, he will reach for it and hook it across to his right side with the stick transversed and held in the left hand.

In the case of the centre forward the chief medium of a pass is the push and scoop strokes.   The ability to make these strokes quickly and naturally must be acquired.   The manner of making them is described in the chapter dealing with the elements of the game.

When nearing the circle, the centre forward needs to summon all the dash of which he is capable.   And if he shoots at goal let him follow up his shot with energy in the hope of catching the rebound from the goal-keeper, or so flustering that player that he fails to clear.   If another forward has shot at goal, the centre will follow up the shot, although he will occasionally be wise to hang back on the

CENTRE FORWARD, S. H SHOVELLER, FOLLOWING UP SHOT BY INSIDE LEFT, R. G PRIDMORE

chance of trapping the return hits of the defence and so maintaining the attack.

Many centre forwards, good in mid-field, are wretched finishers. They reach the circle by much cleverness, but once within its precincts they become inept and seem incapable of getting the ball into the net. The dash which brings them to the circle must be continued inside it.

Just one warning to the centre forward before leaving him. Let him eschew one-handed play. Here and there a centre forward may employ this ugly method with success, but such cases must be very rare. A capable back or half-back should experience little difficulty in depriving the one-handed player of the ball. The use of one hand only means loss of power and of control.

CHAPTER VI

IN PLAY—THE FORWARD LINE (*continued*)

INSIDE RIGHT

A LTHOUGH the qualifications for, and the duties incident to, the positions of inside right and inside left are very similar, it is seldom that one and the same player is equally at home in either. But possibly this is because, in these days of specialising, players are never given time to test their versatility or to accustom themselves to a change of position. It is usually only by way of a *pis aller* that a player is moved, say, from inside right to inside left. It would be easier for an inside left to turn his shirt and become an inside right than *vice versa*, because he would be exchanging an acquired style of play for one that is natural.

There can be no question that in all respects, save feeding the wing, the inside right fills the easier position. He can dribble, pass to his centre, and shoot naturally, without any of that twisting of the body and straining of the wrists which is required of inside left. Since it is natural for a player to hit from right to left, inside right may find that passing to his wing is the chief difficulty of his position. And so he may be tempted to neglect this player, the very thing above all others that he must not do. There are two considerations with regard to this wing player which inside right needs to ponder well, and act accordingly. Outside right is probably one of the two speediest forwards in the line, and, secondly, likely to be

more often unmarked than any of his confrères, because
of left half's tendency to drift inwards.   So how great the
responsibility of inside right, and how great his privilege
and opportunities !   In mid-field he must be concerned
much more about outside right than about the centre
forward.   Here, in mid-field, the opposing left back is not
yet near enough to threaten inside right.   So the latter,
avoiding the centre half by veering slightly to the right,
faces the task of getting the ball past the opposing left
half to outside right.   And this is where acumen steps in,
or in many cases makes no appearance at all.   If it is
impossible to get a good pass to the wing, inside right
must dribble on himself till the possibility presents itself ;
and by a good pass is meant a pass which will result in
ground being gained and in the attack being prolonged.
It is not a good pass which reaches the wing simultaneously
with the half-back, nor is it a good pass—seldom, at least
—which is hit back instead of forward.

It is the essence of stupidity and bad play for inside
right to persist, as so many do, in passing out to his wing,
despite the fact that the left half just as persistently
intercepts the pass.   But this stupidity is among the
commonest of the many faults of intellect encountered on
the hockey field.   And yet there is a good motive at the
back of it.   It is evidence that inside right wishes to do
his duty by the wing forward, and it is evidence also of
unselfishness ; and unselfishness is a large part of the
the make-up of an inside right.

As the game nears the circle, and as inside right closes
in towards his centre, he will give more of his attention to
this player.   If the ball is in possession of the right-
wing player, inside right must watch keenly for the express
centre which is sure to come, field it with his stick and
dribble on, or, if in the circle, essay a swinging shot, or
leave it to the centre forward, whichever seems best, whether
of these courses or of the many others which lie open
to him.

Combination between him and the centre forward must be of the intimate order. The finest combination of inside right and centre probably ever seen is the Logan-Shoveller combination. Paired together in Club, County, Divisional, and International hockey, Logan and Shoveller have such an intimacy with one another's methods, and such a perfect mutual understanding, that telepathy is almost suggested. Their play is an object lesson in combination. And yet perhaps it is scarcely the model for young players to copy. Their combination is at times a little exclusive. The right wing occasionally gets neglected. Probably this is in the interests of the particular game in which these two players are taking part,—geniuses they should be styled,—but as a general thing exclusiveness of this sort is not in the interests of a game. Other considerations apart, the most effective combination in hockey is certainly that of Logan and Shoveller. And inside rights may learn from Logan's play what backing up is, what supporting a centre forward is, what it is to manœuvre for receiving, as well as giving, a pass, and what it is to shoot.

When one of Logan's shots hits the goal-post, one expects to see the post fall in two, so vigorous is his shooting.

More opportunities for shooting at goal come the way of inside right than any of the other forwards. He must be a good and a severe shot, and he must shoot on sight. He will do more actual shooting and less finessing than the centre forward. Most of his shots will be from right to left, and the harder these come the better. It would be all easy sailing for him in the circle were it not for the fact that the defence will so often tackle him on his left side and, generally, hamper him. If the tackle is not technically illegal, it frequently results in what, albeit not obstruction in the eyes of the umpire, is obstruction so far as inside right is concerned. Anyhow he is put off his shot, and his opportunity is spoiled. When inside right, about to shoot, perceives a player on the point of tackling him from the left, he may be sorely tempted to turn that player's tackle into a foul by giving him his left shoulder and causing him to touch it before touching the ball. No doubt he sometimes falls before this subtle temptation; but even if it is not strictly illegal his action cannot be suffered to pass as "cricket," although, perchance, it will have the secret sympathy of many a good player and true.

Much cleverness and stick-craft are less essential to inside right than to the other inside forwards. So long as he is unselfish, quick on to the ball, fast, courageous in charging down the hits of the opposing left back, and a daring and accurate shot, he should rise to distinction in his position.

OUTSIDE RIGHT

The easiest position in the field, and one from which players have often graduated for the other forward positions. Many a player now occupying some other position began his hockey career as a right-wing forward. Possessed of a good eye, an athletic physique, and a certain knowledge of the rules, and one who has never handled a hockey stick before will make a respectable showing at outside right. Before hockey had become the scientific game it now is, pace was deemed the sole qualification for a right wing— pace and the ability to centre hard. If a new player was upon the market, the inquiry would be, "Can he run?" and if the reply was in the affirmative, he would be at once installed as a right-wing forward. This was the lot of many an undergraduate down from the 'Varsity for the vacation in those days when hockey was beginning to filch recruits from the football ranks. Pace seemed to be the one criterion, the one test of fitness for a wing position, especially the right wing. Club captains deemed any additional qualification superfluous, and a token that fate had destined the player for another position. And as for a player with unusual pace being named in connection with a vacancy in the back division, the suggestion was absurd.

5

It was quite a comedy, the system on which the players were sorted and the team pieced together. The pace all in the forward line, the small players at half-back, and the heavy-weights at full-back. The system was crude and full of pitfalls, but there was truth in it, and the mark was often hit.

Time stands still in some things, and outside right remains to-day what it was then, the easiest position in the field, while those who fill the position are still the speediest members of the team. But in other respects a great change has been wrought, and the right wing must now be resourceful to a degree if he is to defeat the clever half-back play opposed to him. Besides pace and the ability to hit hard, he must be a cunning dribbler and an adept at that one device above all others which a right wing must employ for outwitting halves and backs. The device is to hit the ball to the right of the opposing back or half-back, and then to run round him on the other side and join the ball. Over and over and over again will it occur during a match that this is the only absolutely right procedure for the right-wing forward to adopt. Neither captains, coaches, nor text books on the game sufficiently emphasise the value and absolute necessity of this mode of attack for an outside right. Its effectiveness, when the device is properly understood and cleverly practised, is so great and so patent, that one marvels at the paucity of players whose game it informs, and at the backwardness of captains and others in insisting upon its use and utility.

All young players, not only right-wing forwards, but the occupants of every position in the field, should be thoroughly taught this device. Constant practice will bring a cleverness and a development which make the device doubly effective. The prince of right-wing forwards, W. M. Johnstone, an Irish player, is an expert at this device. He has reduced it to a fine art, and any one watching him play will see what a great part of his game it is, and imagining him deprived of the right to use it, would

OUTSIDE RIGHT E F. EDGE PARTINGTON) OUTWITTING LEFT HALF-BACK BY HITTING BALL TO THE
RIGHT OF H M AND RUNNING ROUND ON THE OTHER SIDE

understand how the deprivation would deplete his game. Johnstone will run down with the ball, and as he approaches the left back will edge himself slightly to the left, while allowing the ball to be well out on his right and just within reach of the left-hand lunge. Thus he himself is to the left of the back and the ball to the right of that player. At the right moment Johnstone dabs at the ball with his left, and as he is already half past the back, quickly gathers the ball again on the far side, and is away on his free run to the enemy's lines. *Ars est celare artem*, and nothing of his intentions is apparent in Johnstone's manner.

In order to make this device possible and profitable, outside right must leave enough room between himself and the touch-line. If he does not, he will hit the ball into touch. In his endeavour to defeat the back by this device, he must avoid playing the ball too fine—that is, too straight. His hit past his opponent must partake of the diagonal. Otherwise it is certain to be intercepted. The most irritating fault outside right can commit is, with only the back to defeat and then a clear dash for the circle, to leave the ball at that player's feet, either because he hung on to the ball too long, or because his hit to the right of the back was not wide enough. A right wing who is much given to this device may overdo it. The defence will anticipate his intention. Here is an opportunity for resourcefulness on the part of outside right. He must vary his tactics, and practically the only variant is a pass the other way, to inside right. This change of tactics to satisfy the need of the moment marks just the difference between a good and an indifferent player.

Although for the sake of the above device outside right must sometimes play several yards—say four or five —from the touch-line, he will at other times benefit by reducing this distance. By playing near the touch-line he increases the difficulty which the defence will always experience in tackling him. One specific reason for keeping near the touch-line would be a left half-back with a

tendency to drift to the centre.   The opportunity for
racing down the line unimpeded is thus secured, and the
simple task of merely passing in just prior to the left back's
tackle is all that outside right must accomplish.

If he beats the defence, he will pass in when nearly
opposite the circle, sometimes a little later, just according
to circumstances—that is, just according to whether or not
there is a clear avenue for his pass.   And this final centre,
if he is far out on the side line, must be hit very hard.
The secret of getting pace on the ball is timing rather than
brute force, and a correct follow-through.   So many right
wings leave their final centre too late.   They take the ball
almost on to the goal-line before dispatching it to their
inside forwards ; and when they do dispatch it, as likely as
not it is at the wrong angle, across the goal-mouth instead
of back to the edge of the circle.   One fault breeds
another, and right wings who take the ball too far are just
the players to mishandle their centres.   Now and again
outside right is compelled to take the ball nearly to the
corner flag—compelled because he is engaged in a duel
with the left back or left half, and cannot get in his pass.
But he has a possible alternative, one that many a right
wing seems to be wholly unconscious of.   He may pass
back to the right half, who should be there supporting him,
a few yards in his rear.   Such a pass should be feasible,
because unexpected by his opponent, who is striving to
prevent a side and not a backward pass.   If he cannot
yet get rid of the ball in a profitable manner, he must
prevent his opponent doing so, and he must keep the ball
in play.   It is a criminal offence for outside right to hit
the ball over the goal-line,—a wanton sacrifice of an opportunity,—and yet how frequently it is done !

Outside right will increase his usefulness to his side by
varying his game as far as possible.   An occasional bolt
for the circle will be effective, if for no other reason than
because of its unexpectedness.   The defence will be taken
by surprise.   And on another occasion outside right must

be in or near the circle if he would be in his proper place —the occasion of a corner hit from the other wing.   He will take up his position on the edge of the circle, and he must see to it that an intentness upon the passage of the ball marks his conduct.   The ball will not infrequently come to his edge of the circle.   He must field it with his stick, and shoot without hesitation.   In a whole season he may not score more than a couple of goals.   This need not disturb him.   It is no reflection on his proficiency. The fact is that even when outside right does reach the circle his chance of scoring is remote.   He generally has to shoot from a difficult angle.   In or near the circle the quality of dash is essential to this player, as it is to all the forwards.

A duty he must perform in the case of a corner hit from the left wing is to field the ball if missed by the other forwards.   Having regard to the fact that the ball is hit from the goal-line and will therefore be travelling outwards, it will be necessary for him to stand a few yards outside the circle and on a level, or slightly behind, the other forwards.   If the ball has been hit correctly, he will field it outside the circle.   His part is to return it at once to the players on the edge of or inside the circle.

In taking a corner from his own wing, he must hit very hard, keeping his eye glued to the ball, paying great attention to the follow-through, and aiming at the centre forward. The aim must be adjusted first, so that the eye need not be lifted from the ball.   And if by some evil chance he misses the ball, fails to touch it, he may whack at it till he does.   Hockey is not golf.   Mention is made of this because players—ignorant players, of course—have been known to refrain from a second attempt at hitting the ball, under the belief that their attempt would have been punishable.   If, however, the ball is so much as touched, a second hit before another player has touched it is illegal.

In the case of a penalty corner, outside right will moderate the vigour of his hit.

Before the present roll-in rule, the duty of rolling-in devolved upon outside right. Now the half-back performs this function, and outside right must toe the 5-yards line. A good variety of combined tactics is possible, but the simple roll down the line gives outside right the best chance to use his pace. Wing forwards are apt to be very remiss in matters of defence. Occasionally they are bound to help their back, while they must always worry the half-back or back who has filched the ball from them.

Easy as the position is, good right-wing forwards are comparatively rare—a wholly unaccountable circumstance. It is many years since England had a really great player in this position. A famous right-wing combination of the late nineties was that of C. H. M. Ebden and J. H. Horne, a product of Cambridge University. The former played on the wing, and with his hockey skill suplemented by fine athletic qualities, was the beau ideal of an outside right, and a type of which nature is anything but prodigal. W. M. Johnstone has already been mentioned, and if only every young candidate for proficiency at outside right could study at first hand the play of this famous exponent, there would soon be less scarcity of good right wings in the land.

INSIDE LEFT

So much of what is true of one position is also applicable to another. Therefore the danger of repetition. But repetition is not always a thing to avoid. It is sometimes beneficent—the hammer rap that startles the attention and emphasises what is important. Thus, when considering inside left, a position of close similarity to centre forward, repetition is first inevitable and then wise, and wise because the avoidance of repetition might lead the unwary reader into the mistake of supposing that certain qualifications necessary for a centre were not necessary also for an inside left because mention of them had been omitted from the treatment of the latter position.

To the average player who has tried the various positions in the field, inside left is the one he finds least comfortable and most awkward. What makes it thus is the necessity it imposes on the player of much turning of the body from left to right before anything profitable can be done with the ball. Especially is this so when the circle is reached. The ball is to the player's left and the goal to his right, and consequently shooting a difficult matter. And in this connection a fault to which inside left is very prone is the blind obstinacy of persisting in an endeavour to shoot when a shot is certain to be fruitless, and when the right course is to pass back or in to his centre, or to his left wing, if that player chances to be close to the circle. When a pass comes to him from the right, or when he is square to the goal with the ball on his right side, then it is both easy and fitting for inside left to shoot. And yet in spite of his difficulties in the circle, perhaps because of them, inside left—a good inside left, that is—scores many goals. The explanation lies here, that so many of his tries for goal are in the nature of a push stroke from left to right across the goal-keeper and towards that player's left hand—the most difficult shot with which a goal-keeper must deal. For the right execution of this stroke—and the stroke will be as necessary in mid-field as in the circle—inside left requires strong and supple wrists.

If the ball is too far to his left and his body turned too much that way, this diagonal push stroke is impossible, and inside left must cast about for an alternative. The only one to hand, apart from hitting the ball to some one else, is the reverse stroke, so successfully employed by T. Pethick—the most resourceful inside left of all time. But this stroke is difficult and Pethick a wonder, which to the average player must mean that the stroke is only a last resource. As Pethick was ambidextrous—the past tense is used in view of his retirement from first-class hockey—his reverse stroke came with sting and accuracy from his stick. He scored plenty of goals that way, and not a few with his left hand alone. H. R. Jordan, another famous inside left, is so cunning in his control of the ball that he seldom suffers it to be outside the scope of the push stroke, and thus seldom exploits the reverse stroke for actual shooting, although his reversed stick is busy enough during one of those tortuous dribbles for which he is noted.

When Pethick and Eric Green played side by side for Staines and England, then was seen a left-wing combination, brilliant, remarkable, and for effectiveness never matched. Unlike so many left-wing pairs, these two brilliants were always in touch, never so separated as to be no longer a combination. Even when the game took Pethick away from his partner to the circle, he was not unmindful of Green, who, like the wise player he is, himself closed in, ready to have the ball tipped on to him in the event of Pethick finding no avenue for a direct shot. Intelligence of this sort is the very essence of combination. Inside left is so dependent upon his wing partner that he is shorn of much effectiveness if that player is not in complete sympathy with him. This is why personal friends usually combine so well. Each plays for the other's hand as well as for his own, not blindly and without premeditation, but advisedly, in fulfilment of a well-thought-out plan, discussed and elaborated off the field. One would like to see far more of this in hockey — friendships off the field as combinations on the field, and councils of war preceding victorious play. No team was ever great that would not have been still greater had *esprit de corps* been stronger and social intimacy among its members. The failure of many an International team is the lack of personal intimacy amongst its members, several of whom are probably meeting and playing together for the first time. Who would look for the finest sort of combination from such a heterogeneous circumstance? If there is to be combination of the first water, there must be real comradeship among the players. Pethick and Green were "Tom" and "Eric" to one another off and on the field, a fact which throws a pleasant little sidelight—despite the smile of the reader who lacks imagination—on one of the causes of their effectiveness in double harness. When members of a team use the Christian name in calling to one another on the field, it is pretty certain that here is a team with *esprit de corps*, with a good record, and with a right to enjoy their hockey.

This is less digression than appears, because inside left occupies such a central position, with a player on either side of him, that any lack of mutual confidence and understanding between him and the fellow-members of his team will abridge his personal skill.

In mid-field play inside left must, speaking a little loosely, follow one of three courses—pass to his wing, pass to his centre, or dribble on himself. If the last, it must be merely as a means to an end—the end the scoring of a goal, not self-advertisement. An individual dribble must be abandoned the moment the end in view is more likely to be attained by the medium of a pass. And what are the signs of such a moment? When the centre half is about to tackle him from behind, and the right back from in front, inside left is at the moment when a pass is the right thing. The situation is clearly one that demands a pass to his centre. This will be a diagonal push pass to a point a few feet in front of the centre forward, so that the latter may take it at full dash. But let inside left have a care of one thing. If he leave his pass till the back is almost on him, and if his centre is ahead of him, his pass may find that player in an offside position. Or the right back might deliberately run in to put the centre forward offside. In either case, inside left must hold back his pass.

If the way to his centre is blocked and to dribble on is fraught with danger, he must pass to his wing, and that he can do only if the right half is out of the way, or if a pass hit well ahead could be reached by outside left before it crossed the side line, or before one of the opposing side could reach it. If there is no immediate opening to his wing, he must create an opening by dribbling towards the half.

This will either lure that player inwards or push him to retreat. If the former, inside left will soon find a way round him for a pass ; and if the latter, he must retain the ball awhile, or possibly send it to the attendant left half. There is always a way out, but he must be definite and instant.

The crucial stage of the attack is the near approach to the circle, when the three middle forwards need to be near together, and when dash and combination are essential and the harbingers of success. But dash is so likely to upset combination and to result in individual scrambling after goals. Let inside left beware of this tendency, and another of the dangers of dash—the hitting of the ball too far in front. His endeavour must be to ally dash with control. Let him also avoid dribbling to the left of the goal, and nearly to the goal-line. Many goals are lost this way. A corner hit from the left will be fielded by the centre forward for inside left, who will take the shot—the best of all methods.

At the half-way bully inside left will stand close to his centre, not more than two or three yards away. At the roll-in from touch, whichever side is taking it, he will stand at the 5-yards line, careful to mark an opponent if it is defence, and quick to place himself in communication with the roller-in if it is attack.

Upon inside left, as upon inside right, devolves the task of rushing the opposing backs. This requires not a little nerve ; but it is encouraging to note that good backs will seldom hit into a player, and that the nearer inside left gets to the ball the less likely is he to get hurt. This latter consideration should lend wings to his feet. Akin to this somewhat unenviable duty is that of following up shots at goal in the hope of catching the rebound from the goal-keeper, or of trapping his clearing hit or kick, or of flustering him into a blunder. And here emphasis should be laid upon the importance of the three inside forwards following up one another's shots.

Finally, inside left must be quick and wristy, an adroit

handler of his stick, and careful to avoid the body obstruction which his position makes so easy of commission.

OUTSIDE LEFT

The position is an interesting one to discuss because of its many difficulties. Few players perform these with facility or distinction. Outside lefts are manufactured by the gross every year, but very few indeed are masterpieces. In ladies' hockey, where most clubs have a special coach, either some old International or some former games mistress of a girls' school, or some qualified instructor, good outside lefts are fairly plentiful. Left alone, they would have muddled along and played according to the light of nature, with success only in the case of genius, but, carefully taught the duties and methods of their position, they fall into a style of play which, if stereotyped, is at least free from the *gaucherie* and active mistakes of the untutored. In men's hockey it is different. Save for a chance word of advice or admonition from the captain, there is practically nothing that can be called coaching. This is a grave defect. Of course, there is the usual interchange of ideas on all things hockey by the players, in the train on the occasion of an out-match, in the dressing-room, or wherever they may chance to foregather; but of practical coaching none. So players must learn on the field by personal experience, and from the play of others. Experience is an excellent school, but in the case of outside left most emphatically it should be preceded by individual instruction.

There is a conventional type of playing at outside left which players lacking enterprise and creative ability follow like sheep. They become horribly stereotyped. It is down the wing to a given point, then a right turn, and, no matter what the circumstances, an almighty slog into the centre. The harder the hit, the greater their pleasure and self-complacency. This is the eternal thing that discolours so much club hockey. Want of thought, too great impulsiveness, and obsession with the idea that a terrific bang to the circle is the be-all and end-all of outside left play, form the root of this common tendency.

Watch that great player, the greatest of all outside lefts, Eric Green, and mark how he nurses his opportunities, instead of dissipating them by too conventional practices, and makes his famous right-angled hit from touch-line to circle only when wisdom dictates, not because it is the fashionable thing to do.

The very essence of intelligent hockey is to diversify one's methods. An outside left who becomes stereotyped must also become increasingly ineffective. His opponents come to know exactly the when, the what, and the how of his action. So they can easily either anticipate it or make provision against its effectiveness.

In lieu of his right turn and bang to the centre, let outside left now and then try a dead stop, so that the pursuing player shall overrun him, and then either a pass of moderate pace to inside left or a continuation of his own run, or let him try a dash for the circle. Let him ring the changes on these and any other alternatives prompted by circumstances or by his own resourcefulness and strategic brain. No player will ever be great as an outside left who cannot pass in to the centre while going at top speed. This is the most difficult accomplishment required of him. It is done by means of body turn, a half right turn of the body from the hips up. The position of the feet and legs is almost the same as though the hit were straight down the field. The stick is not taken far back, the stroke being essentially one of the wrist and forearm, but with plenty of follow-through. It is a quick shot, otherwise it would not be necessary, and correct timing is its complement. Eric Green—a household word wherever modern hockey light shines—is the greatest exponent of this stroke.

If the player who makes this shot well is also a cricketer, he is certain to have an offside shot past extra cover, so akin are the two shots.

ERIC GREEN MAKING HIS FAMOUS CENTRE FROM OUTSIDE LEFT WHILE
RUNNING AT TOP SPEED BY MEANS OF A HALF RIGHT TURN OF THE BODY

And the time to get rid of the ball by means of this shot is a stride or two before the 25-yards flag is reached—provided, of course, that attendant circumstances do not render this inopportune. If they do, then outside left must try a full stop, a deliberate right turn, and a hard hit into the centre. The object of his centring at the point advocated is that the inside forwards may take his pass at full speed, a circumstance far more likely to result in a goal than if they had to wait stationary for his pass on the edge of the circle. On this account, taking the ball down to the corner flag, although often necessary and desirable, is not a commendable practice. Should outside left find himself near the corner flag, or near the goal-line outside the circle, he must pass back to the inside forwards, waiting just inside the circle.

To minimise the difficulties of his position, outside left must play near the touch-line, always within that and the 5-yards line. When he gets a fast bumpy pass, let him field it with his hand—the safest of all methods, provided time does not press. Often a pass will come fast and ahead of him which will be wasted over the side line unless with stick reversed and extended in his left hand—the most telescopic means at his disposal—he can stop the ball. A strong wrist is necessary for this, quickness, and much practice. An alternative stroke is the same thing with the right hand; but the disadvantage attaching to this is the fact that the right shoulder and right side of the body may shut out the sight of the ball.

Outside left must be an adept at the two-handed reverse stroke. It is often the last resource left to him. And the beauty of it is that this stroke is best and most easily made when the player is going at top speed. It is really a wrist flick with the point of the stick. Irish players seem to employ it more and better than English. F. M. Hewson, a distinguished Irish left-winger, is the first exponent of this emergency stroke: not that it is an emergency stroke in his case; it is an active part of his

game.   In the few minutes of practice which usually
precede an International match, Hewson will run down the
field and practise this stroke at the expense almost of all
others, thus clearly showing that he at least regards it as a
valuable asset of his play and a stroke that requires and
deserves much practice.   First-class players will sometimes
belittle the importance and need of this stroke, but that is
because they cannot make it effectively themselves, and
therefore do not find it useful.

Every outside left should practise assiduously to perfect
himself at this stroke—not with a view to its usurping the
place of the orthodox hit, but in order that when the
occasion arises for its use it may be made with confidence
and effect.   And not even constant practice will assure
certainty.   The player who brought it off successfully time
and again one day, will break down over the stroke as
often the next.

Outside left is in constant peril of putting himself
between an opponent and the ball.   He is in full view of
the umpire, his every twist or turn cruelly exposed, and
ready to be interpreted as obstruction.   So he must be
very careful.   Circling round the ball from right to left,
besides being bad hockey and wasteful of time, is the
shortest possible cut to a penalty.   Hitting between the
feet is another short cut.   In fact, he is never really safe
unless facing towards his opponents' goal.

In one respect outside left has a decided pull over
outside right.   As it is easier to hit to the left than to the
right, outside left will, in the normal order of things, receive
more passes than outside right, although the growing
proficiency in the push stroke is minimising this advantage.
This pleasant fact should go far to console him for the
many limitations and difficulties of his position.

CHAPTER VII

IN PLAY—THE BACK DIVISION

GOAL-KEEPER

THE post of goal-keeper is still with us ; it has withstood the trend of circumstances, and refuses to become the anachronism many have sought to make it. And what are the forces that have imperilled the retention of the goal-keeper in hockey ? For utilitarian purposes, and in some cases because of the difficulty in securing good goal-keepers, numbers of clubs have from time to time adopted the three backs or the four half-backs system. In recent years the practice has become all too common, to the detriment of hockey. And among the converts to this heresy are some of the leading Metropolitan clubs—Staines and Southgate, to name two signal examples. Small wonder, then, that goal-keepers have at times trembled for their avocation. But the arguments against these heretical systems are so much more urgent than those for that they are never likely to become general, and certainly never to obtain in International matches.

And seeing that this question so nearly affects the goal-keeper, it will not be irrelevant to touch upon it here.

From the spectator's point of view, the four half-backs game (and the three backs game scarcely less) is an absolute spoil-sport. Under the good old-fashioned disposition of the eleven players, a hockey team is like a machine, and a first-class team like a machine in good working order. But when such a team meets the four half-backs game, the result is as often as not dislocation and a machine no longer smooth-working. The inevitable answer to this will be that such was the very result aimed at by the opposing team. But the edge of this answer is turned when it is shown, as it easily can be, that the four half-backs work the self-same disorder in their own team as they do in that of their opponents. The tendency is for combination to suffer, and for the game to degenerate into a scramble, a rabble, a congested medley, which parodies hockey at its best, and irritates spectators by robbing them of their enjoyment.

If hockey is to become popular as a spectacle, it must cleave to the orthodox disposition of the players. Furthermore, it is a fallacy to suppose that any real advantage is to be gained by abolishing the goal-keeper and substituting for him an extra back or half-back. That some teams have done this and imagined it to pay is no argument in its favour. Because a thing succeeds, it is not therefore necessarily right. Given two teams of equal strength, the one with and the other without a goal-keeper, and the former will always win. Provided the circle can be reached, goal-scoring is made comparatively easy when no gloved and padded defender stands between the posts. Twelve feet of undefended space would be at the absolute mercy of such quick and deadly shots as Logan, Shoveller, and Pridmore, England's three inside forwards on so many occasions, and joint scorers in the Olympic contests of 1908 of some 20 goals. And even if one of the backs does drop back into goal in an emergency, misunderstandings are certain to arise, and in the nature of things he cannot prove so reliable as a regular goal-keeper.

So the goal-keeper is likely to remain one of the permanent institutions of hockey.

When regard is had to the manifold hardships of goal-keeping and to the uninspiring nature of the goal-keeper's duties, it seems strange that players are so ready to fill the post. In many cases, indeed, this readiness amounts to enthusiasm, and there are goal-keepers who entertain the same ardent affection for their office as do backs, forwards, and halves for theirs. They practise and train for the special requirements of their position with the utmost zest, and bear with equanimity the idle afternoons they chance to spend between the posts. So there must be excitements and rewards—as indeed there are—in goal-keeping which are not apparent to the lay eye.

But it will be well for the sake of those who purpose becoming goal-keepers to paint the dark side of the picture first, not to discourage them from their intention, merely to prepare them against disappointments. To be fore-warned is to be forearmed.

A goal-keeper gets many and hard knocks. His position is one of danger. The enemy's guns are turned full upon him. He is the centre of their hottest broadsides. Whether shots are at long or at short range, travelling slow or flying fast, he must do his best to stop them, interposing hand or foot, stick or person. Then his comrades-in-arms often accentuate the perils of his position. In their proper eager-ness to resist the attack they throng the goal and interrupt his view of the ball. For his own safety's sake and that of his goal it is essential that the goal-keeper should have a clear and unimpeded vision of the ball all the way from the stick of the attacking forward. Nothing is so likely to result in the dual disaster of injury to the goal-keeper and the defeat of his skill as this imperfect and interrupted view of the ball. Against really good forwards the dangers of goal-keeping are far less than against third-rate players, because the former place their shots to right and left of the goal-keeper, often with a gentle, persuasive push, instead of hitting into him with brutal directness.

And while the goal-keeper is exposed to so much danger, he is himself a grave source of danger to his opponents, and not infrequently to his own comrades, if this is any consola-tion. His flying hits, often rising head-high, and his lofted kicks, are a menace to the whole circle. He must remember, however, that the better the goal-keeper the less dangerous

6

the game he plays, because it is bad hockey to hit or kick into a player. The object of the goal-keeper must be to hit or kick the ball clear away to a place of safety. One of the surest signs of bad hockey is this barbarous practiçe of hitting into players. It is thoughtless and brutal, and never necessary, although occasionally excusable, and sometimes, in the case of the goal-keeper, practically unavoidable. Unfortunately it is not confined to goal-keepers, but is a malpractice into which all players of reckless and slogging propensities are apt to fall.

In addition to dangers from ball, stick, and person of his opponents, the goal-keeper is subjected to all the rigours of the weather. He will experience the whole gamut of meteorologic vicissitudes, from a drizzling rain to a howling blizzard. But provided the inner and outer man are adequately fortified, he will find his calling a bracing and healthy one.

In view of the dangers and rigours to which the goal-keeper is exposed, his equipment is a matter of the first importance. Assuming that the temperature is what it should be in the hockey season—low rather than high—he must be warmly clad. Nothing saps the courage and energy from a player so much as coldness and numbness in body and limbs. A thick vest, a flannel shirt, a substantial sweater, and a muffler should resist all save the bitterest cold, provided circulation is aided by sentry-go from goal-post to goal-post, or by the more vigorous exercise of running to and from the edge of the circle. To keep the hands warm, comfortably, but not tightly, fitting gloves should be worn, the material of that sort which will allow a firm grip of the particular handle the player affects. Cricket pads are now worn by all good goal-keepers, and over a pair of thick stockings will keep the legs sufficiently warm. Both gloves and pads, besides preserving the goal-keeper from cold, prove a most valuable defensive asset, enabling him to stop with impunity shots which would otherwise cause sore or broken bones. The boots worn by

EQUIPPED FOR GOAL-KEEPING—H. WOOD, A FAMOUS ENGLISH
GOAL-KEEPER

some goal-keepers are fearsome things, amorphous masses of leather, corrugated with strips of cane or indiarubber, fashioned to resist the hardest of shots and hardest of balls. Whether such boots handicap more than they help or no, the goal-keeper should see to it that his boots are strong and well guarded on the inside, as he will be required to stop many a shot with this part of the foot.

Needed for strong rather than delicate work, his stick should be heavy, anything from 23 oz. upwards.

Thus fully accoutred the goal-keeper may set out to play the game. And in the following attempt to instruct him a blunt and imperative method is employed.

Stand in the middle of the goal, if anything rather to the left, so that the right hand, right foot, and stick may guard the greater part of the goal, and stand, in play, at least a foot over the goal-line. This latter necessity is obvious. Hold the stick in the right hand. Concentrate the attention upon the play, and as the opposing forwards approach the circle move towards the side where the ball is. Thus, if it is with the attacking left wing, move to the right of the goal. When the forwards enter the circle let vigilance be redoubled. If a shot comes from the edge of the circle, it will, or should, be a fast one. Keep cool and take your time. Indulge not in a flying hit, but stop the ball with hand or foot and hit it hard away to the touch-line. If the shot is a bad one, a slow one that comes lobbing along, beware! This is the sort that so often scores. Treat it with respect. Get well in front of it, and, above all, hold back the flying hit you are so tempted to indulge. Is the shot from the right wing, move to the left and face the shooter squarely, and if from the left wing act accordingly. The angle at which the shot is taken will decide you as to how far to the left or right you move.

When the forwards shoot at close quarters, spread yourself out, ready for shots to right or left of you. Decide on your action at once, and act promptly. Hesitation spells a goal. You have many defensive agents—hand, foot, leg, body, head, stick; be prepared to use them all! Good forwards place their shots. Try to anticipate their intention. If you are cunning enough you may even practise little deceptions upon them. Such forwards as Shoveller will practise deceptions upon you. He will come close up to you and persuade the ball into the right-hand corner of the net, when by all the laws of common sense and anatomy he ought to have shot into the left-hand corner. But Shoveller is a genius, and so superior to such trivialities as common sense and anatomy. Unless you are a genius yourself, do not attempt to meet a genius with his own weapons. Stay-at-home goal-keepers are fair game for forwards who shoot at short range. "To attack is to defend" is a well-worn aphorism, but one that goal-keepers do not practise often enough. So go out of goal more often to these clever, pushful forwards who finesse the ball into goal rather than shoot it there. No one has played against forwards of this school, the English school, and, of course, the best school, more often in representative matches than E. P. C. Holmes, the Irish goal-keeper. And frequently during the course of a match does this very original player deem it best to venture forth and meet the English attack. But he picks his opportunities and occasions for so doing. Nothing is more fatal than indiscriminate rushing out of goal. When a forward has got clean away by himself, and is bearing down on the goal all unmolested, go out to meet him, and the farther the better. It is your only hope. Do not waver, but do not rush headlong at him. If you do, he will quietly hit the ball to one side of you and run round on the other, and a goal will result.

Then beware the flying hit. Use it only when delay is dangerous, or when you can get nothing else but your stick in the way of the ball. For this you need a good eye, as you also do if you are to be a successful goal-keeper. When you do essay this flying hit, do so with confidence. Let there be no half measures, no tentative tap. Bang at the

GOAL-KEEPER CLEAR NG BY KICKING—A METHOD FOR EMERGENC ES

ball heartily, but control your stick, despite the customary leniency of umpires to goal-keepers.

Use your feet. Remember that you are privileged to use your feet in a manner permitted to no other player. Your privilege, however, is limited to the circle. Outside this area you are, in respect to your feet, as other players; so never roam too far afield. All good goal-keepers kick the ball, and where the forwards are quick to follow up their shots it is perhaps the safest method of saving. But whether you hit or kick the ball, keep your eye upon it—an elementary but necessary injunction, so seldom is it really observed.

When your side toe the goal-line for a corner, see to it that not more than one other player beside yourself stands in the mouth of the goal. On the occasion of a penalty corner the number in goal should be not less than three.

Do not concede a corner unless every other way of saving a goal is closed to you. It should be the last resort. Deliberate hitting over the goal-line results in a penalty corner, taken 5 yards from the near goal-post, and with good shots among the opposing forwards a goal is highly probable.

Penalty bullies are rare. That is well if it implies what it seems to imply—universally clean and scrupulous hockey. In reality it means that umpires are chary of imposing so drastic a penalty. But players must not take advantage of this.

The goal-keeper must never incur a penalty bully. To do so is an almost certain goal, as the foul will usually take place right in front of goal, and the goal-keeper unversed and unpractised in the art of "bullying" will stand little chance against the picked champion of the other side. Then he is put at a still further disadvantage by the fact that he may not use his feet during the progress of a penalty bully. Should he so far forget himself as to do so, the umpire must give a penalty goal against his side. So do nothing to incur a penalty bully.

And remember that goal-keeping is not solely defensive. You can and must help your side to attack. Pass, when it is safe, to one of your own forwards, that one whom you consider to be in the most favourable position for attacking. In most cases this will be a wing forward.

As a final piece of active advice, always get a little preparatory practice before a match. You will never want for players to shoot at you. The practice will loosen your joints, warm your blood, get your eye in, and give you confidence.

The Backs

There is a popular delusion that a back need not possess pace. The truth is that unless he does he can never rise above mediocrity. It must be his first qualification. Is a forward losing the keen edge of his pace, then shunt him to the half-back line or still farther back, was formerly—and probably still is—the accepted policy in places where hockey light shone but dimly. In truth the extent of a player's deterioration came to be measured by the position he occupied. It was a sort of graduated scale, a player's tenancy of the post of goal-keeper marking the last stage in his decay. Players who had arrived at this last shift would taunt their friends with " You're coming, you're coming back ; you'll soon be with us." Nor are prominent clubs entirely free from this tendency. Veterans who have become stiff of limb and slower by several yards in fifty than they were, are retained in the team as backs, or extra backs, or flying halves with a roving commission, but no suggestion of flight in their movements. It may be that the committee have not the heart to pass sentence of eviction upon them, or that there are no young players to take their place ; but there it is, and the impression is created that the rear-guard is the place for encumbrances, and that pace and quickness are not the *sine qua non* of a back. There is just this reservation, however, that many a veteran back who has lost something of his youthful pace makes good this deficiency by virtue of his experience and judgment, and is thus often of greater value to his side than a younger player who is fleeter of foot but less experienced. One consideration which makes the possession of pace so important for a back, and which may easily be overlooked, is the fact that he must go in to meet forwards already at top speed, and if he fail to check, or if he overshoot them, must face about and pursue them. What chance would a slow-footed back have in such circumstances? So a back needs to be speedy, quick at turning, and fast into his stride.

Then he must be a powerful hitter, not a slogger, but hard and clean on to the ball, with plenty of forearm, and that final snap of the wrists which adds sting to the stroke. It is so easy for a back to degenerate into a slogger. There are many painful instances on record of such degeneracy. To watch some backs, no one could imagine that a rule existed forbidding the raising of the stick either in its backward or forward swing above the shoulder. During the past few years the Irish backs have earned for themselves a considerable reputation for " sticks." No doubt the umpiring in Ireland is to blame, but whatever the cause, there it is, as the Irishmen have learnt to their cost when visiting England, because English umpires, of whom M. Baker has long been king, and G. H. Morton a worthy second, insist on a strict observance of the rules. On the occasion of their visit to England in connection with the Olympic Games, the Irish scarcely transgressed at all in this respect, and the brothers Peterson, hitherto arch-offenders, so curbed their sticks that they seldom drew the whistle.

It is urgent, therefore, that a back should cultivate a lawful style of hitting. As to the back swing he must exercise restraint, while as to the forward swing he can obviate the risk of " sticks" by turning his hands and wrists over from right to left at the end of the follow-through. H. S. Freeman, regarded as among the finest exponents of back play, does this to a very noticeable degree, and the Petersons hardly less, that is judging from their play in the Olympic contest.   But it is possible to hit hard and fairly without employing this method.   Although a back should be a hard hitter he must temper this power with discretion.   He must not hit so hard that forwards cannot reach and gather his drives—or passes, as they frequently should be.   After watching a debauch of hard slogging by backs in a country match, on a rough ground, it is as delightful as it is educating to see a first-class back, skilled and self-contained, despatching gentle passes in lieu of wild hits to his forwards, backing them up and pressing home the attack.   That is hockey. The other may be enthusiasm, but unfortunately, or rather fortunately, it is not hockey.

It is essential, too, that a back should field well with hand, foot, and stick, be *au fait* with all the strokes of the game, and understand the art of dribbling; not that he will find it desirous to use this last-named at all frequently, but his mere knowledge of it will greatly aid him in coping with those whose part it is to exploit it.   The extent of a back's dribbling is seldom more than a few swift passes with his stick and then a quick clear.   And everything preliminary to the clearing stroke is unnecessary if the clearing stroke is possible without it.   It constitutes just so much delay.   With the rules regarding "fouls" so strict, the devices open to a hockey player are very limited.   How, for example, shall a back in possession of the ball and with an opponent charging him down evade the latter?   The method *par excellence* is for him to tap the ball gently to the right of the on-charging player and step quickly to the left, rejoining the ball when the danger—as represented by the on-charging forward—is past, as it instantly and inevitably will be.

What is true for one player is often true for another, and to the back as to the goal-keeper the warning must be —beware the flying hit.   On a bumpy ground the risk is too great, or when the ball is a foot or more from the ground.   A team who possess a back prone to the flying hit are a team of many anxious moments. And what burdens such a back imposes upon his partner! The latter must leave the protection of his own territory to cover these wholly unnecessary indiscretions.

And where shall the backs stand, how far behind the half-backs? is a question constantly asked. There can be no final answer to this question. Circumstances must decide the conduct of the backs in this respect. Slow backs will, of course, stand farther from the halves than fast ones. In attack the backs will do well to lessen the distance between themselves and their forwards so as to crowd in the attack and maintain its continuity. When their forwards are in the circle they should be well up and over the half-way line. And let them always bear in mind that the heavier the ground the nearer should they play to their forwards. Still, although the best way to defend is to attack, there is a danger lest in obeying this maxim the backs hamper the halves and clog the wheels of combination. And if the backs be slow they incur the additional danger of being outdistanced by fast forwards. On the other hand, by standing too deep they allow the opposing forwards to get well into their stride, and to approach too near the circle before attempting to check them. And akin to this is one fatal mistake into which backs are liable to fall—and half-backs too. It is that of retreating before oncoming forwards, instead of going in boldly and un- hesitatingly, but not impetuously, to meet them. To retreat is to bring danger ever nearer to the goal and to curtail the scope of beating off the attack, while to advance is to multiply opportunity. This habit of retreating and retreat- ing before forwards is among the commonest faults seen on the hockey field. Tackle the moment you can is good advice for any back. There are occasions, of course, when to tackle is to invite disaster. But such occasions are perfectly obvious. The right moment for tackling, for darting in to rob the opposing player of the ball, that the back must decide for himself. And he can help himself to this decision by keeping his opponents under close observation. Moreover, he has this in his favour, that his movements and intentions are far less evident to his opponents than theirs are to him. A forward dribbling dare not lift his eyes from the ball; his vision is accordingly limited, and a wily back will often come upon him unawares. This is what a back must aim at. Then a back must often decide on a race for the ball, whether he can get there before the forward or no. And it is not every good player who can successfully judge distances.

The position of his opponent's body and a quick glance at his eyes will often enable a back to anticipate the direction of the former's pass. If it is to the back's right he will thrust out his right foot or his stick, but seldom the hand at close quarters. If the pass is a wide one, the stick held at the end of the handle with the arm fully extended is the only way to stop the ball. The stick may he held in either the right or the left hand. If in the latter, the stroke used will be the " lunge." Alan Jenkins, the finest back that ever came out of the West, employed this " lunge " most effectively on such occasions, while H. S. Freeman invariably affects the right-hand method. If the pass goes the other way, to the back's left side, he will use his left foot, or stick transferred, or the right-hand " cut:" This last stroke is a dangerous one to use in tackling a forward, by reason of the strong likelihood of a foul that it invites.

Dalliance with the ball beyond what is necessary for purposes of outwitting the opposition is fatal in a back. Forwards may toy with the ball and little harm accrue, but disaster will inevitably overtake the back who indulges in " gallery " asides. " Get rid of the ball at once " is a sound principle for backs. Instant action, indeed, must be their guiding star. Finally, the backs should not stand too far from one another, lest a fast centre forward should have a clear run for goal.

RIGHT BACK

Competition is so keen nowadays, and the standard of play so high, that to win distinction a player must specialise. In the old days a back was a back, and no one troubled about such fine distinctions as "right" or "left." If a player was a hard hitter, and possessed certain defensive qualities, he was labelled "back" and put in that position, either right or left, according to circumstances, but not necessarily according to his own preferences, if he had any. Selection committees, or whatever the authority that chose the teams in those days, picked the best individual players and thought lightly of selecting one accustomed to play on the right for the position of left back. This sort of thing was of frequent occurrence, especially in the provinces. Nor was it an altogether mistaken practice. A player's excellence is not always confined to only one position. A good back will not infrequently make an admirable half, and *vice versa*. Indeed, there are instances of players who have filled almost every position on the field with ability and success. One of these versatile players in the short space of three seasons did duty for his county as outside right, outside left, centre forward, right half, and right back. But this was many years ago, and times have greatly changed. No player is granted the opportunity of evincing such versatility. Here and there may be found a player, such as J. H. Pattison, Hon. Secretary of the Army Hockey Association, and as fine a back as any in the country, equally proficient at right as at left back, or one who fills the position of left half as creditably as that of centre half, or a forward who feels as much at home in an inside berth as on the wing. But in first-class hockey such cases become increasingly exceptional. The tendency is ever more and more to specialise. And this is so with backs, although perhaps not to the same extent as in the case of the other places in the field. At one time England's two foremost exponents of back play—H. C. Boycott and H. S. Freeman—were both right backs.   Versatile and resourceful players as they were, neither could play as effectively on the left.   Despite this, however, they were played together for England, which proves nothing except the faith of the Selection Committee in their ability.   This instance is recorded to show, even though it be indirectly, the need for specialising.

It is customary for the right back to play farther up the field than his partner.   Therefore, if one of the two lacks pace it certainly must not be the former.   Pace, as has already been stated, is essential to backs, but especially essential to the right back with his additional ground to cover.

Now the constitution of a hockey team and the disposition of the players are such that in defence the right back will have one player and only one under his immediate surveillance.   This player is his opponents' inside left.   There are no odds at hockey; each player has his *vis-à-vis*, and theoretically a game of hockey is a series of encounters *à deux*.   And it is well to have a theory; it aids discipline, and often proves a corrective memory.   But theory and practice are two different things, and the exigencies of actual play are apt utterly to confound the former.   So, although inside left is his first and particular charge, the right back will not confine his activities to this player.   He will often be called upon to go across and tackle the outside left, and not infrequently to thwart the intentions of the centre forward, especially if that player is of nomadic habits.   And in some special emergency he may not be out of place even on the far right wing.   If a goal is thus saved, no one can charge him with vagrancy, seeing that the saving of goals is the sole objective of defence, just as the scoring thereof is of attack.   Despite this, there is a disposition on the part of certain captains who are determined sticklers for theory and orthodoxy, to growl at players for getting out of position, no matter what the circumstances.   To quote an extreme instance of this—one of these hide-bound captains rebuked a centre half for leaving his conventional sphere of operations to stay the progress of an outside left who had eluded and

A LEG T MATE TACKLE ON THE LEFT

outdistanced the rest of the defence. And this despite the success of the centre half's misdemeanour (?). Nor is this an isolated case, so tyrannical is orthodoxy. This is the fetish that stifles individuality and enterprise. So captains will further the interests of the game in general, and of their team in particular, if they grant more discretionary powers and more latitude to individual players.

As the right back should have as much as possible of the game to his right hand, he should keep slightly to the right of his centre half, or about midway between the opposing centre forward and inside left. In these days of strict umpiring and clean hockey the right back must be wary as to his tackling. So far as tackling the inside left goes, this is simplified by his playing to the left of that forward. In setting out to tackle this player, his object is either to rob him of the ball, or to make him get rid of it, or to spoil or intercept his pass. And it is important to note that if the right back merely makes his opponent pass the ball he has done well, because he has compelled what is far more likely to break down than individual effort, to wit, passing among the forwards.

Quickness and picking the right moment for darting in are the means by which he will rob inside left of the ball; and it will be a matter solely for the stick. For spoiling, that telescopic "lunge" with the left hand or the right hand thrust will be most effective, while for intercepting passes to the centre forward he will use his left foot or his stick reversed. These are the difficult passes to deal with. The passes which go to outside left are much more readily intercepted. And when the right back has trapped the ball and cheated his opponents of it, what shall he do with it? Hit it hard away to the touch-line, if he cannot safely pass it to one of his own forwards, being careful to gain as much ground as possible, and keep the ball as long in play as possible for outside right. Those right-angle slogs out of play are seldom other than unnecessary. Constant hitting out of play is bad hockey, and peculiarly irritating to spectators. A gentle pass to the centre or right half is often a telling substitute for the customary clearing hit. This is all in defence. When his own forwards are attacking, and he has gained possession of the ball through stopping a break away by the opposing front line, he must refrain from hitting it out of play, or too vigorously. Let him pass quickly, because quickness is the essence of the contract, either to the centre forward or inside right, his special charge in attack, but very seldom to the outside right if the forwards are near the circle. To pass to the wing in such circumstances is to give the defence time to block the circle and hamper shooting. For attacking purposes, the right back, as also the left, will often need to use the " push " pass. So let it be one of his acquirements.

When a " corner " is being hit by his own side, he should stand farther to the right in order to intercept the clearing hit of the defence towards touch. And should the right back charge out to the edge of the circle when a " corner " is hit by his opponents? This none too pleasant task belongs to the forwards, and the backs should let it alone, if for no other reason than for this, that " too many cooks spoil the broth."

LEFT BACK

Human nature being what it is, there is nothing surprising in the assertion made by right backs, that, despite the popular idea to the contrary, theirs is the more difficult of the two back positions. Their main contention in support of this assertion is that they have the bulk of the game on their left, whereas left backs have the bulk on their right. But somehow practice does not square with this theory, and in watching a hockey match the impression is that the lot of a left back is more awkward than that of his partner The former so constantly finds himself running towards the touch-line with the play on his left, obliged to use the difficult reverse stroke, or unable to tackle for fear of a foul.

AN ILLEGAL TACKLE ON THE LEFT. THE HALF-BACK (IN SWEATER HAS TOUCHED H S OPPONENT BEFORE THE BALL

Unfortunately for themselves, right backs cannot give the only proof which would establish the truth of their assertion—and we have two such distinguished right backs as H. C. Boycott and H. S. Freeman unable fully to repeat their prowess at left back.

Now, seeing that in defence the left back is responsible for the opposing inside right, he is clearly out of position unless the outside right is some way to his left, and as this wing player is probably the speediest member of the attack, and as it will often fall to the left back to bar his progress, the difficulty of the former's position is obvious. It is so easy for him to foul outside right. That is one thing he must avoid. And if he avoids doing that, and secures the ball, he is in all probability so placed that he can either use only the reverse stroke or else hit out of play, and not much ground gained. Should he be pursuing the wing forward, he must run round and tackle him from the touch-line or right side. This entails loss of time, and he must needs be very fast to overhaul the fugitive. And let the left back make generous use of the privilege, still retained in men's hockey, of hooking sticks. This will often be his only means of interfering with outside right's final centre. If he sees there is no chance of his overtaking this speedy wing player, let him choose the shortest cut to his normal position. He may be just in time to intercept the hit-in, or to harass one of the other forwards in his efforts after a goal. But whatever course he adopts, he must never abandon hope or endeavour. As, however, inside right, rather than the wing, is left back's special quarry, his duties in connection with that player must form the special subject for consideration. He will do well to play somewhat to the left of his charge. The benefit thus accruing will be twofold: he will be able to tackle instantly without manœuvring to avoid a foul, while he will be advantageously placed for intercepting passes from inside to outside right. There is no defensive stroke like the left-hand " lunge " for quickness or for taking an opponent by surprise. Left back will find it invaluable

in spoiling inside right's intentions.   Those who saw Alan
Jenkins, the famous West of England left back, play, will
recollect how frequently and effectively he used this " lunge."
Indeed, no one ever played this stroke so well or turned it
to such good account.   But then Jenkins was ambi-dextrous,
and the stroke came as readily to him as the right-hand
thrust did to E. V. Jones or Freeman or Boycott.   On the
occasion of the South *v.* West match at Bristol in 1901,
Jenkins, playing at left back for the latter division, gave
frequent demonstration of the spoiling qualities of the
" lunge."   Over and over again, when the situation seemed
past redemption, he would flick in with his patent " lunge "
—it was nearly his monopoly in those days, although fairly
common now—in the nick of time and frustrate Shoveller's
goal-scoring intention.   And here it may be noted incidentally that Jenkins was a far greater back than the authorities ever gave him credit for being.   True, by way of a
sop to the claims his admirers had for years put forward on
his behalf, he was given his " cap " against Scotland ; but as
his game was then past its zenith, this tardy recognition of a
grand player's merits came too late to give much satisfaction
or to serve any useful purpose.   This " lunge," which is so
telescopic, so quick, so unexpected, and so much safer for
its exponent than the right-hand thrust, must then be a part
of left back's stock-in-trade.   And he must be a deft handler
of his stick, prompt to reverse it and use it that way either
with left hand or with both hands.   If inside right essays a
pass to his wing, left back will often be limited to one chance
of intercepting or diverting the pass, namely, to the stroke
in which the stick is held at full length in the left hand
with the toe of the stick pointing to the ground.   A strong
wrist is essential to this stroke, which is not really a stroke
at all, but merely a means of stopping the ball when outside
the ordinary means of doing so, or of gathering it from the
left and hooking across to the right side.

Left back must remember that he is part of a machine
and work in unison with left half, and especially watch for

the moment when the latter will compel the wing forward to make his centre.   Then is left back's great chance, and if he is the alert player he must needs be would he command success, he will appropriate the pass that was meant for another—his enemy inside right.   In attack, left back will limit his hits down the field—hits which will be of the nature of passes in their intention — to the centre forward and inside and outside left.   Rare occasions there may be when a hit to the right wing is expedient, but these are too infrequent to need special consideration.   And left back must guard against hitting too hard and hitting over the touch-line.

And let the final word to this player and to his partner be an exhortation to self-restraint and judgment.   Without these qualities no back is ever truly great.   H. S. Freeman is a perfect exemplar of these qualities.   It is a liberal education in back play to watch him keeping himself and his hits under control, and exercising judgment in easy and difficult circumstances alike.

CHAPTER VIII

IN PLAY—THE BACK DIVISION (*continued*)

THE HALF-BACKS

AND that is just what they are, *half*-backs and *half*-forwards as well. Their play is an admixture of back and forward play. They hit like the backs, but not so hard, and they finesse like the forwards, but not so much. They are the first line in defence, and the second line in attack. Generally speaking, they are the busiest members of the team, while their duties are more varied than those of their comrades-in-arms. As the strength of· a chain is in its weakest link, so the strength of a hockey team is in its half-back line. Any weakness here has a crippling effect upon the whole side. A weak half-back will spoil the opportunities and efficacy of the forwards, and throw the back division out of gear. If circumstances necessitate the inclusion of one or two inferior players in a team, they should not be half-backs. By reason of their central position the half-backs best supply deficiencies, so let them be a good and reliable trio. Possibly the best place for an inferior player is at wing forward ; not that wing forward is an unimportant post, but because it is a post that can be more easily and more naturally neglected than any other. Too many matches illustrate the neglect, the careless, but unintentional, neglect of wing forwards. Nothing is easier or more common than starving wing forwards. And, of course, if these players are below the standard of the rest of their team, their starvation is the right course to adopt.

But in these days there should be such an *embarras de choix* of players as to render inferiority an obsolete circumstance. The story of English supremacy at hockey is a superlative line of halves behind a superb line of forwards. Confirmation of this responds to a backward glance at the hockey of the past ten years. During this period English hockey has been rich in half-backs, of whom the most renowned are R. E. Knowles, H. C. King-Stephens, J. N. Burns, F. F. Blatherwick, F. C. Stocks; while to-day the best traditions of English half-back play are carried on by the twin-brothers L. M. and J. Y. Robinson,—the former of Cambridge, and the latter an Oxonian,—E. W. Page and A. H. Noble, to name a few of the many gifted halves to be found in English hockey. And the play of a first-class modern half is so different from the rough-and-ready methods of earlier days. Then it was chiefly stern defence and vigorous hitting, the player disregarding the niceties of the game, and using a stick suited to the hard hitter but too heavy for quick and easy handling. The modern half-back game is an altogether scientific business, in which hard hitting, albeit frequently necessary, plays a minor part. Instead of hitting hard, the half-back will, perchance, pass the ball quietly to one of his forwards by means of that " push " stroke so indispensable to the make-up of a modern half, or, if that is not possible, will manœuvre for an opening before despatching the ball, or, as an alternative, will pass to one of his backs. And this last device might well be employed far oftener than it is. Want of thought being the root of most bad hockey, any bad hockey played by half-backs who employ this device will at least arise from some other cause. As the modern half-back is also the model half-back, it will help on the purpose of this chapter to set forth his virtues and qualities here. Not, of course, that there ever was a half-back so perfect as the one depicted. He is fast and agile, a storehouse of energy, and absolutely untirable. He is watchful as a hawk, and swoops down upon his opportunities as unerringly as that bird upon its prey. His watchfulness is of that sort which eventuates in what is sometimes called intuition. Then he is versed in all the tricks of dribbling, and knows how to bring them to nought when exploited by an opponent. Every stroke in the game and every turn and quip of the stick respond to his nod. Of course he is fearless, and also unselfish. So much for this paragon.

Before treating of the half-backs individually, it will be well to resume for a brief space the general reflections with which this subject was opened. The half-backs form the backbone of the team. In a marked degree this trio of players bear the strain and stress of battle. In defence and attack alike they are at the heart of affairs. No space for idleness is theirs. And much of their work is of the order called "donkey," uninteresting and unobtrusive. If their opponents are attacking, they will be busy tackling, worrying, and intercepting passes. If, *per contra*, the attack is with their own forwards, they will be backing up the latter, despatching passes, intercepting the hits of the defending side, and eluding the vigilance of some hostile forward or half-back. So they need to be of exhaustless energy and well trained, sound in wind and limb. To play at half with continuous zeal from end to end of a hard, fast game is possible only to the trained player. Halves require to be nimble of foot and quick to turn. So much of this turning is asked of them. One moment they are facing the game, the next it is behind them, and they must turn to pursue it. More of the dodging which obtains in Rugby football is required of the halves than of any other player. So none of your heavy-footed, clumsy players will do for this position.

The normal and theoretical position of the half-backs is about a *dozen yards* behind the forwards, this distance tending to lessen in attack and increase in defence. But dogmas as to the distances which should separate players are impossible in hockey. It is a matter which the exigencies of the moment and the discretion of the players must decide.

BLOCKING THE AVENUE FOR A PASS

It is all-important that, when their side is attacking, the halves should be between their own forwards and the opposing forwards.   Thus placed they will be better able to appropriate the hits of the defenders, and to crowd in, and maintain the continuity of, the attack.   And it is surprising how much ground three watchful halves can take under their tutelage.   They can make it almost impossible for the defenders to clear.   Given an eager and intelligent watchfulness, and the physical readiness of those about to start for a race, and there is very little ground between touch-line and touch-line that the halves cannot guard. When driven beyond the half-way line and compelled to defend, the halves must retreat and take up their position between their own backs and the enemy's front line.

If there is one fault more than another that halves are prone to commit, it is that of hitting too hard.   In attack this fault is especially serious.   Instead of the ball being passed to a forward at a reasonable pace and a proper angle, it is slashed wildly over the goal-line, and a golden opportunity is lost.   Although among the most elementary of faults, it is not unknown in first-class hockey.   Indeed, it is far too common, with this reservation, that it would seem, at least, to be less so were the fielding of forwards safer.

An important duty that falls to the half-back is the taking of free hits near the circle.   And here promptitude is the essence of the contract.   The hit may be taken the moment the penalty is awarded, provided there is no transgression of the rule governing the free hit.   The hit must be taken at the place where the infringement occurred— although there is much laxness in this respect—while no player of the attacking side may be within 5 yards of the ball.   Those, and the prohibition as to "scooping," are the only conditions to which the free hit is subject.   True, the rule says that no other player than the striker shall be within 5 yards of the spot where the free hit is made, but unless the defending side gain some advantage by one or more of their members being within 5 yards of this spot, the umpire, by virtue of his discretionary powers, is not compelled to sound his whistle.

Should the half-backs ever go into the circle in attack? is a vexed and oft-repeated question. They certainly should not make a habit of it. For the most part it is bad play, but now and then a sudden and unexpected dash into the circle by a half-back is very effective. It takes the defence by surprise. The wing halves have fewer opportunities and less need than the centre half for entry into the circle. The latter hovering on the edge of the circle in support of his centre forward will happen upon occasions when a shot at goal is obviously the best move.

In defence, the exigencies of the game will often necessitate the presence of the half-backs in the circle. But here, again, the less they are there the better, so important is it that the backs should be unhampered and the goal-keeper obtain a clear view of the ball. This does not refer to the centre half, who, if he is to fulfil his duty of marking the opposing centre forward, must accompany that player into the circle.

CENTRE HALF

The centre half is entitled to the priority he here receives. His is the most important position in the half-back line—possibly in the field. He is the very pivot of the game, its heart and centre. He dominates the game to a greater extent than any other player. The springs of the attack are to be found in him, while he is the chief rock of defence—the rock on which many a promising forward movement splits. To his office the centre half must bring boundless enthusiasm and energy. Unless he is bubbling over with these he has mistaken his calling. These qualities are a *sine qua non*. And withal he needs must be hardy and well trained, determined and fearless. There must be a keenness about him that stops just short of selfishness. Many a centre half is accused of selfishness whose fault is nothing more nor less than superabundant energy. The centre half cannot be too great a glutton for work, provided such gluttony does not lead to poaching on the preserves of the wing halves. His enthusiasm and his avidity for work are two of the prime essentials of a centre half; but they must not degenerate into their corresponding vices.

Another abstract quality he must sedulously cultivate is that of watchfulness. It is impossible to overestimate the importance of this. Nor will ordinary watchfulness do; it must be eager and unremitting. One cannot play at centre half in a jolly and jaunty fashion. It is a serious business requiring acute concentration. The centre half's habit of mind and body must be one of intentness and alertness, a hot and incessant alertness, that is never taken unawares. He must watch his opponents with feline insistence, deciding what their intentions are and acting accordingly. And it is surprising how accurately a watchful centre half will anticipate his opponents' intentions and how quickly he will bridge the space that separates him from the destination of the ball. It is safe to say that no centre half has ever attained distinction without the practice of this watchfulness.

The chief physical attributes of a centre half, in addition to endurance, are a good eye, quickness, considerable dodging powers, and strength of wrist.

Endowed with the necessary mental, temperamental, and physical equipment for the position, the player will, on such a foundation, build confidently that knowledge and practice of the special duties and requirements of a centre half which will make him an efficient exponent of this central position.

The true learner is he who learns *ab initio*, starts with the A B C of his subject, content to walk first and run later. No one can leap-frog over the period of learning and novitiate straight into proficiency. And in the case of the centre half especially fulfilment comes only after much striving.   So let the aspirant after honours in this position learn his lesson humbly and patiently, and from the beginning.   And here let emphasis be laid upon the value to a learner of watching the play of first-class exponents.   There is no more thorough, and certainly no pleasanter, way of learning hockey.   More may be learnt of centre half-back play in an afternoon by a close study of the methods of E. W. Page and L. M. Robinson, for example, than by a month of ordinary club practice.

The two cardinal facts which must inform, before any others, the mind of the centre half are these, that *in defence* his paramount duty is to cling like a leech to the opposing centre forward, and *in attack* to support and nourish with passes his own centre forward, save when that player is too closely marked.   If this were the limit of his knowledge, so vital is it, he would be already more than half-formed for his position.   Just as a careless attitude towards these two duties brings disaster, so does the strict performance of them bring safety and success.   Let the centre half then realise their importance and make them the bed-rock of his game.

If the opposing centre forward happens to be an unusually clever and dangerous performer, the centre half must exaggerate his duty, and dog this player's footsteps and hamper him at every turn.   How many centre halves have set out with this resolve in the case of S. H. Shoveller and have failed!   But then Shoveller is a genius, and would elude the vigilance of half a dozen centre halves. In the circle the centre half must see to it that his charge is never more than a stick's length away.

In attack the centre half must transfer his attention to his own centre forward, and his energies to keeping that player and the inside forwards well supplied with passes.   But his activities are much wider than these two main duties.   He has a share in looking after the three inside forwards in either team.   Although his operations are theoretically confined to the middle of the ground, he

CENTRE HALF-BACK L. M. ROB NSON, INTERCEPTING PASS FROM CENTRE FORWARD TO INSIDE RIGHT
W TH LEFT HAND CUT

in reality hunts very far to the right and left of this. His is a roving commission. At one moment he will be helping a needy brother on the right, and anon he will go to the assistance of his colleague on the left. But let him be quick to return to his own particular territory. Absorbed with the idea that he is pass-bearer to his centre forward, he runs some risk of neglecting the inside forwards. The latter are chiefly dependent upon him for their passes. Occasionally it will chance that none of these three forwards is favourably placed for receiving a pass. His plain course then is to hit the ball hard out to one of the wing forwards.

A perfect understanding must exist between the centre half and the half on either side of him. They must not go for the ball, two of them at the same time. When this was done in the old days of Rugby football, the captain's warning cry would be " same side "—perhaps it is still the cry. It will facilitate matters and allay any doubt if the centre half cries " mine," or " yours." And incidentally it may be remarked that centre half is the ideal place for the captain of the team.

At the initial bully the centre half will stand immediately behind his centre forward slightly to the left of him, and anything from one to three yards away. Many centre halves stand close up and convert the bully into a mêlée The practice is not to be commended. If the opposing centre forward gets the ball he will probably do one of two things, either pass to inside right or inside left. This the centre half must frustrate, and so nip the attack in the bud. The left-hand " lunge " will best check the pass to inside left. while the right-hand " cut," or the stick held at the full stretch of the left arm, will interfere with the pass the other way. L. M. Robinson is particularly quick and clever at this last method. And this business of interrupting the intentions of the opposing forwards and of constantly harassing them is a large part of the centre half's occupation. He must compel these forwards to pass when they do not want to, if he cannot prevent their passing altogether.

When his own forwards are in possession he must go down the field in close attendance on them. It is rare, but effective, for the centre half to attach himself to the front line as a sixth forward. Thus the defence is outnumbered and taken by surprise.

The centre half must be an adept at the various kinds of "push" and "scoop" strokes. These strokes he will use both in attack and defence, but chiefly in the former. He could not possibly be first-class without them. And the ability to play the ball on the volley must be his. Hockey is such a quick game now that players must either improvise strokes or else remain unresourceful and mediocre.

Great players come and are quickly gone, superseded by younger players. They have their day, but it is a short one, except here and there where a veteran holds his own with the rising generation. F. F. Blatherwick of Cheshire was a few years ago England's most finished and scientific centre half. But, alas! his skill no longer helps England to win matches. Were young players of to-day able to take him as their model, we should speedily have a race of sterling centre halves. Another characteristically English centre half was H. C. King-Stephens, very sound in his methods, adroit at extricating himself from difficulties, and remarkably accurate at hitting the ball without first stopping it, this last an achievement which players would do well to emulate.

LEFT HALF-BACK

As compared with other positions in the field, that of left half-back is poorly served. Players who perform here with distinction are few and far between. And, having regard to the fact that demand creates supply, a contributory reason for this may well be the inveterate paucity of good right-wing forwards. But the root-cause of the

CENTRE HALF-BACK, L. M. ROBINSON, PASSING TO FORWARDS BY MEANS OF SCOOP STROKE

scarcity of accomplished left halves is the many difficulties inherent to the position, and the consequent reluctance of players to qualify for it.   For the more showy and attractive positions in the field there is never any dearth of candidates.   In truth there is a general scramble for them ; players endowed, probably, with few and meagre qualifications for the positions, proferring themselves as centre halves, centre forwards, right-wing forwards, etc.   But for the unpopular post of left half-back the candidates are ominously few.

So here is an open door to hockey fame, and if they would pass through it youthful aspirants must specialise as left half-backs.   And they will speedily discover that its difficulties are, first, exaggerated, and then that they supply the chief pleasures of the position.

The left half is in much the same case as the left back. His main difficulty is the fact that, although the greater part of the game is to his right hand, much of his own work is inevitably on his left.   He is constantly finding himself either so placed that he cannot drive the ball and yet keep it in play, or on the wrong and unassailable side of a speedy wing forward.   His dual endeavour then must be first to obviate, as far as possible, these besetting difficulties, and secondly to acquire a resourcefulness which will enable him to surmount them.   And nothing will aid his first endeavour so much as the practice of playing near the touch-line.   And yet the practice receives scant observance at the hands of left half-backs.   Their universal tendency, indeed, is to drift from the touch-line and gravitate towards the centre of the field.   This is the common fault of left half-backs.   In the case of tyros this fault is rampant.   So that left half-backs are themselves largely to blame for the difficulties of their position, while they manufacture trouble for their side and throw the defence out of gear.   And all this because they do not grasp the importance of, nor yield obedience to, the maxim " Lie well out on the touch-line." A moment's reflection and the simplest intelligence will comprehend what effect the observance of this maxim is bound to produce. But the left half must not be an extremist. Obedience to this maxim is to be tempered by discretion. The left half who " freezes " to the touch-line, while of limited value to his side, is at least preferable to him of widely wandering habit.

In defence the left half's specific duty is marking down outside right; in attack nursing outside left.

If his two charges play hockey aright, they will, generally speaking, confine their activities to the 5 yards between the touch-line and the intersected line marked for purposes of the " roll-in." So it must be the endeavour of the left half to operate as much as possible within this 5-yards space. In defence he should incline rather more to the touch-line than in attack. So far as outside right is concerned, the left half's duties are simple. He must tackle that player, and either rob him of the ball or make him pass it to inside right. The fulfilment of these duties is almost a regular certainty if the left half plays near the touch-line and has pace. He leaves his opponent so little margin for outwitting him. When he has deprived him of the ball he must beware lest outside right return the compliment, as a good outside right will endeavour to do. So he must be brisk and " nippy," and part with the ball quickly, but not to the opposing right half eager to trap it. If there is no thoroughfare to outside left, he must pass to inside left or centre forward.

Should he tackle outside right on his left side, a thing he will not infrequently be called upon to do, he will find the right-hand " cut " an invaluable stroke to employ. It requires to be made with an iron wrist and great decision if it is to be effective. A player who illustrates this stroke with much efficacy and frequency is A. H. Noble, England's left half-back for the past few seasons. He runs alongside his man until he sees an opportunity for cutting in with his stick without seriously risking an illegal tackle. This stroke is Noble's speciality, just as the " job " was Merton

LEFT HALF-BACK CHECKING OUTSIDE RIGHT BY MEANS OF RIGHT-HAND CUT

Barker's, the left-hand lunge Alan Jenkins', and that thrust with the right hand H. S. Freeman's. And thinking of his defensive duties, what a worrier the left half must be. He must never give up, never relinquish the task of harassing outside right, and, no matter how far in the rear, never abandon the pursuit of him. Although he may be far inferior to outside right in pace, the left half need never despair of overtaking him, seeing that the latter is hampered by having to control the ball, while there is always the possibility of his blundering or overrunning it. So let him persevere in his stern chase, always remembering to run on his opponent's right in order that he may tackle him the moment he overhauls him. And if this is at the eleventh hour, just as outside right is about to shoot, it will be a case of hooking sticks. If the stick is already uplifted, and the forward swing about to be made, the left half must insert his stick underneath so as to meet his opponent's stick in its descent. This method of spoiling a shot or a centre is as effective as it is irritating to the player against whom it is employed. Should the wing forward vary the orthodox run down and right-angle centre when opposite the circle by leaving the touch-line and making a dash for the circle itself, the left half must do the same. In the event of the left half deciding that his opponent has gained too big a start, and that pursuit down the touch-line is futile, he must cut across and take the place of the left back, who will try to check outside right. This latter player must not be allowed to go unmolested in order that theory may be satisfied. In any case the left half's action will tend to stiffen the defence, and if he is too late to intercept the wing's centre, he may be in time to interfere with the actual shooting. Never should a wing forward, or any forward, indeed, be permitted to career along, his progress unarrested, because he happens to have eluded the player immediately responsible for him. Somebody must tackle that forward, and that without delay. And the left half should ponder this, for often it is his duty to tackle other forwards than the wing.   In some matches, possibly by reason of a weak left back, he will find himself in conflict with inside right almost as often as the wing.   But even so his work will be easier and pleasanter if it is grounded on the principle of keeping near the touch-line.   It will now and again chance that his wing opponent is a player of unorthodox methods, of nomadic but misguided habits—such are all too plentiful. In these circumstances he must abandon his principles.   To sum up the left half's defensive requirements, he should be an adept at the right-hand " cut," the left-hand " lunge," and the " reverse " stroke, quick with his feet and stick for fielding purposes, an untiring worker, and a chronic worrier. Some left halves employ the " job," and a clever and useful stroke it is, but one that is native rather than acquired.   It is especially useful when the half is attempting to rob the wing forward of the ball from the latter's left side.   Or there is that left-hand stroke used with such efficacy by L. M. Robinson, and illustrated in this volume.

When in the performance of his attacking duties, the left half must guard against hitting over the touch-line, hitting too hard, and playing into the hands of the opposing right half-back.   No fault that a left half can commit is more annoying to his own side or to the spectators than that of hitting the ball out of play over the touch-line. Except in the direst of straits it is bad hockey.   A left half who does this intentionally, or thoughtlessly, when there is a better alternative at hand, is a very poor player indeed. Many courses are open to him in lieu of hitting over the side line.   If forced to act immediately with the ball on his left, he can use the " reverse " stroke, or he may even play the ball between his feet, having a care to it that in doing so he is not guilty of obstruction.   Then he can endeavour to manœuvre himself into the position that will enable the regulation hit.   Somehow or another he must keep the ball in play in attack.   The necessity challenges a player's resourcefulness.   And almost worse than the practice of hitting over the touch-line is that of hitting over the goal-line. When passing to the wing forward the left half must see to it that the ball goes to that player's right hand. A pass to the left side is very awkward to gather, besides throwing outside left out of his stride. And, especially at close quarters, it is possible to pass too hard. Passes, then, must be at a proper angle, and not unduly fast. The worst charge one can level at players is that they do not think. And nothing is so indicative of want of thought as hitting so that the ball goes to foe instead of friend. The left half must be a thinker, and before hitting must locate that watchful right half and avoid his clutches, and any other player who may be in the intended line of fire.

No finer model of a left half-back could be held before the eyes of young and ambitious players than F. C. Stocks of Oxford, the South, and England. To watch him play was to take a free and illuminating lesson in hockey in general and in left half-back play in particular. Peihaps he did not adhere so closely to the touch-line as the left half is here admonished to do,—and in writing of him the past tense is used because he has taken no prominent part in the game these two years. But there was a touch of genius about his play, and such a fact excuses a player from the rules binding the common herd. Stocks fielded so cleverly with stick, feet, and hands, and had such a gift of anticipation, that his enterprising methods in no way partook of folly. Young players could not have a better model, with this reservation, that in so far as *genius* is concerned it is dangerous to copy that.

RIGHT HALF

In many respects the right half is the right back over again. A modification here, an exaggeration there, and a few additions, and the former's game does not differ greatly from the latter's. So those who wish to study right half-back play should make a parallel study of right back play. The right half will not operate so near the touch-

line as the left half.   With so much of the game necessarily
to his left, he must, without dislocating the machinery of
his team, keep as far to that side as possible.   And if
any one requires exactitude to the somewhat vague " as far
as possible," then the right half should seldom be to the
left of the opposing inside left, while he should never leave
more space on his right than he can conveniently and
quickly cover.   So common is the failing of half-backs to
desert their post and follow the game, that teachers of
hockey must hammer in the need for greater self-restraint
in this respect, and for a stricter observance of the theory
of half-back play.

There is one circumstance, however, in which a half-
back is not to be censured for straying afield.   When he—
the right half-back for example—tackles an inside forward,
and that forward commences a diversion to elude his
clutches, he must stick to him even if it takes him far from
his usual sphere.   Generally speaking, it is a mistake to
break off in the middle of a movement and relinquish it to
some one else.   A wise captain recognises this, and forbears
to rebuke a player for getting out of position in such
circumstances.   Apart from these special circumstances, the
tendency of the right half still is to drift towards the centre.
This tendency is, of course, the outcome of a desire to have
more of the game to his right hand.   Now the special
function of the right half is to mark the opposing outside left,
intercepting passes intended for him or tackling him when in
possession of the ball, and to feed his own right wing.   By
drifting too far from the touch-line, the right half makes it
much easier for inside left to get his passes out to his wing,
and leaves semi-marked the latter, possibly the speediest
player on the field.   And if the right half is bitten with
this tendency to drift, he will fall an easy prey to the wiles
of an inside left who lays baits to lure him away to the centre,
in order that he may secure an easy opening for a pass and
a clear field for his wing.   But he must distinguish between
what is intentional deception on the part of inside left and

the honest effort of this player to shake him off. Seeing that inside left is the right back's special quarry, the right half-back cannot be justly blamed if that player breaks through the defence.

The pursuit of the wing forward is a simpler matter for the right than the left half. No running round his opponent, resulting in loss of time, is necessary for the former. He is always on the assailable side of outside left. Directly he gets within stick's reach of him, and before he comes within his vision, the right half must lunge out with his left hand or thrust out with his right and spoil his opponent's centre, or disturb his run. And in sprinting after this forward let the right half be on the look-out for a device common to outside lefts. As the attacking player nears his opponents' lines, and just as his pursuer is about to overhaul him, he will suddenly stop dead, face towards the centre of the ground, and hit the ball hard at right angles to the touch-line. Unless the right half is expecting this sudden halt, he overshoots his opponent, the latter thus being given a clear way for his pass. If the right half does not overshoot him, outside left will probably start dribbling back towards his own goal. There is no fear of his turning round on the ball, as in the old days. It is that final centre to the edge of the circle, so often begetting a goal, which the right half must make every effort to hinder. If outside left has taken the ball down nearly to the goal-line, his hit-in will generally be diagonal to the edge of the circle opposite the goal. So if the right half has failed to run him to earth, he may hang back on the chance of trapping this centre. But should outside left avail himself of his un-marked condition and make a dart for the circle, the right half should be into him like a flash, because few shots are more deadly than those made from an unexpected quarter and at a sharp angle. A right half needs to be a very quick player, because his chief business is with a player of quick and uncompromising methods. Fortunately for right halves, outside lefts who can make their centre while travelling at

8

top speed by means of a half turn of the body and a wrist and forearm shot are few and far between.

To intercept passes from inside to outside left is, with the aid of due watchfulness, comparatively easy. An enterprising and intelligent right half, blessed with a good eye and flexible wrists, will often convert a pass labelled " outside left " into a pass for his own outside right, and that without stopping the ball. No more difficult shot can be essayed in hockey, but it is often well worth the trial and the risk. Hitting the ball while it is in motion is not common enough with halves and backs. They are too prone to stop, before attempting to hit it. The right half is presented with more opportunities than any one else of hitting the ball when it is on the run. Let him meet it boldly with his stick-swing in to meet it. Confidence is essential if success is to attend the effort. J. N. Burns, among the very finest right halves England has ever had, is an adept at this bold method of playing the ball. His is a beautiful, free, cricket shot. When pressed by his opponents, he does not stop the ball and then endeavour to clear it, after the humdrum method in vogue, but meets it full, no matter how fast it is coming, and hits it, not somewhere in the direction of the opposite goal, but with unerring aim to one of his own forwards, thus performing at one and the same time the dual act of defending and attacking. Such quickness is the essence of successful defence, and this method of Burns's deserves many imitators. But this method is not to be commended in the case of a bumping ball or a rough ground.

The right half's duties in attack are simple and clearly defined. His prime duty is to sate outside right with passes. Then any passes he has to spare he must give to inside right. His judgment, however, must brood over these duties and temper them according to the exigencies of the game. Many a right half is so obsessed with the idea that his office is to keep outside right in passes, that in season and out of season he tries to get the ball to this player. That the latter is carefully marked, that the opposing left half is directly in the line of the ball and bound to intercept the pass, that inside right is much better placed for receiving a pass, is not at all suggestive to him of the futility of hitting towards outside right, or of the wisdom of hitting somewhere else.   A little thinking and a little looking before hitting, and this fault would be less painfully present in the play of right half-backs—not that it is the monopoly of this position.   The right half who takes in the situation at a glance will sometimes do wisely to ignore his charges so far as to pass to the left wing Not in every game, perhaps, but in many, each forward in the line will receive a pass or passes from the stick of the right half.   It is essential that passes to outside right should be so dispatched that he may take or overtake them at top speed.   And they must be hit along the ground, in order that outside right may field them with his stick.   Undercutting, lifting, or chopping passes must be avoided by the right half.

Almost as numerous as the right halves who overfeed their wing forwards are the right halves who neglect them. This neglect is generally due to the fact that it is easier, for the majority of players at least, to hit from right to left than the reverse.   From right to left is the more natural direction.   And players do what is natural to them more willingly and better than that which costs them more effort. Strong wrists and a proper use of the forearms are necessary for the hit from left to right.   It is a cricket shot, a drive to extra cover.

As outside right is in the team solely for purposes of attack, and is, if he responds to the requirements of his position, aggressive and fleet of foot, the right half must back him up continuously and closely, seldom being more than 10 or 12 yards away in attack, and must keep on sending him passes.   He will not need to use the " push " and " scoop " passes nearly so often as the centre half.   His passes will usually take the form of a clean, quick hit.   And let him remember that when his own inside forwards are in

or near the circle his passes should, in ninety
of cases. be directed to them.

Players who, having the necessary qualificatio
search of a position which is at once easy and of
possibilities, cannot do better than settle down
half-back.

CHAPTER IX

INTERNATIONAL HOCKEY—A COMPARISON OF STYLES

ALTHOUGH England's hockey supremacy has been successfully challenged only once in the history of International encounters, the honour of winning the first International match ever played belongs, not to England, but to Ireland, while the distinction of instituting International matches is enjoyed by Wales. If the historian would be a faithful annalist, he must admit, however reluctantly, that England gave no encouragement to the early desire of Wales for the institution of International matches between the two countries. It was very different in the case of Ireland, and when Wales broached the idea of an International match to that country the idea received all the warmth of an Irish welcome. The ground of England's refusal to entertain the proposal of a match with Wales was the weakness of Welsh hockey, and the inevitable one-sided nature of an English-Welsh match. Commenting on England's attitude towards a refusal of the proposal of Wales, C. Connah, one of the moving spirits of Welsh hockey, says: "Granting that we were too weak, surely a match might have been arranged, if only for the encouragement of the game; and apparently no thought of the disappointment this decision would give to the players who were struggling so hard to give the game a footing in Wales, crossed the mind of the English Association. Looking at these facts, the refusal to give the struggling Welsh players a helping hand was scarcely to the credit of the English Association, and a direct contrast to the way the gallant Irishmen treated the innovation."

In no way discouraged by England's lack of sympathy, Wales pluckily went forward, the fruit of their pluck and enthusiasm being realised on January 25, 1895, when Ireland were encountered at Rhyl, the birthplace of Welsh hockey. The result of that match was a win for Ireland by 3 goals to nil, the lightness of this defeat proving a wonderful stimulus and encouragement to Welsh hockey. That was how International hockey began its career. This new departure infused fresh vitality, hope, and ambition into Welsh players, and each succeeding year witnessed a definite improvement in their play. But as they improved so did the Irish, and their supreme ambition of overcoming the latter has not yet crystallised into fact.

It was not till three years later—in 1898, to be exact—that England deigned to play Wales. The match took place at Kersal, Manchester, England winning by 7 goals to nothing. Strive as they have done, Wales have never yet succeeded in overcoming England. The limit of their success has so far been to get within 2 goals of a draw. This occurred at Bath in 1908, when England, on a ground decidedly inimical to their close and clever methods, won by 4 goals to 2. On this same ground once before England were in danger of tarnishing their great reputation. Wales dislike a mushy, muddy ground far less than do England. The superiority of English over Welsh hockey is great and undeniable.

It is only against Scotland that Wales have met with definite success. They played them first in 1903, winning that year and the next, and drawing in 1905. Since then Scotland have had the upper hand, but only just.

In point of pace and vigour, and qualities of pluck and determination, the Welsh players compare favourably with those of any other country. But they want for the superlative dash of the Irish and the Scotch, while in point of cleverness and stick-craft they lag far behind the English.

The wonderful hand-to-hand combination which is the proverb of Welsh Rugby football, is sadly missing from Welsh hockey. Now and then, two or even three members of the forward line will exhibit a familiarity with one another's methods and an intimacy of combination which approximates nearly to the wonders of an English forward line. But such excellence is rare and ephemeral. Welsh forwards lack finish. They miss the finer points of forward play, and fail to appreciate the scientific possibilities of the game. Their hockey is good, remarkably improved during the years of. the twentieth century which have already run their course, but there is not that patent of nobility about it which is so clearly stamped upon English hockey. Individually their forwards are often capable of taxing the best defence,—T. W. Pearson, of Rugby football fame, was a forward of whom Wales were proud, dashing and, despite his great pace, very clever at controlling the ball,—but collectively the Welsh are crude performers beside an English line. And it is the same with the half-backs. They play keen, robust, sturdy hockey, are dauntless—they would not be Welsh were they otherwise—and tireless tacklers. Their passes, however, are the hits· of backs rather than the pushes of the English style. That finessing and making of openings, that diagonal passing by means of the wrist push and scoop, so salient a feature of Irish and English—more especially English—half-back play, is seldom an adornment of the play of Welsh halves. Isolated instances there are, but nothing more, of Welsh players who have attained to this effective and finished style of play. As a whole, the half-back play is raw, and would suffer by comparison with the half-back play of the majority of English first-class counties. A like disabil·ty is found in the backs—they lack polish and resource. In virile qualities they leave nothing to be desired. They hit hard and cleanly, and tackle and spoil as well as may be, but come short in the finer points of the game. Welsh goal-keepers are a courageous race, and more than one

International match has witnessed a period of Welsh inspiration between the goal posts. And small wonder that Welsh hockey is not on the same high plane as that of England and Ireland, when the conditions surrounding it are so little favourable to progress and development. Clubs—that is, good clubs—are few and far between, distances are great, while the ameliorating influence of playing against first-class English clubs is denied to the Welsh. Just as frequent encounters with Welsh Rugby football has moulded the play of the leading West of England Rugby football teams to the wonderful Welsh pattern and raised it nearer to the Welsh standard, so would inter-club hockey matches between the best English and the leading Welsh clubs bring the play of the latter nearer to the high English standard. Save for an occasional visit of a team on tour, such as the old Rossallians or Penfields (Staffs), Welsh players get no opportunity of whetting their skill against that of first-class English clubs. Welsh hockey is shut up to itself and dependent upon itself. All the important lessons are learned in International matches, when players are too busy to pay much attention to lessons. In the interests of Welsh hockey, and also as a medium of a very enjoyable holiday, one or more of the crack English clubs might tour Wales during, say, the Easter holidays.

The same year that saw Ireland defeat Wales in the first International match ever played, also ushered in the initial meeting of England and Ireland. This match took place at Richmond, England winning by 5 goals to nil. Save for a draw in 1898, the fourth year of these matches, England kept on winning steadily down to 1904, when the palm of supremacy was, not altogether unexpectedly but only temporarily, snatched from their grasp. On their native heath at Dublin, and led by W. M. Johnstone, the most famous Irish player of all time, the wild Irishmen beat England by 3 goals to 2. This match will remain ever memorable in the annals of hockey, first for its thrilling nature, and then for the unique fact that nine of the Irish team were members of one club, to wit Palmerston, and that five of these nine were members of one family, to wit Peterson.   The defeat of England was the ambition the Irish had set before them, and had now successfully realised after many years of eager striving.   Since that famous victory Irish hockey appears to have gone back. But it must come again.   Who that knows the national characteristics can doubt it ?

Scotland, the youngest of the four countries in hockey experience, challenged England first in 1903.   Save for a drawn game at Glasgow in 1904, when the visiting country were poorly represented, England has always won, but in hollow fashion only once—namely, in 1905, at Surbiton. On that occasion England were irresistibly brilliant, and piled up 9 goals, while their opponents drew a blank.

Ireland were before England with their International match with Scotland, playing them first in 1902.   Until 1907 Ireland enjoyed an easy superiority over the Scottish players.   But seven is a momentous number, and that year the match, played on Scottish soil, resulted in a draw.

So the order of the countries on results, and on merits, is England, Ireland, Scotland, Wales.   It may appear to the cursory observer that Scotland's progress and development have been more rapid and more marked than that of Ireland and Wales.   But Scotland started the game much later, and it is obvious that progress is far more rapid in the novitiate than in a later stage.   Despite this qualifying circumstance, however, there can be no denial of the fact that Scotland's advance in the game has been quite remarkable, and seems to rebut, to some extent at least, the idea, at one time very prevalent, that hockey could be built only on a foundation of cricket, because the Scotch, like the Irish, are no great cricketers.   To disarm any possible resentment at this assertion, let me hasten to add, while the Scotch, as a race, are not famed for their skill at cricket, there are many individual Scotchmen, and Irishmen too, who have earned renown on the cricket-field.

Having passed a criticism, not too ungenerous, I hope, upon Welsh hockey, I will pass to a comparison of the styles and play of the other countries.

Between England and Ireland a spirit of keenest rivalry has always existed. The former, excepting the year 1904, have always held the whip-hand. And why? Because of their superior hockey. And what are the elements which form this superiority? That is a question which the comparison of English and Irish styles will strive to answer.

The opinion of the vanquished, when sane and impartial, is entitled to a specially respectful hearing; and there can be nothing but respect for the views, on the relative merits of English and Irish styles, of so great a player and so sound and just a judge of hockey form as W. M. Johnstone, a player of possibly more International hockey experience than any one in the world. His opinion, written expressly for this chapter, is interesting and illuminating. He says: "In comparing English with Irish hockey, one is faced with two vastly different styles, just as one is in the case of other games. Take, for example, Rugby football! There one sees an Irish team winning a match by loose forward rushes, which completely demoralise and bring to nought the scientific attack of their opponents. The irregular and heterodox methods which may, and often do, prove effective in Rugby football, are impotent in hockey, as the Irish know to their undoing. The Irish style of playing hockey is desultory, consisting as it does of wild individual forward play—play which beats in vain upon the scientifically equipped teams of England. Hockey is essentially a scientific game, a fact which accounts for England's almost uninterrupted supremacy over Ireland. I saw the Irish-English match in Dublin in 1908, and though the ground was in a terribly soft condition, the cohesion of the whole of the English team and the perfect and practical understanding which existed between each member was altogether admir-

F NA OF THE OLYMPIC HOCKEY CONTEST IN THE TADIUM—ENGLAND *V.* IRELAND

ENGLISH FORWARDS AWAITING A CORNER HIT

NAMES, LEFT TO RIGHT—S. H SHOVELLER, G. L AN (E. W. PAGE, CENTRE HALF, A H. N ILF, ILFT-HALF), R P DA RE

ERIC GREEN

able and an outstanding feature of their play. It was not the forward combination alone—though that made one tremble for Ireland's chances—but the union of the whole team. They played together as one man, and on several occasions converted a hot Irish attack into a still hotter English one, confirming the truth of the saying, ' Attack is the strongest form of defence.' One naturally asks why the Irishmen, knowing the importance of scientific combination, do not set themselves to acquire it. Well, my answer is, that owing to bad grounds and wet climate it is almost impossible to do so. After all, we are human, like other people, and so we adopt and develop a style of game which pays best in Ireland, but is—and we are the first to admit it—of an inferior quality to that played in England. I think, too, that our national temperament, just as is the case in cricket, must be held to some extent responsible for our style of play. An Irishman does not display that careful patience which, speaking generally, is so characteristic of the English. I had great hopes that we were steadily improving our position year by year, and when, in 1903, we lost by only 1 goal at Surbiton, succeeded the next year by a win in Dublin, that we had reached the summit of our ambitions, and could now put ourselves on an equality with England. Alas! these hopes have not been realised, as subsequent results clearly show; but without being thought over-optimistic, I believe that we will ere long assume the honourable position we more or less forfeited in 1907, 1908, and at the Olympic Games, and that these lean years will give place to years of plenty, and that we shall not have to wait the prescribed period of scriptural patience."

Ever since the inauguration of International matches between England and Ireland, the same difference in styles has existed, and this although the English style has been completely transformed since that far-off first match at Richmond in 1895. In those days combination did not centralise. The centre forward was an isolated figure, a unit, a player of individual parts, and the wings hunted in couples. And who that can recall the skill of the Westrays as a wing combination can doubt the effectiveness of this method? But it gave way to a better, and one that was more expedient. Whichever the particular method, however, combination, a scientific and premeditated combination, has always been, in more or less degree, the keynote of the English style, just as individual effort and reliance on personal brilliancy and dash have formed the chief part of the Irish game. So far as forward play is concerned, the Irish readily yield the palm to England, but not so in half-back play, in which department they claim to have had players fully the equal of England's best. On this subject W. M. Johnstone writes: "In spite of what English critics say, I hold that R. F. M. Clifford, early associated with Irish hockey, was the equal of any half-back produced by England, such as Merton Barker and E. W. Page. With Clifford I would couple S. C. D. Harrison, the finest right half that ever donned a green jersey. Did Ireland possess such players now, the margin of victory in England's favour would not be what it is." There was a cleanness, a finish, and a dexterity about the play of the Irish half-backs mentioned above that is all too rare nowadays. There was all the necessary delicacy about their play, but none of the effeminacy, or something very like it, with which not a little modern half-back play seems to be touched. It was a splendidly robust type of game, the game of those Irish halves of a past generation.

It is natural enough that Ireland should produce backs to bear comparison with the best in the world. The slashing, hard hitting, and enterprise possible, and often necessary for a back, appeal to the Irish temperament. W. B. Dobbs, O'Connor, and the Petersons form a quartette of backs hard to beat. But the Irish backs err on the side of over-severity in their hitting. The grounds on which they play, heavy or rough, or both, and the general style of play adopted in Ireland, must be held responsible

AN IRISHMAN'S SHOT AT GOAL A PERFECT FOLLOW-THROUGH

for this, and the indifferent umpiring. Irish backs hit too hard to be as useful to their forwards as they should be, and as English backs are. Pace on the ball seems to be their main objective, although O'Connor must be excepted from this indictment; he was a beautiful hitter, and never a slogger "Hit hard and hope for the best" is, one imagines, the principle on which the Irish backs model their play. Self-restraint is not a feature of Irish back play. And just as the Irish are more individual, more daring and more piratical in their back and forward play, so is it with their goal-keeping. An Irish goal-keeper—judging, that is, from the player seen most often in England and Wales, namely, E. P. C. Holmes of Cliftonville, Belfast—takes delightful risks, runs out of, not only the goal, but also the circle, to meet an oncoming forward. Such a daring procedure is seldom seen in England. I have seen Holmes, a picturesque figure in his white flannel trousers and stocking cap, take the ball past the 25-yards flag before relinquishing it to one of his confrères, and this daring, almost impudence, in an International match!

Scotland are in very different case from the other countries. Hockey—that is, modern hockey—is a comparatively new game to the Scotch, so new indeed that their International experience of the game dates only from the second year of the twentieth century. So their hockey style and reputation are yet to build. Their ranks are not fed from the public schools and Universities, as in England and Ireland, because the Scottish schools devote their winter energies almost entirely to football, and only here and there to hockey, and then in but a mild way, while to undergraduates of the Universities the game has not yet appealed at all strongly. And then Scottish affections are given so loyally and so naturally to golf, that hockey can win its way only by forced marches. Hitherto the game has drawn its recruits chiefly from those who are the flotsam, as it were, of other sports, players who, having perhaps earned distinction on other fields, and having lost the keen edge of their skill and enthusiasm, turn to hockey for consolation and an outlet for their athletic energy. But hockey is worthy the very best a country can give it, and there are signs that the Scotch are beginning to realise this.

The play of the Scottish International teams is far more like that of the Irish than of the English. The style of the last-named is the growth of long years, a national style which it has taken decade on decade to produce. The Scotch have made extraordinary progress, and they are quick to learn, but hitherto their guide has been the light of nature rather than any clearly defined and scientific ideal. They do better against England than against Ireland. They cannot play the Irishmen at their own game, although they try to, while they do not attempt to play the Englishmen at a game which is outside their capacity. Their dash is grand, of the sort that sweeps opponents off their feet, and where the players are on the right side of thirty their pace and quickness tremendous. In the race after England and Ireland they have out-distanced Wales. Their aptitude for the game is decided, and if the conditions of the game were more like those obtaining in England, they would soon come nearer to the latter in style and proficiency than even the Irish. Temperament plays so important a part in games, that almost prophetic remarks may be risked with no other data than a knowledge of this circumstance. Thus the caution and mental sobriety of the Scotch are far more likely to lead to a methodical and scientific style of play than is Irish impetuosity.

And the Scotch have left their beginnings far behind, and already their game has taken on an orderliness and method quite English.

INTERNATIONAL HOCKEY—GERMANY *V.* SCOTLAND AT THE STADIUM.   A RUN BY THE SCOTTISH FORWARDS

CHAPTER X

UNIVERSITY HOCKEY

By L. M. and J. Y. Robinson

Oxford

HOCKEY at Oxford may be justly termed a new game, but its newness does not prevent its being an exceedingly popular form of Oxford sport, and undoubtedly the game has come to stay. Whereas a few years ago men up at the University played hockey for exercise or merely as a "by-game" apart from their chief form of sport, at the present time hockey is undoubtedly specialised in. The fascination which exists in hitting a hard ball with a bent stick, the great pace of the game, and above all the increasing skill which each year accrues to it, appeals to the sporting instincts. It is not now played as a game which in some slight measure supplies the joys of football when the latter is no longer possible; it is played for its own intrinsic worth, and we of Oxford worship our God of Hockey as zealously as do the devotees of any other winter sport.

Hockey was started at Oxford in 1890 in quite an unofficial manner. The Parks, the home of so many games, welcomed a small band of eager players who doubtless indulged in the delight of slogging a cricket ball in the wildest manner, irrespective of whom the ball would finally reach. But so great was their enthusiasm, and, evidently, so marked their skill, that in this initial season they accepted the challenge of Cambridge to battle. There seems to have been some difficulty in finding eleven men to play, although the match was played at home, but no difficulty at all in defeating their rivals; for Oxford claimed a meritorious victory by 2 goals to 1. One can imagine the curious concourse of spectators, the zest of players, and the extraordinary enthusiasm of the victors. The fillip of this "famous victory" to Oxford hockey was at once apparent. The O.U.H.C. was founded, elected officers, received subscriptions, and proceeded on the even tenor of its way, not always victoriously, it is true, but ever more prosperous.

At the present time we have five grounds in the Parks at Oxford, which were originally intended for the members of the Club, and are still used by them to a certain extent. But the enormous growth of the game has necessitated the providing of a ground for each college, and consequently the members of the University Club are greatly diminished. Of the more prominent of the colleges may be mentioned Balliol, Magdalen, Keble, University, Trinity, and Exeter. The League system is not in vogue at Oxford, but during the latter half of the season the colleges compete fiercely for premier position. Of late years, Oriel, Trinity, University, and Magdalen have won this position. The all-round cleverness of the best college teams is a remarkable feature at the University, and makes the choice of the University team each year a matter of increasing difficulty.

The Inter-University match is naturally keenly contested, and the margin of victory never very large. When one side obtains the lead, the nervous apprehension of forfeiting it will act as a drag upon its attacking skill, and instead of aggressive tactics the players will concentrate their energies upon preventing their opponents from filching their lead. The victories seem to run in batches, Oxford winning for several consecutive years, and then the tide of fortune running for Cambridge.

The Oxford University Occasionals Hockey Club

L M AND J. Y. ROBINSON—FAMOUS HOCKEY TWINS, AND JOINT AUTHORS
OF CHAPTER X

deserves mention. The object of the Club is the rewarding of those players of more than average ability but whose skill is not of sufficiently high order to win them a place in the University team, although all those who do get their "half-blue" are given their "Occasionals" too. The Club thus gives additional interest to the game by increasing the keenness of college matches. The Occasionals also arrange fixtures with outside clubs; the annual tour in the North being a special feature, carrying the University style through the country.

As to prominent players who have left their mark on Oxford hockey, A. L. Smith deserves first mention as the father of Oxford University hockey. He is now Senior Treasurer of the O.U.H.C., and all honour is due to him for his untiring efforts in that office, of which his tenure has lasted fourteen years. The late Honorary Secretary of the Hockey Association, H. M. Tennent, is an old Oxonian. He is the life and soul of the Occasionals Club, and his wonderful powers of organisation, and his unflagging interest in the Club and all its affairs, are mainly responsible for its honourable position and continued prosperity. His personality and skill as a player raised the O.U.H.C. to splendid efficiency during his term of office. It was during his captaincy of the Oxford team that the University was awarded the "half-blue."

It seems almost superfluous to mention the famous family of Stocks, who have left their mark on both Oxford and English hockey, three of their number having played for Oxford against Cambridge. Their fame is world-wide. A. L. F. Smith is another famous Oxonian who played for England at centre forward. At his best he played a wonderful game, and was capable of winning a match off his own stick. Then there is C. S. Hurst, the Captain of the team in 1907–8, a fine, fearless player, possessed of the most perfect hockey style, and certain to win the highest honours. Many another famous player could be mentioned whose skill and clean hockey have helped to build up the prestige which Oxford University enjoys in the ever-growing world of hockey.

CAMBRIDGE

Hockey has been played at Cambridge for twenty-five years, and is now established as one of the principal games of the University. It is the newest of the chief games, and stands high in University favour, although its popularity cannot be compared with that of football and cricket.

Under the auspices of the University Club, a League has been formed with three divisions, in which twenty-one teams take part during the Lent term. Every college has a team, some more than one, while all the colleges save two belong to the League. The League is mainly responsible for the dominance of hockey in the Lent term. Although played in the winter term, hockey is regarded as little more than a *pis aller* before Christmas. In addition to the college teams, there are various clubs, not directly connected with the colleges, which are well supported.

In common with other games, hockey started its University career in a humble way. It was introduced in 1883 by some members of Trinity College who played the game among themselves. Clare followed, and these two colleges engaged one another in casual matches. By degrees other colleges took it up, and interest increasing, the standard of play rose, and in a few years matches were arranged with some of the London clubs.

It was in 1890 that the University Club was first formed with a view to arranging an annual match with Oxford.

The first Inter-University match was played this year at Oxford, and resulted in a win for the home team.

The Cambridge colours at this time were red and green ; blue was not yet worn, since the game was not recognised by the Blues Committee.

Of the first four matches played, two were decided at

Oxford and two in London, and in each case Oxford proved victorious.

In the early days of the game at Cambridge, the grounds were bad, and improvement in the play consequently retarded; but with the improvement in the grounds came corresponding improvement in the play, and in 1894 the standard of University hockey was considered high enough by the Blues Committee to warrant the granting of the " half-blue." From that concession the fortunes of the game at Cambridge mounted. The recognition of the game's merit was not enjoyed by Oxford, and the stimulus of a " half-blue" proved so effective in the case of Cambridge, that after drawing the matches of '95 and '96 they carried all before them till 1900, when the belated honour of the " half-blue" was granted also to Oxford. Curiously enough, this stimulated the Oxonians in like manner, and for half a dozen years Cambridge were forced to play second fiddle. Then came three successive years of victory for Cambridge, and in 1908 a full " blue" was granted to Cambridge.

It is remarkable how the results have been influenced by official encouragement given to the game—a fact which would seem to justify the honours bestowed. Although the full " blue" has not yet been granted at Oxford, there is every hope that it will come within the next few years. Cambridge themselves are every whit as anxious for this as Oxford, since the interest and importance attaching to the University match are enhanced if the teams are on equal footing, while, indirectly, every recognition of the game's merit wherever given, and especially if given at Oxford, would help forward the game at Cambridge.

Although Cambridge have produced ·many fine players in the past, chief among them Ebden, Horne, and Raynor, Internationals all, it is only since about 1905 that Cambridge hockey has come prominently to the front. In 1906 five of the University team played in the Southern trial match, while the following year the same number were invited to take part. The University team of 1908 was generally considered the best combination in the country. True, they were beaten by Hampstead, but this was merely the luck of the game, and not any superiority on the part of their opponents. Among their victims that year were such powerful clubs as Southgate, Northampton, and Blackheath. In all they registered the enormous total of 147 goals. The chief factors in their success were H. J. Goodwin, E. F. Edge Partington, J. F. Ireland, and A. F. Leighton.

No account of Cambridge hockey would be complete without mention of H. G. Comber, who was associated with the novitiate days of the game, being Captain of the University in 1893 and 1894, the latter year being the occasion of the granting of the "half-blue." He was again Captain a few years later, under exceptional circumstances, when none of the previous year's team were able to play. He has held for many years the office of Honorary Treasurer of the C.U.H.C. He has guided the Club successfully through times of stress and difficulty. His able finance has set it upon a firm basis, while his personality and his position in the University have greatly contributed to the promotion and popularity of hockey at Cambridge. To him more than to any other single individual is due the honourable position which the game occupies among the sports of Cambridge.

The Schools and the 'Varsity Style

The hockey style obtaining at the Universities is distinctive, and unlike that of the great majority of other clubs. The reason is not far to seek. It is only within the last few years that this particular style has developed, and it is without doubt due to the increasing popularity of hockey at the public schools. Till now Marlborough has been the leading hockey school, and it would not be inaccurate to say that the style of Marlburians is still distinctly recognisable on the hockey-field. A. M. Horsfall of Oxford and J. F. Ireland of Cambridge are typical examples. It is a neater and more finished style than others. There are, of course, other schools where hockey has been played for many years, notably Rossall; but there the game is quite different, and consists chiefly in dribbling and combined rushes in such a way as to exclude the finer points of the game. Uppingham and Felsted have also produced several well-known 'Varsity players, such as C. S. Hurst, C. C. Mountfort, and J. L. Beaumont, but it can hardly be claimed that the standard of hockey is quite so high at these schools as at Marlborough. Marlburian players have been prominent in 'Varsity teams ever since the game was started, and in the last few years at any rate they have formed on an average half of both 'Varsity sides. As in Association football it is almost impossible for an amateur to get sufficient control of the feet to be a skilful player unless he learn the game at a public school, so in hockey, unless one has learnt as a boy to control the stick, one cannot have complete mastery over the ball. Moreover, in a school where a game is young, the same skill is not attained as in a school where it has been played for some years, since the standard of play throughout the school rises as the game grows older, and boys learn more from each other than from the best coaches. Now, the game was played at Marlborough before it was taken up at the 'Varsities, and therefore it is natural to find Marlburians occupying so prominent a place in 'Varsity teams. Doubtless, as the game grows older in other schools, a like standard will be reached; and the prospect of hockey is bright at the Universities for this reason, since the standard is likely to be far higher when the captain has many schools to draw from. Hitherto many have found places in 'Varsity teams, and even captained them, who never got into the Marlborough team; and it is probable that in some years Marlborough could have beaten the 'Varsity teams. But this will not be the case in the future, owing to the fact that hockey is being so widely taken up in the public schools. Marlborough, Rossall, Uppingham, and Felsted have been mentioned as the most prominent: Hailebury, Cheltenham, Wellington, Malvern, and Repton among others have taken to it lately. The Oxford Occasionals and the Cambridge Wanderers—clubs composed of the best University players—do their utmost to encourage the game among the public schools by sending good teams to play them; and the greater the number of schools, the higher the standard of hockey will be, not only in the 'Varsities, but all over England.

The style, then, which originated chiefly at Marlborough, and has been carried to a higher pitch at the 'Varsities, is one in which the stick is used to the exclusion of hand and foot. So far it was carried by the best players of the public schools; the 'Varsity players, with more experience, developed the principle. The stick alone is used by every member of the side except the goal-keeper, since in the hockey of to-day there is no time to use hand or foot, and with practice as much certainty, and far more skill, can be obtained with the stick as with the hand. When the ball is bumping, the straight part of the stick is used, and not the curved part. For ordinary purposes the stick is held in both hands, but for intercepting passes one obtains a far longer reach by transferring it into the right or left hand, as the case may be. For stopping balls which rise, the stick is used rather than the hand for two reasons: first, because a longer reach can be thus obtained, and secondly, because one has no time as a rule to use the hand.

Two strokes, known as "the shove" and "the scoop," are seen more at the 'Varsities than elsewhere. The shove stroke has three advantages over the ordinary hit. It does not take so long to make, since the stick need not be lifted at all; it is far more difficult to intercept, because the opposing side cannot easily tell where the ball will go; and it is far easier for the person for whom it is intended to take it, partly because it can be placed more accurately, and

TO STOP A BUMPING BALL

partly because it comes to him at a convenient and uniform rate. The scoop stroke, to which many objections have been made, but which has now been expressly legalised, is very much akin to the shove stroke, but raises the ball by means of a flick of the wrists. It is even more difficult to intercept than the shove stroke, and a half can sometimes lift it over the opponents' heads and drop it at the feet of one of his forwards. He can even, when running towards his own goal, " scoop " it past a pursuer to his own forwards by turning the stick round the ball. The universal use of the stick and these two strokes chiefly distinguish 'Varsity hockey from that of other clubs.

As to the methods of 'Varsity hockey, they are as follows :—The forwards make use of what is known as the " short-passing game." There is very little individual dribbling, but the ball is passed to and fro quickly ; often the three inside forwards go down the field without passing it at all to the outsides. This style of play has been adopted perhaps more by Cambridge than by Oxford. H. J. Goodwin is a very able exponent of it. It is, however, liable to abuse. It may result in dallying with the ball without any ground being made, and chances have been missed by passing backwards and forwards where a rush perhaps would have resulted in a goal. The other abuse to which it may lead is that of neglecting the wings, thus losing half the power of attack, and at the same time cramping the game and making it easier for the opposing defence to intercept the passes. But these two abuses are not necessary consequences of the short-passing game. The outsides may and should be used, and the game be kept open, while the attack is varied sometimes by an individual dribble, sometimes by a series of short passes. The advantage that the short-passing game has over the dribbling game is that it is far more difficult to stop. The halves and backs, by a method which will be described later, can always stop a dribbler, but they cannot be sure of intercepting short passes. It may fairly be claimed that the short-passing game has been carried sometimes to excess by the 'Varsities, but the principle is right, and if occasionally varied by dribbling, it cannot fail to be the most effective mode of attack.

The short-passing game, then, is the most prominent feature of the attack.   The methods of the defence are perhaps still more unlike those of other clubs.   They have been practised and brought to the front during only the last three years.   The principle shortly is this: the two backs and three halves form one line to oppose the five forwards; each marks a particular man, the backs the two inside forwards, and the halves the centre and outsides, and each concerns himself only with his own particular forward.   To ensure the success of this method it is necessary for all the defence to be fast.   They can then go as far up the field as they choose, keeping as far as possible in one line.   The halves do not follow closely behind their forwards; it is sufficient to keep just in front of or close to the men they are marking.   It is useless to go up farther, since no good player hits without passing to one of his own men; consequently, if the halves were close up behind their own forwards, they would leave the opposing forwards unmarked, whereas if they keep a few yards in front of or at the side of the forwards they are marking, a pass can be intercepted and sent up again at once.   In the case of the backs it is useless to hang back, since if they do the two inside men are always unmarked.   They must remain close to the men they are marking: then the opposing halves will find it difficult to pass to any of their forwards—the ball will be intercepted; if they hit in front, the defence, if reasonably fast, can easily overtake a forward who is hindered with the ball.   The one essential, then. for a defence under this system is quickness—quickness of stick to intercept passes and send the ball up again at once, and quickness of foot to overtake a forward, should he break through.   For the forwards quickness of foot is not so necessary, for they can scarcely hope, when impeded by the ball, to outpace the defence, and they rely mainly upon passing and upon varying methods of attack.

The most difficult point in this system has been found to be that of dealing with an opposing half who dribbles up and tries to draw the defence away from one of the forwards they are marking. If he succeeds in doing so, the system fails; therefore it is best for a half not to leave his man unless he is absolutely certain of getting the ball, but for one of the forwards to tackle back and force the opposing half to pass. Forwards as a rule are not eager to do so, but in the 'Varsities it is possible, since they are always in good training.

As to the individual methods of defence, a man rarely rushes at an advancing forward. It has been found more profitable to wait for him to make an indiscreet move. The half or back therefore retreats with him, never letting him get past, until the forward either passes, or in attempting to dribble past hits the ball too far in front, and puts it in the power of the half. The forward cannot therefore dribble past, while, if he passes, his pass is intercepted either by the half who is marking him, or the back or half who is marking the person to whom he passes. The defence always has this advantage over a forward, that a forward must keep his place, while a half or back can always place himself between the forward and the ball. He should therefore always be able to intercept a pass.

These, then, are the main characteristics of the 'Varsity style, which has made such progress of late years—a progress which has been so great that for several seasons the two 'Varsities combined have been equal to the pick of the rest of the South.

CHAPTER XI

HOCKEY IN OTHER LANDS

By Philip Collins

THE title of this chapter is a fairly comprehensive one, and it may be as well to commence by enumerating the countries outside the United Kingdom in which hockey is played.

The game is played in France, Germany, Denmark, Holland, and Belgium of the European countries; in India it is immensely popular; in Western Australia, New South Wales, and New Zealand it is spreading; while the Transvaal are taking to the game as keenly as they have taken to cricket.

In Canada there are two sorts of hockey played—ice hockey and field hockey; the former hardly coming within the province of this book, the latter (quite in its infancy) being practically hockey as played in England. The game is popular amongst Englishmen resident in Egypt, while it has now spread to Turkey, being played in Constantinople at the English High School there. Before going into fuller details in connection with the Continental countries, it should be mentioned that in addition to Ireland, Scotland, and Wales, the Channel Islands, where there are several strong clubs, are included under the head of the United Kingdom, as also is the Isle of Man, in which there are a few clubs.

Dealing first with France, the game was introduced there in 1897 by Mr. E. P. Denny, who, as Principal of the Anglo-Saxon School, thought it would be an excellent game for his pupils.

In Paris itself the game rapidly became popular, and in April 1898 the Union des Sociétés Françaises de Sports Athletiques, which controls every amateur sport in the country, formed a special Committee to look after the interests of hockey. It was not until after Easter 1899 that a match against an English team was played, but from that time onwards two or more teams have visited Paris practically every year, and French teams have frequently made short tours in England.

There are about twenty clubs affiliated to the U.S.F.S.A., which organises series of district and national championships and various cup competitions. The principal clubs in Paris are the Racing Club de France, the Club Athletique International, and the Sporting Club Universitaire de France. Outside Paris there are clubs at Roubaix, Le Havre, Lille, St. Servan, Rheims, and Lyons.

With regard to the game itself, in France the players are very greatly handicapped by the absolute impossibility of finding level grounds: a "hit and rush" style of play is therefore indulged in, which, while effective on bumpy grounds, when tried against the scientific methods of English teams on our level turf is of very little use. Some of the more prominent French players have made short stays in England, and played the game near London.

Judging by the great improvement they have shown after short experience of the game on level grounds, the ruling body in Paris would be very well advised if they made strenuous efforts to improve the quality of their grounds. The obstacle in the way of this is the cost, since hockey matches do not draw the same gates in Paris as the football matches do, so that, while some of the leading football clubs have stretches of turf that many of our clubs would be proud of, the hockey players have to be content with fields which have not been properly laid down, but merely rolled out as level as possible, and as a general rule this does not mean much.

Germany started playing hockey two years later than France, namely in 1899, although bandy had been played there much earlier.

During the winter months the continued frosts render the game impossible, and skating and ice hockey claim the attention of every one. In the spring of the year mentioned above, it occurred to some devotees of ice hockey that, when the ice had gone, they might continue their game on grass, and this they accordingly proceeded to do. A few of their players had already, during visits to England, learnt something of the rudiments of the game, and when once started in Hamburg, it speedily became popular.

The members of the Uhlenhorster Hockey Club of that city can rightly claim to be the pioneers of the game in Germany. This club was founded in 1901, and soon afterwards started their Easter Hockey Weeks, which are now an established institution. Two good club teams from England and one from France are usually invited to go over and play a series of games with the teams of two or three of the leading German clubs which visit Hamburg for this purpose. These annual meetings have done a vast amount of good for the game in Germany, and have resulted in a very rapid improvement in the standard of play. This was clearly shown by the performance of the Uhlenhorster Hockey Club team under the captaincy of Herr A. Brehm, that visited London for the Olympic Games of 1908, and were only beaten by Scotland by 3 goals to nil, while they defeated France by 1 goal to nil. In Herr H. B. Nilsen, the President of the club, they have a thorough enthusiast, who, in addition to being one of its founders and first players, is still one of its keenest supporters. Thanks chiefly to their annual Easter meetings and the lessons learnt at them, the Germans have a somewhat better idea of the English combined method of play than the Frenchmen, though it is true they are still

GERMANY'S TEAM IN THE OLYMPIC HOCKEY CONTEST

much handicapped by the difficulty of finding really level grounds.

Their principal clubs, besides the Uhlenhorster, are the Berliner, Harvestehuder, Eilbecke, and Bremen Clubs, while in all there are about fifty or sixty clubs in the country. As yet they have no recognised governing body, but, with the game spreading as it undoubtedly is, the foundation of one is only a matter of time. They play under the rules of the game, for the time being, authorised by the Hockey Association; cup competitions are allowed, the three chief ones being those promoted by the clubs of Hamburg, Berlin, and Frankfurt.

A very encouraging feature is the number of spectators that their club matches attract, as many as three hundred being a fair attendance—which number, it may be remarked, compares very favourably with the numbers seen at a good club game in England. It should also be mentioned that the spectators are of the right sort, all enthusiasts who take a keen interest in every point and feature of the game.

A Berlin Hockey Association has just been formed, and though at present it controls only the actual clubs in Berlin and the neighbourhood, its power will no doubt increase. It has approached the Hockey Association with a view to entering into some sort of agreement on the question of rules, etc., as that now in existence between the Hockey Association and the Union des Societés Françaises de Sports Athlétiques.

The next Continental country to be dealt with is Denmark The players of Denmark can claim that they have authentic evidence of their country being probably one of the first to play the game of hockey—in the old altar pot referred to and illustrated in the historical chapter of this book. The game of modern hockey was only actually started in Copenhagen in 1900, but since that date it has spread slowly though surely.

In the summer of 1908 it was decided to form a governing body to take control of the game, which had hitherto been played under English rules. There are at present about fifteen clubs affiliated to the Danish Hockey Association. The rules of the game have been carefully translated into Danish, and the players over there are now trying to arrange for annual Easter Weeks, from which no doubt they will learn a great deal, and improve their methods of play, in the same way that their German neighbours have done.

The principal clubs are the Copenhagen, the Orient, the Rungsted, the Frederica, the Elsinore, and the Haste Horkey Clubs.

A cup competition is recognised by the Danish Hockey Association, and the attendance of spectators at matches reaches as much as four hundred. The Association takes the very wise precaution of remaining an entirely amateur body, quite distinct from any football or other sports organisation.

Hockey has been played in the Netherlands, or Holland, since 1890, but the game is not the same as that played in England. The rules are practically identical, except in two points, namely, the kind of ball used, and the fact that it may be hit with either side of the stick. The ball used is considerably larger than a hockey ball, and is made of rather thick rubber, hollow, not solid. Several attempts have been made to persuade the Dutchmen to alter their rules in these two respects, but without any effect, so that no International matches between Holland and England can be played.

In 1898 the Netherlands Hockey and Bandy Association was formed, and there are affiliated to it something over thirty clubs. These clubs play a League competition amongst themselves, the six leading ones being the Amsterdam, Haarlem, Rotterdam, and Hilversum Hockey Clubs, and the Haagsche Hockey Vereeniging and Haagsche en Bandy Club, O.D.I.S. The game is certainly spreading, although large gates are not yet obtained at any matches.

It was early in 1900 that hockey was first introduced into Belgium, and for the next five or six years it was played there under Dutch rules; then English teams began to tour the country, and eventually the Brussels Hockey Club took the initiative and adopted English rules. Since then the game has made very fair progress, though, as the Belgians are not as a nation particularly fond of strenuous exercise, its spread has not, perhaps, been quite as rapid as might be wished. Antwerp has the Beershot Athletic Club, with a membership of nearly fifty players, and every year it holds an Easter Hockey Week, in which Dutch, German, French, and Belgian teams take part. English teams also visit the city, but do not actually take part in its competition. There are two clubs in Brussels, the Brussels Hockey Club, and one at Bruges, while one or two others have recently been formed in outlying districts.

It is a good sign that one of the schools near Brussels is starting the game.

Austria, though keenly devoted to Association football, does not appear to have taken up hockey to any great extent. There are, however, one or two clubs in the country who play occasional matches with some of the South German clubs.

Turning to the Colonies—in the Empire of India the game is on a very different footing from elsewhere. There is no Indian Hockey Association or anything of that kind, though a very large number of tournaments are held every year in different parts of the country.

It is said that there are altogether nearly two thousand hockey teams, but though some of them play quite a good class of hockey, their reputation is entirely local, and it is impossible to name any team as being the best. An All Indian Hockey Tournament is held every year at Allahabad, which attracts a large entry; and there are also tournaments in each Province, besides inter-regimental competitions and a Native Army Tournament. The rules of the game recognised by the Hockey Association are those observed, and any points in dispute as to their interpretation are referred to that body.

The natives are exceedingly keen on the game and very quick on their feet, but, owing to the fact that there is no organising body, it has not yet been possible to send a team to play in England. There is, however, some prospect of an Indian Hockey Association being formed beiore long, and it will not be surprising if an attempt is then made to arrange for the visit of an Indian team to England.

Hockey in West Australia is of very recent origin, but there are now five or six clubs in the colony, and a very fair team could be picked from them. The chief difficulty is the eternal ground question : they have only two level grounds, one at Perth, and the other on the Fremantle Oval, and great keenness is displayed in the various matches played at these places. It is hockey under difficulties, but the enthusiasm of the players and the spirit in which the game is played speak well for its future in that part of the world.

Although hockey has been played spasmodically in New South Wales for some years, it was not until 1905 that it can be said to have definitely taken root. In that year Mr. Rabett and a few other enthusiasts founded the Corinthian Hockey Club. The formation of this Club was quickly followed by that of the Barbarians, the Pilgrims, and the Sydney Grammar School (past and present) Hockey Clubs.

By the commencement of 1907 these clubs were putting two, and in some cases three, teams each in the field, while several new clubs sprang into existence. The result of this was that, in July 1907, a meeting was held at Sydney under the chairmanship of Mr. A. M. Hemsley (an old Middlesex player) at which the New South Wales Hockey Association was formed. An Association so young as this cannot, of course, have much history, but it may be mentioned that its rules, so far as cup competitions and amateurs are concerned, are based on those of the Hockey Association, and there is every sign of its becoming before long a very powerful body in connection with amateur sport in the colony.

The New Zealand Hockey Association, with its headquarters at Christchurch, is a comparatively recently formed body; but is doing much towards furthering the interests of the game. There is also a Ladies' Hockey Association with headquarters at Wellington. Owing to their isolated position, the hockey players of New Zealand have had no chance of showing their worth against any outside teams, though strenuous efforts have more than once been made to induce an English team to undertake a tour there. Up to the present the distance and expense have made this impossible, but no doubt in years to come such a tour will be undertaken. It will give an immense impetus to the game both in New Zealand and in the Australian provinces, which could be visited at the same time.

Having now dealt with Australia, it is time to consider the position of the game in South Africa. Hockey is making great strides in the Transvaal, and, in addition to the Transvaal Hockey Association and the Transvaal Ladies' Hockey Association, there is an Independent Umpires Association. The headquarters of these bodies are at Johannesburg, while Bloemfontein and Pretoria each have their local organisations affiliated to the central Association.

Cup or prize competitions are forbidden under their rules, but the country is divided into leagues, in each of which the clubs play a series of matches on the "League" system. These "Leagues," as they are called, really correspond more to the English County Associations, and are all affiliated to the Transvaal Association. The principal ones besides those already mentioned are those with headquarters at Pretoria, Potchefstroom, Klerksdorp, Standerton, and Kroonstad, and the Western Transvaal League. The game is played under English rules, except that the ground is larger, being 110 yards by 70. There does not seem to be much difficulty about obtaining fairly good grounds,

10

though they are not, of course, of the green turf description of English ones. They are, however, level, and there being practically no grass, are very fast.

The scattered positions of the towns and the expense of travelling such long distances have, up to the present, made it impossible to arrange any matches between a combined Transvaal team and any of the other South African colonies. This, however, is only a matter of time, and there is a chance of a start being made in this direction before very long.

The game is also played in Natal, Cape Colony, and Orange River Colony, but as none of these colonies has a governing body, it is simply a case of playing friendly games between local clubs.

An effort is being made, as mentioned above, to start a series of matches between each of the South African colonies, and should the effort bear fruit the natural sequence will be the foundation of a ruling body in each colony.

Turning now to Egypt, during the months of December, January, and February each year there is a recognised Hockey Tournament, promoted at Cairo by the Cairo Hockey League, whose headquarters are at the Turf Club, Cairo. The two leading local teams are the Khedival Sporting Club and that composed of the staff of the Ministry of Education, the remaining teams being principally those of English regiments stationed in the country.

It is a far cry from Egypt to Canada, and, as can easily be understood, the game is played under very different circumstances in our North American possessions. There ice-hockey is, one might almost say, one of the national games; it is played, however, in a very different spirit from that usually connected with the game of hockey. In a recent report of the speech made by the President of the Ontario Hockey Association, one notices the following headings: " Referee baiting," " Habitual roughness," " Men off (*i.e.* hurt) in the first half," " Sharpening sticks," and, finally, " Mobbing frequent " !

The speaker deals with the subjects at some length, and

then goes on to say that they can at any rate congratulate themselves that things are not so bad in their district as in Eastern Canada, where the previous year four deaths occurred directly through rough play in hockey matches! It is only fair to state, however, that things have greatly improved of late, and that there are now a large number of genuine amateurs playing the game in the " cleanest " possible way.

"Field hockey," as the English game is called in Canada, is not often played. Occasionally a few players from the Old Country organise games in the neighbourhood of Winnipeg, Vancouver, and Victoria, but, with the ice available, they all sooner or later abandon them for the certainly faster, and possibly even more exhilarating, game on the ice.

Just a few words must be added, by way of summary, to point out that, unlike any other outdoor game, except possibly cricket, hockey is known and played in every part of the civilised globe where games are played at all. Football is, of course, played in most of the countries mentioned, but if it were possible to take a census of the numbers playing these three games in the countries in question, it is pretty safe to say that hockey would take pride of place.

CHAPTER XII

LADIES' HOCKEY

SENTIMENT has nothing to do with the inclusion in the present work of a chapter on ladies' hockey. Such a chapter is essential to that idea of completeness which the author has striven to compass. By their prowess on the field of play, and by their ability in the councils of hockey, ladies have long since established their right to an honourable place in any history of the game. Here and there, perchance, may be found male ignorance and ill-humoured prejudice to deny them this right; but such must be very rare, and certainly unworthy a thought. Any real knowledge of hockey as it is to-day includes the admission that the game is admirably adapted to athletic womanhood, and that ladies play it with remarkable skill and science. Would it be the paramount winter game at practically every ladies' school and college in the land were it not suited to the gentle sex? While as to ladies playing hockey skilfully and scientifically, for visual proof of this it is only necessary to watch a match between two first-class counties, or visit Cheltenham during a Territorial week, or Richmond on the occasion of an International encounter. The initial sensation of those who for the first time witness a match between two first-class ladies' teams is amazement,— amazement at their speed, their combination, their power in hitting, their dexterity with the stick, and their application of the science of hockey. Any previous scepticism as to the hockey ability of ladies is for ever dispelled. Wonder and admiration form the reigning thought. And if

A LADIES' INTERNATIONAL MATCH OF TO-DAY. ENGLAND *v.* SCOTLAND AT RICHMOND BEFORE 3,000 SPECTATORS

the match is an International one, between England and Ireland, say, the amazement is all the greater, so brilliant and dashing is the play. Not, of course, that International matches always provide the best exhibitions of hockey, but when the picked eleven of one country is pitted against the picked eleven of another the chances are that brilliancy will out. The Old Deer Park, at Richmond, each year the *locale* of an International match, has proved the grave of many a doubt as to the proficiency of ladies at hockey.

And, the play apart, what a wonderful sight have these International matches become! Whereas in the early days of these encounters the spectators numbered a few hundred, now they throng the ground in as many thousands. Richmond holds the record with three thousand odd; that was in March 1908, on the occasion of Scotland *versus* England. In Dublin, too, as many as two thousand spectators will assemble for an International match, while Raeburn Place, Edinburgh, has known fully fifteen hundred enthusiasts. Nor are these crowds composed solely of members of the fair sex. They invariably contain a generous ingredient of the male element. And what unrestrained enthusiasm prevails! *Carte blanche* is the order of these occasions, and liberty of tongue, and a continual accompaniment of shrill cheers is the music which inspires the players to heroic deeds.

And if ladies play hockey well, they organise the affairs of the game possibly better. The parent Association, the All England Women's Hockey Association, is a model of what an association should be, and Miss M. A. Julius, its Honorary Secretary since 1905, a genius endowed with all the qualities necessary to the successful occupancy of such an office, and having the well-being and furtherance of the game thoroughly at heart. Miss Julius is enterprising too, and has many ambitious schemes for the future, schemes which will widen the scope and influence of the A.E.W.H.A. She believes that where there is no progression there will be retrogression. And so Miss Julius will never rest until every club in England and every ladies' school and college

is affiliated to the parent Association, and until the latter is
as perfect in every imaginable detail as human ingenuity
can make it.   Although the A.E.W.H.A. has never yet
been affiliated to the men's Hockey Association, nor is ever
likely to be, nor indeed has any desire or need to be, the
attitude of the latter towards it is one of admiration and
respect.   It was not always thus; this desirable attitude on
the part of the men is a product of recent years.   When
the ladies launched their Association some fifteen years
ago, the Hockey Association gave them a cold shoulder,
refusing either to recognise or help them.   In no wise discouraged by this want of male sympathy, and animated
by a spirit of independence and determination, the ladies
pushed forward into a future which was to yield them a
harvest far beyond their rosiest expectations.   Little did
those far-off pioneers of the A.E.W.H.A.—Miss L. M. Faithfull, Miss E. G. Johnson, Miss C. Lawrence, Miss Guinness,
Miss Tatham, Miss Jameson, to name a few—think that
their stumbling efforts, in the teeth of opposition and prejudice, would one day result in a proud organisation with
three hundred clubs under its ægis, and a weekly paper to
chronicle hockey views.   Although a private venture, the
Hockey Field (now styled the *Hockey Field and Golf Green*)
is regarded as the official organ of A.E.W.H.A.   The existence of this paper and its growing prosperity are at once an
indication of the importance of ladies' hockey and then of
its progress.

But it will be both orderly and interesting to trace
chronologically the career of ladies' hockey from its birth
onwards, noting the chief landmarks by the way.

Although a little desultory hockey, played with rude
ash sticks and string-covered ball, was indulged in by the
women students of the Oxford colleges before the year
1887, this may be regarded as the year which witnessed
the dawn of ladies' hockey in England.   So that as a game
for ladies hockey is little more than twenty-one years old,
barely out of its infancy.

To Molesey belonged the distinction of having pioneered the game, the Molesey Club being the first ladies' club ever formed. The first captain of this club was Miss Piper, who afterwards became Mrs. D'Oyly, and played for England, the South, and Surrey, being at her best a sound and resolute back, clever at breaking up an attack, and a powerful hitter. Even now Mrs. D'Oyly occasionally assists her county—and it is assistance—and shows by her clean and scientific hockey that players of the past generation compare very favourably with players of the present, despite the overwhelming privileges of the latter.

Molesey's example was followed the next year by Ealing. Both these clubs have long since been disbanded, and the present East Molesey and Ealing Clubs bear no kinship to the two clubs who gave English ladies' hockey its happy send-off.

The hockey fever spread to Wimbledon, where a club was formed under the able captaincy of Miss Margaret Clapham, whose sister, Miss E. Clapham, was subsequently such a brilliant member of the English team. This club has held on its way ever since, surviving all the many and trying vicissitudes of fortune. If its teams have not always been up to the standard of the strongest Southern clubs, at least it enjoys the honour of having for two years, 1904 and 1905, supplied England with a fast and dashing centre-forward, to wit Miss M. Theed. Probably there never has been in ladies' hockey such a fleet-footed, swift-striding player as Miss Theed, nor a forward so dangerous near goal. There have been cleverer dribblers, and forwards far better in combination, but never one who went so hard and straight and unflinchingly for her objective.

After the formation of this trio of clubs, ladies' hockey for several years seemed to hang fire. It made no appreciable advance. No fresh enthusiasm was kindled; no new clubs sprang into existence. It appeared as though the promoters of the game had pinned their enthusiasm to a cause devoid of vitality or merit. But any such fear was

soon to be dispelled. In its early days hockey did not
commend itself, except to those who knew its possibilities,
as a game for ladies. The conditions under which it was
played, and the erroneous notions commonly held about it,
precluded any recommendation. The grounds on which it
was played were very rough, while the popular and untutored
conception of the game was a stick and a ball and a hit.
Nor was this conception an entirely false one, because in its
novitiate hockey had nothing highly scientific about it, and
was little more than a hitting and a chasing of a white ball.
Add to this rough-and-ready method of play the uneven
state of the grounds, and the result was of necessity a game
big with the element of barbarity. Small wonder, then,
that parents held their daughters back from participating in
hockey. It was a rough and dangerous game, a game to be
avoided. So thought the many. But the little company
of pioneers pressed on hopefully, feeling assured that a game
of such scientific possibilities would one day win through to
popularity. Before that came to pass, however, hockey
lived many hard days, battling against the odds of prejudice
and propriety and regiments of other foes. These chasten-
ing days overpast, hockey appeared stamped with its true
character, a game of great merit, and *par excellence* a game
for the gentle sex. Slow at first, the process of evolution
quickened, and with the improvement of hockey its spread,
and anon the game was sweeping with the resistless rush of
a prairie fire over England, Ireland, Scotland, and Wales.
Enthusiasm for the game once kindled, there was no staying
its progress. And the passing years have only served to
strengthen the hold hockey has obtained upon the affections
of the gentle sex. Parents, guardians, and principals of
schools and colleges, so far from being hostile to hockey,
give it their cordial approval. It now occupies the first
place in the athletic curriculum of practically every ladies'
school and college in the land. Miss Faithfull, the principal
of the Cheltenham Ladies' College, one of the first girls'
schools in the kingdom, is president of the A.E.W.H.A.,

a fact which speaks for itself too clearly to need elucidation.

But to resume the narrative of the career of hockey, the year 1894 is the next landmark. Up to this year the three clubs mentioned, and limited play at Oxford and Cambridge, constituted practically the whole of English hockey. In Ireland, however, the game was in better case; and in the Christmas holidays of 1894–95 the Alexandra College, Dublin, invited an English team over to Ireland to play a series of matches. Miss Jameson captained the visitors, who were drawn from past and present students of Newnham College, Cambridge. Four matches were played, three of them being drawn and one lost. Unimportant in other respects, this little tour was epoch-making, in that it sowed in the English mind the idea of the A.E.W.H.A. The Irish boasted a Ladies' Hockey Union, and were most anxious that there should be a similar organisation in England, in order that International matches might be arranged. The project was discussed by the leaders of English hockey, but without any definite issue. For the second time an impetus was given to the game in England by the Irish, who brought over a team to meet an English eleven raised and captained by Miss E. G. Johnson. The match was played at Brighton very late in the season of 1894–95, on April 10, and resulted in a draw, neither side scoring. If science and combination were not conspicuous features of the play, zeal was in abundance, and English hockey received a decided fillip.

The immediate outcome was the formation of the English Ladies' Hockey Association, and from that Association's first meeting on November 23, 1895, hockey stepped forth boldly as a ladies' game. Now it was all progress. The game had come to stay. It began to assert itself. Grounds improved, and this was succeeded by an improvement in the play. As this happened prejudice waned and hostility to hockey, and players and clubs multiplied. International matches were instituted, and became annual

events.   Territories were formed—North, South, Midlands,
West—and inter-territorial matches played.   County teams
were started, and soon such a spirit of keenness and rivalry
was informing inter-county matches, that these encounters
became, and still remain, the most interesting and exciting
form of the game.   And the A.E.W.H.A., as the parent
Association was subsequently designated, waxed mightily,
displayed a courageous and an independent temper, and
finally severed their tacit allegiance to the Hockey Association by making a drastic change in the rules of hockey.
This will be referred to later.

In Ireland, too, the game marched forward apace; while
Wales, caught by the contagion, formed an Association in
1898, Scotland following suit a couple of years later.   And
since then none of these countries, save Wales, has looked
back.   Whether it is the polemic temperament of Wales,
or whether some other cause, Welsh hockey has not run too
smoothly, nor advanced as it should have done.   In truth,
some four or five years after the formation of the Association
in Wales, the game in the Principality visibly declined, and
the subsequent split between North and South Wales caused
a still further declension.   Happily, however, signs of a
revival showed in the season of 1907–8, and, stimulated
by the example of the other countries, and by the help
which they are always ready to give, Wales may yet
produce players worthy the steel of England, Ireland, and
Wales.

The impromptu encounter between scratch teams
representing England and Ireland, played at Brighton in
1895, and already referred to, laid the foundation-stone of
International hockey and of the rivalry between these two
countries, which has endured ever since.   Every year since
1895 have English and Irish teams met, the former visiting
Ireland the even years, and the latter visiting England the
odd ones.   Including the 1895 match, the matches played
number fourteen.   Of these England claim nine wins and
Ireland three, while two have been drawn.   The first Irish

MISS E. G. JOHNSON, ONE OF THE PIONEERS OF LADIES' HOCKEY, AND ENGLAND'S CAPTAIN ON MORE THAN A DOZEN OCCASIONS

victory occurred in 1896, on the occasion of England's initial visit to Dublin, the measure of the latter's defeat being 2 goals to nil. That was the first year of Miss E. G. Johnson's long tenancy of the post of English captain. Eight years in all was she England's captain, while she was also a member of the team when Miss Heneage and Miss Clapham captained England respectively in 1897 and 1898. After a draw in 1897, England had a run of nine successes, broken by one defeat in 1902, this occurring at Dublin to the extent of 5 goals to 1. Then in the year (1908), for the third time in the history of these matches, England suffered defeat on Irish soil by 4 goals to 2. Despite the defeats England has sustained, there is no denying the superiority of English to Irish hockey. In all the finer points of the game English ladies are superior. They combine better, are more resourceful, and more polished than the Irish, and handle their sticks with greater adroitness. When the Irish have beaten them it has been, not by better hockey, but by greater dash and a resistless impetuosity, characteristic of Irish athletics. On home soil, and stimulated to heroic endeavour by their cheering compatriots, the Irish are apt to be very dangerous. In one department of the game the Irish need not bow to English supremacy, namely in hitting. They are clean and hard hitters.

To Scotland, England has never yet succumbed, although the 1905 match, played in Edinburgh, was a draw, while at Raeburn Place two years later, before a record crowd for Scotland, the English ladies only just squeezed home by 2 goals to 1. All this reflects very great credit upon Scotland, the youngest of the hockey countries. Their matches with England commenced in 1902, Glasgow being the venue of the inaugural encounter, and the result a win for England by 4 goals to nil. In 1904 they visited England for the first time, and found the home country too good for them by 7 goals to 2. But they rendered an attractive account of themselves, and won a popularity with the spectators which has each year increased.   Miss A. Jones, their nimble-footed centre forward, especially took the fancy of the spectators, her speed and quickness on to the ball. and individual skill, earning much delighted applause.   It is interesting to note that of the, two elevens who did duty for their respective countries on that occasion only two players took the field at Richmond last year (1908) when England met Scotland, namely Miss A. Murray for the former and Miss A. Jones for the latter. And what a reception the Scottish ladies were afforded on this their latest visit to England!   Escorted on to the field of play by a trio of Highland pipers, and uniformed in becoming plum-coloured skirts and blouses, they made an imposing entry into an arena thronged by thousands of spectators.   Add to this the English team following close upon their heels, and clad in scarlet skirts and white blouses embossed with a red rose, and there is a picture of what an up-to-date ladies' hockey International match is.   Of the seven matches in which they have met the Scottish ladies, England has won six, the remaining match being drawn.   In pace and dash and vigour in hitting the Scottish ladies compare very favourably with their English sisters.   But in the science of hockey they are very decidedly inferior to the latter.   The short passing game, a feature of English forward play, is scarcely attempted in Scotland.   Individual efforts and long passes from centre to wing and wing to centre are much more the vogue.   Until this is remedied, and until a more restrained and thoughtful mode of play obtains among halves and backs, Scotland will continue to bow the knee to England.

The history of International hockey as between England and Wales is brief.   Instituted in 1900, the matches were abandoned after 1902, the cause of abandonment being the overpowering superiority of England.   Only three matches were played, in which England amassed no fewer than 41 goals.   So, rightly enough, the fixture was cancelled, and will only be resumed when Wales exhibit something like International form.

But although breaking off their matches with England, the Welsh ladies have persevered against Ireland and Scotland, not, however, with any definite success. They have played Ireland ten times and Scotland five times, and have lost on each occasion. This is a disheartening record but the Welsh are nothing if not indomitable, and their courage has never faltered, as their optimism has never waned. Their goal-keepers often offer a most brilliant and determined defence. The stubbornness of the goal-keeping is quite a feature of Welsh play. Only one member of the Welsh team who went on tour in 1908 and played against the East at Richmond showed form approaching first-class. This was Miss E. V. Lloyd, a youthful player, whose fine defence at back was the one impressive feature of the Welsh play.

Ireland and Scotland began to play one another first in 1901, victory going to Ireland three times in the first four matches. Then for two successive years Scotland gained the upper hand, only to be deprived of this supremacy in 1907 and 1908. So that of the eight matches played Ireland have 5 wins to their credit and Scotland 2, while one has been drawn.

County and Territorial hockey in England was of later growth than International hockey. There is no occasion to give the dates and details—suffice it to sum up the present situation. There are now thirty-six County and five Territorial Associations, the latest addition to the ranks of the latter being the East Anglian L.H.A., instituted in 1906.

As to County hockey, Lancashire have for long been Cock o' the North; in the South, Surrey vie with Middlesex and Sussex for supremacy, and generally with success; Warwickshire and Cambridgeshire dominate the Midlands; Gloucestershire lead the way in the West; while of East Anglian counties Kent are *facile princeps*.

The competition for places in the County teams is acute, and young players strain every nerve to compass their ambition. Although good enough in theory, and characteristic of the method with which ladies manage their hockey affairs, the County trials do not always result in the best teams being chosen. For one thing, the trials are held early in the season, while players are short of practice; for another, the desire of each player to catch the eye of the Selection Committee engenders selfishness and prevents combination, which places at a disadvantage those players whose qualities are sterling but unobtrusive; while finally, oppressed by the importance of the occasion, players, through nervousness, fail to do themselves justice. But the worst feature is seen after the team has been chosen—the absolute finality of the transaction. Once a team has been chosen, that identical team must play throughout the season. Like the laws of the Medes and Persians, it changes not. This at least in theory, although there is a growing tendency to pick the team afresh for each match, and on current, not historic, form.

A collateral development of the game is the hockey tournament. The credit of its creation belongs to the West of England. Under the auspices of the Western Counties Association, and under the able management of Colonel W. Leir of Ditchett Priory, Bath, a tournament was instituted at Weston-super-Mare in 1901, and such success attended the venture that it became an annual event. At first it was intended solely for the seven Western counties—Cornwall, Gloucester, Somerset, Devon, Dorset, Wilts, Hereford, but subsequently, and with the primary object of making the number even, an eighth county was invited—namely Sussex. This tournament excites great interest in the West of England, and for ten days, the period over which this hockey carnival extends, hundreds of eager spectators flock to Clarence Park, the venue of the meeting. Its ameliorating influence upon Western hockey, and the widely-spread reports of its special enjoyments, have prompted others to a like enterprise, and now tournaments are held by the East Anglian

Association, by Kent, and by Herts, while club tournaments are fairly numerous.

Territorial hockey started late in the nineties. The
South have the best record, and in ten years have only
once succumbed to the North, their chief rivals. During
the past few years the Midlands have been very strong,
especially in forward play, and have generally supplied
the English front line with one or two of its members.
Perhaps the finest centre forward England has ever boasted
came from the Midlands, namely Miss Phillpotts, who played
for England for the last time in 1901, when her comrades
of the forward line were Miss M. Bryant, Miss H. Carver,
Miss Loch, and Miss Pennycuick. Then in the three
Miss Greens of Bedfordshire—one of them is now Mrs.
Boycott, wife of H. C. Boycott, the celebrated hockey
International and one-time English captain—the Midlands
possess a trio of rare hockey merit. The Miss Greens
are renowned for their fleetness of foot, and have each
one of them played for England.

The West are the weakest of the territories. They have
produced some fine backs—Miss B. Kelly, Miss I. Carroll.
and Miss Chris Baldwin—the last-named a young player
still in her teens, who has twice been reserve for England;
but in forward play they fall below the standard of the
other territories. With so strong a county as Kent to draw
from, and with the game rapidly developing in Suffolk,
Norfolk, Herts, and Lincolnshire, the fifth territory and the
newest, the East, are likely to produce teams equal to those
of the other territories.

If a ballot were taken to decide who was entitled to
the place of honour among famous lady hockey players, the
result would surely find Miss E. G. Johnson at the head of
the poll. As a centre half-back Miss Johnson has never
had an equal. Although she still plays for Surrey, and is
worthy a place in the Southern and English elevens, her
game has lost something of its effectiveness, because it is
impossible for any one to play through as many seasons of

vigorous and first-class hockey as Miss Johnson has done without the keen edge of her game becoming blunted.   But as the self-same qualities which made her name and her fame are still to be found in her game, it is possible to write of Miss Johnson in the present tense.   Forwards who play in front of Miss Johnson never starve.   Her hand is lavish in supplying them with passes.   She is the least selfish of half-backs, and understands her *raison d'être* as a centre half far too well to indulge in that showy, but often time-wasting, dribbling affected by so many modern half-backs.   But what is even more noticeable than her unselfishness is her lightning detection of the forward who is in the best position for receiving a pass and making an attack, and then the instant flash of the ball to that player.   In this she is a model.   Her gift of anticipation is another feature, and remarkable enough to be mistaken for intuition.   It is, however, simply the result of great watchfulness ; and the moment she decides what her opponents' intentions are, which way they mean to hit or pass the ball, she acts accordingly.   Small wonder that she is an arch-breaker-up of attacks.   Then Miss Johnson has a long and telescopic reach, very useful to herself, but very disconcerting to her opponents, while she is an adept at the " lunge."   Ladies, with a few notable exceptions, seldom make good leaders. Miss Johnson is chief among the notable exceptions. She is an ideal captain.   Her moral effect on the team under her is remarkable.   She fires them with her own confidence and enthusiasm, and puts a wise restraint upon blame while being generous with praise.

In addition to Miss Johnson, other half-backs who have left their mark upon the game and are worthy to be enrolled among heroines of the hockey field are Miss Stocks of Leicestershire, the sister of many hockey-playing brothers, Mrs. Armstrong of Surrey, who first won International distinction as Miss Bell, and Miss B. Hawtrey of Kent, niece of the distinguished actor, Charles Hawtrey.   Of Miss Stocks it is necessary to write in the past tense, as she has not for many years taken part in representative matches.

She was a left half, superlatively clever, and resourceful to a degree. Her play suggested an early training in the school of mixed hockey, so vigorous, quick, and skilful was it. As a maker of openings for her forwards she has probably never been equalled. Although she could hit hard enough when occasion required, and without any prefatory dallying with the ball, her more usual method was first to elude her immediate opponents, and then to present her forwards with the ball by means of a quiet pass. Miss Stocks, her dexterous play and her wonderful head of hair, will long be remembered by those who saw her on the hockey-field.

Mrs. Armstrong was playing for England in 1899, and was still playing for her country in 1908, although in the latter year only as a reserve. But whereas in the former year she played as a half-back, in the latter she played as a back. Her proper position, the position in which she shines most, is that of right half-back. She excels at fielding with her stick, and the same quality which enables her to do this, namely a good eye, enables her also to hit the ball when it is travelling fast. She possesses great pace, and this endowment, together with her effective manner of using the "lunge," makes her a most difficult half to defeat. In conjunction with Miss Johnson she has for many years formed the backbone of Surrey hockey.

Miss Hawtrey's inclusion in this list of celebrated players will not pass without question. A fine natural player, hitting the ball with all a man's power, and the essence of energy and pluck, she suffers from one somewhat serious defect, which, however, is more apparent than real— she is slow in her movements. Any limitations this may impose upon her game are balanced by her many splendid athletic qualities. Left half-back is the difficult position she has filled for England, although her special *métier* is centre half. Miss Hawtrey is a fine cricketer, too, has

11

made her centuries, and thrown a cricket ball some 70 yards.

The two finest exponents of back play among English ladies are undoubtedly Miss A. Carver, a Northern player, and Miss A. Murray, of Sussex, both left backs. The former has retired from the game for some years, but at her best she was a fine free player, clean and hard-hitting, and a host in herself.

Miss Murray is of a different type, a clever and finished player, who has a genius for extricating herself and her side from difficulties. For the past few years she has been the soundest spot in the English defence. Her resourcefulness and her coolness in outwitting impetuous forwards are impressive features of her play. She is a model for all young players.

If for no other reason than that she has done much, very much, to promote hockey in the North, and has captained the English eleven for the past two seasons, Miss F. A. Mack deserves enrolment in this list. But she is a fine player, a right back, who plays the most scrupulously fair and correct hockey. A noticeable feature of her game is her habit of deferring her effort till it seems almost too late and then of effecting a surprising and brilliant save.

Of goal-keepers, Miss Horner of Essex takes the palm. Uninviting a position as that of goal-keeper is, ladies take to it readily enough, and fill it conspicuously well. Few of them use their feet or come out of goal to the extent they should. Miss Horner took all manner of risks, a splendid eye enabling her to indulge in flying hits at the ball— a practice which in most cases would have resulted in disaster. She preferred her hands to her feet for fielding the ball, and exceedingly safe they were.

Coming to the forwards—Miss Phillpotts has already been referred to. She is described by Miss E. G. Johnson as the finest centre forward England or ladies' hockey has ever known. She was a well-equipped player, not brilliant in this department and weak in that, but armed at all points,

very fast, and very quick, and very clever; individual if
occasion demanded, but equally good in combination.

Miss C. Evans, a product of Cambridge University, and
subsequently the reformer of Kentish hockey, was a centre
forward on scientific lines; but she had her limitations.
Her play and methods never failed to exercise a beneficial
influence on the forwards who played with her, and a
forward line with Miss Evans in it was sure to exhibit
some very pretty hockey. The last time she figured in an
International match was in 1907 at Richmond, and
England's 7 goals to 3 victory over Ireland on that
occasion was largely due to Miss Evans's skill. Owing
to considerations of health, Miss Evans has retired from the
game, and thereby has left a blank in Kentish and English
hockey.

No one will dispute the title of Miss M. Bryant to be
inscribed the best right-wing forward known to ladies'
hockey. She played for England first in 1901, when she
was a schoolgirl in her middle teens. So she is now in her
prime. Her allegiance was, at the beginning of her career,
given to Sussex and the South. Subsequently she migrated
to Lancashire, and has now thrown in her lot with that
county, while in Territorial encounters she represents the
North—very much to their benefit. Her pace and quickness
are extraordinary for a lady, and her shooting of masculine
power. She is thoroughly versed in the dribbler's art, and
her practical demonstrations of this are the wonder of
International matches no less than her feline agility.
Every known stroke and every trick of the stick are of her
armoury. Spectators love to see this wonderful little
player in possession of the ball—she is so frequently the
author of sensations. And if she does romance over-much
with the ball and occasionally carry individual effort to
excess, these are days of such arid devotion to combination
and collective movements that a departure from convention
is like an oasis in a desert.

And just as Miss Bryant stands alone in her position,

so does Miss L. M. Pennycuick in hers—left-wing forward. She played for England first in 1899, the same year as Miss Lottie Dod, the most versatile of sportswomen. Her International début was an unqualified success, and she was by good judges of form recognised as a player of no ordinary talent. Three years at Newnham College, Cambridge, although preventing her appearance in International and Territorial matches, proved of the utmost value in forming and developing her game. She enjoyed the singular good fortune of being for two years under the wise captaincy of Miss C. J. Gaskell, and of playing alongside Miss Loch, the most delightful and unselfish of forwards. This was the "Newnham trio" of fame, feared by foes, and long to be remembered as the best combination of centre and left wing ever seen. On leaving Cambridge, Miss Pennycuick resumed her old position in the South and England teams, helping them to victory for several seasons. Owing to scholastic duties, she is once again lost to first-class hockey.

Outside left is admittedly the most difficult position in the forward line. The touch of genius in Miss Pennycuick enabled her to surmount the inherent difficulties of the position, and create a method for playing there which remains a model for all time. Her beautiful centres, executed while going at top speed with a half-right turn of the body, her clean and judicious fielding with her hands, and her perfectly hit corners were among the more salient features of her game. A small player, like ·Miss Bryant, she never found her lack of weight and inches any bar to the efficacy of her play.

One of the most dangerous forwards who ever played for England was Miss K. Rodger. Her rise to distinction was rapid. Member of a second-rate club, she in one season—1904–5—gained her place in the Surrey, South, and England teams. There she remained for three seasons, seasons of many brilliant achievements on her part. Endowed with a fine physique, and without any sense of fear, she was a player of resistless dash, who terrorised her opponents by the directness and severity of her shooting. There never was a player who went so straight for her objective, or banged at goal so unhesitatingly, or gathered goals in such abundance. She seldom played in the season of 1907–8, and was sorely missed by both Surrey and England.

Happily England has a rich reserve of youthful talent, and young players are speedily found and made fit to fill the gaps in County and International teams.

Ladies owe much to mixed hockey. Playing with men sharpens and lends robustness to their game. This form of hockey, however, is neither so common nor so popular as it once was. It has fallen into disfavour, partly on account of the element of danger it engenders. Roughness in games seems to be the chronic and predominant characteristic of certain men, certain clumsy, headlong creatures. Such are the death of mixed hockey. Before parents allow their daughters to engage in mixed hockey, let them make sure that none of the male players is of this order, the order which has not the sense or the ability to temper vigour in the presence of ladies.

At one time — some half-dozen years ago — private mixed matches were very much the vogue in England, being affected by the aristocracy, and even by Royalty.

Much of· this hockey was beautifully primitive and highly diverting. The ladies dressed for spectacular effect rather than for utility, while the men, in obedience to the fancied demands of decorum, eschewed the regulation hockey costume, and arrayed themselves in knee-breeches, high collars, and fancy waistcoats. The weapons of war, the ground, and the manner in which it was set out, often added further to the burlesque. Ignorance of the rules was, of course, rampant, and derision was the retort any one received for objecting to charging and tackling from the left. A hockey-playing member of Parliament tells an amusing story of his first experience of one of these

private country-house mixed matches.   Before the match
he happened to overhear two players, who were to be
among his opponents, discussing the game, its tactics, and
the methods of playing it.   "When I hit at the ball and
miss it," remarked one of them, "I am always careful to
hit one of the other team."   "Why do you do that?" was
the surprised reply.   "Well, you see," was the answer, "if
you hit and miss altogether, it does wrench your arms so."
Small wonder that the eavesdropper was a prey to unpleasant forebodings!   But that was all long ago.   These
are days of enlightenment, and hockey is everywhere played
more according to the book.

Until the year 1907, ladies adhered rigidly to the rules
of the game as laid down by the Hockey Association.
Certain regulations with regard to dress were, of course, a
necessary addition.   In the season of 1907–8, however,
the A.E.W.H.A. showed their independence, and created a
precedent, by introducing a bold and drastic change into
the rules.   They abolished the hooking of sticks.   In
effecting this abolition the A.E.W.H.A. seem to have
been animated by the desire to remove a needless element
of danger from the game, to make the game faster, and
to follow the example of Scotland and Ireland, both of
whom prohibited hooking of sticks.   When either of these
countries visited England, they had perforce to adapt themselves to a practice wholly foreign to them, while on the
occasions of England's visits to Edinburgh or Dublin the
English teams found great difficulty in conforming to
the negative method of their opponents.   For International
purposes, then, the A.E.W.H.A. probably acted wisely;
but it is open to question whether the change has worked
for the good of the game itself.   The right to hit or tip
the sticks up from beneath was retained, and so much have
players concentrated upon this that a new means of defence
is being substituted for the deposed method, of which it is
little other than a variant.   One wise alteration effected
in the rules by the ladies is the introduction of a penalty

for shooting at goal from a corner without the ball first having been stopped motionless on the ground. The punishment for this dangerous and reprehensible practice is a free hit to the defenders.

Ladies in other lands do not as yet play hockey to any great extent. Here and there the game is played in some of our colonies, and in New Zealand they have got the length of an Association.

On the Continent of Europe the game is little played by ladies. In one country, however, ladies have become enthusiastic followers of hockey, although it is not the hockey of English ideas. This country is Holland. In the season of 1904–5 a team of Dutch ladies came over to England and played a series of matches against English teams, under Dutch rules. Despite the disadvantage of strange rules and an eccentric ball, the English players were more than a match for the visitors. Since that time it has become an annual event for a team of English ladies to make a short tour in Holland. They have invariably acquitted themselves with distinction, and upheld the best traditions of English hockey.

To an English way of thinking, the Dutch style is hopelessly destructive of the science of hockey and of all the finer points of the game and its more delicate movements. The Dutch stick is flat on both sides, and both sides may be used for hitting the ball, so that left-handed hitting, illegal in English, is legal in Dutch, hockey. Then tackling from the left, and the resultant charging and use of the body, are permissible in Holland. And the ball! How extraordinary it is! A resilient and lively pudding! Made of canvas, filled with horsehair and lightly compressed, it weighs some 2 oz., and has a girth of about 12 inches.

The oldest club in Holland is the Haarlem Dames Hockey Club, founded in 1898. Other clubs are the Hague, Rotterdam, Utrecht, Hilversum, Nymegen, Velp, Hertogenbosch, and Roermond and Amersfoot.

CHAPTER XIII

SOME FAMOUS PLAYERS AND FAMOUS CLUBS

ONE of the speakers at the great Olympic hockey banquet, held at the Hotel Russell, in October 1908, remarked in his after-dinner oration that there was "only one Shove." This remark drew a mighty and approving shout from the assembled hundreds. From the hoariest veteran—and many a snow-white hair gleamed in that vast assemblage—to the most youthful diner present, from the player of the seventies to the player of the twentieth century, one and all subscribed to this utterance, and to the meaning the speaker intended it to convey, namely, that S. H. Shoveller was the greatest player of all time, the highest and most finished product of the game. No other tribute to "Shove's" genius could have been so impressive as that spontaneous outburst of assent. He has been described as the "prince of centre forwards," which is true; but the description would be no less truthful if it ran, "prince of players." He has been the subject of countless eulogies, while epics galore have been chanted, extolling his prowess. This very pen has more than once essayed to trace the lineaments of his play and personality, but with indifferent success. His genius beggars a faithful portrayal, for he is a son of inspiration. But what is there about Shoveller, apart from his genius, that makes him so wonderful a player? Well, he is as quick as thought, and the most elusive runner and dribbler that ever was. He has a most effective swerve, which he seems able to turn on at will, and a quick-footed dodge which leaves his opponents leaning in one direction while he is away in the other. This knack of getting his opponents on their wrong leg is a valuable factor in his effectiveness. His close corkscrew-runs down the field—he makes no wide détours and takes no keen angles—are a household word, and his pushing the ball through the goal at close quarters is the nightmare of many a goal-keeper. In one of his inspired periods he is equal to defeating, single-handed, the best defence in the world. I once saw him score 7 goals in thirty minutes in a County match. That day he was irresistible. His control of the ball compels astonishment. He seems to caress and persuade it to obedience to his intentions. There is no more pleasing sight in all hockey than one of those sudden and electric runs with which Stanley Shoveller delights his comrades and paralyses his opponents.

"The science of hockey first appealed to me," writes Shoveller, "at Queen Elizabeth's School, Kingston-on-Thames, somewhere about 1893; so I am very nearly a back number. I first played for Middlesex in 1899, and again in 1900, when it was discovered that I had no real qualification for that county. Since then I have played for Surrey. I played for the South in 1901, and for England in 1902." And since the latter date Shoveller has played a very important part in England's hockey supremacy. He was born in the year 1881, so that his career exactly synchronises with the period which witnessed the scientific evolution in the game.

And curiously enough, another Stanley, to wit Stanley Christopherson, was a famous centre forward and a household word in the nineties. He is still the latter, a household word, and one of the great names of hockey as an administrator, as well as a player. Practically one of the pioneers of the game, he has loyally given it his unbroken support, his time and his energies, and in the councils of the Hockey Association has been simply invaluable, and always on the side of wise reforms. He is closely connected with the Wimbledon Club for it was as a member of the renowned Wimbledon team of the nineties that he came into prominence as a player, and proved himself one of the finest centre forwards the game has ever produced. Assuming the captaincy of Wimbledon in 1892, he led the Club to almost continuous victory for five seasons. The strength of Wimbledon may be gauged from the fact that at one time during this period of plenty no fewer than six Internationals were members of the team. As a centre forward, Christopherson was an almost perfect model. He was an adept at feeding his wings—a centre forward was the pivot of the front line in his day, and hard hitting-out to the wings was one of his important resources—and possessed the faculty, so essential for a centre forward, for keeping the forwards together. He was of another school altogether from Shoveller. He 'captained England in her first International match, and added to this honour that of scoring the first goal. As to his administrative services to the game, they have been legion. In 1893 he became Secretary to the Hockey Association, and filled that office till 1899, or during a period of six years, the most arduous in the annals of the game. For this was the period of hockey's rapid rise to popularity. Clubs, County and Territorial Associations sprang up, like mushrooms, in a night, but, unlike that vegetable, remained as a permanent growth. In his official capacity Christopherson was called upon to answer all the thousands of inquiries which such development in the game was certain to generate. He was the butt of every riddle as to the interpretation of the rules, and every question as to the dry details of forming Associations, to say nothing of the more trivial interrogations incident to the position of one who was Secretary of the parent Association. And yet his patience never wore out, and he stayed at the helm until his Association had sailed safely through the rough weather into calmer waters.

England has never wanted for good centre forwards. After Christopherson, P. R. Earnshaw, and after Earnshaw, Shoveller. Earnshaw stepped into Christopherson's shoes, and filled them. He was a brilliant player. Originally a member of the old Putney Club, he threw in his lot with Bromley, and assisted that club to the high position it enjoyed from 1896 to 1902. He stood alone as a centre forward when at the zenith of his skill. Albeit a fine player individually, and capable of brilliant runs, it was collectively that he was so great, his chief characteristic being his unselfishness in passing, and his judgment in choosing the right moment for a pass. The charm of Percy Earnshaw's play was the fact, clear for all to see, that he played for his side first and last, and for himself not at all. Therefore the beautiful bouts of passing which his presence in a team engendered, culminating in one of his terrific shots at goal. From 1896 onwards, until the advent of Shoveller in 1902, Earnshaw was England's " stock " centre forward. Since his deposition by Shoveller he has played full back for Barnes, a prominent London club. Occasionally, lured by the remembered fascination of his old position, he will return to his first love and try to repeat for Barnes what he used to do for England and Kent. But his sojourning at centre forward is short-lived; the position is not one for middle life.

In casting about for a half-back worthy the company of these great centre forwards, the backward eye of the historian will not rove for long before fastening on Merton Barker, the finest left half-back England, or any other country, has ever possessed. Hailing from Radley School, and a keen all-round athlete, it was chance that gave him to hockey—chance in the nature of an accident at football. Joining the Molesey Club, one of the pioneer clubs of hockey, Barker learned his hockey under its tutelage, and, betraying the same aptitude for this new game as he had for every other, speedily developed into a remarkable player. Perhaps the most extraordinary feature of his play was the quickness of his left hand, its rapier-thrust quickness. Then he had an abnormal reach with either hand, and added to this such powerful wrists that he was constantly achieving

the impossible.   His skill at getting a ball, almost out of
his reach, under his control was little short of miraculous.
His methods do not lend themselves to a literary description.
They were peculiarly his own, and would in modern eyes
be hopelessly heterodox.   But they were mightily effective.
Barker represented the South as left half from 1890 to
1897, and England in 1897 and 1898, captaining his
country on both these occasions.   For many years he did
yeoman service for Middlesex.

When the Western Counties Hockey Association sent
a representative team up to London for the first time, in
1901, to play the South, it was generally expected that the
match would be an ill-balanced affair.   Although the raw
West Country lads might, in keeping with their traditional
character, offer a bold and spirited front, they would be
hopelessly out-classed by the clever and experienced
Southern combination.   That was what every one thought
—except the West themselves.   They believed in themselves and their powers.   Nor was this self-belief proved to
be arrogance.   The match was played, and the West
Country " rabble " overran the well-drilled Southrons, and
the measure of their triumph was 4 goals to 1.   The
hero of the day, and the surprise and despair of the South,
was Tom Pethick, the scorer of three of the Westerners'
goals.   His play came as a revelation to London, and the
authorities instantly ear-marked him for International
honours in the near future.   Extraordinary versatility,
skill in dribbling with either hand, in shooting from either
side of the body, and superlative dash were the features of
Pethick's play.   He began playing hockey when a boy;
but his actual hockey career commenced with the formation
of the Avenue Club, Weston-super-Mare, in 1899.   For
three seasons this club, although playing all the strongest
clubs in the West, did not lose a single match, and had a
wonderful goal record, to which Pethick was easily the
most generous contributor, frequently scoring as many as
ten times in a single match.   Somersetshire, the West, and

England have all benefited by his goal-gathering stick. In 1904 he scored 11 goals in International matches. His position was inside left, and his union with Eric Green for Staines and England was rich in combination and goals. Now and then Pethick's play was so bizarre as to partake more of juggling than of orthodox hockey.

Does a player lend greatness to his name, or is it his name that lends greatness to the player? Would Eric Green, for example, have been as great had he borne the name of Richard Browne—and I give him an *e*? That is scarcely, however, a question for the historian to discuss. It must be left to those who dabble in the abstruse and metaphysical.

The historian is concerned with the pleasant fact, which he must give to the world,—although it seems almost superfluous to do so in this case, so world-famed is Eric Green,—that Eric Green is a great player, among the giants of the game. As a left-wing forward he is *facile princeps*, never yet matched in that position. He is renowned more especially for his ability to centre while running at full speed, a feat which he compasses by means of a quick, half-right turn of the body and a wrist and forearm stroke, perfect in timing and follow-through. The stroke is sharp and crisp, and how it hums its way to the centre, travelling at the rate of some hundreds of miles an hour! Eric Green's play of wrists and forearms is wonderful, and his pace tremendous. His right-angled centre from touch-line to circle is a stroke of much celebrity and the terror of his opponents. He is an enterprising outside left, too, and very unselfish—a rare alliance—delightful to play with, an arch-enthusiast and a Trojan for work. He was born at Leatherhead in 1878, and commenced his hockey career at St. Mark's School, Windsor, playing with an ash stick and an indiarubber ball. His brilliant career for Staines dates from 1895. Three years later he was considered worthy a place in the English team, and has represented his country ever since, save on two or three occasions.

Never once has he been on the losing side in an International match, which is a proud record, although it must be remembered that England has been beaten only once. Of the beginnings of his hockey Eric Green says: " I think I learnt most of my game on the tennis lawn at Staines, where my brothers and I were constantly dribbling, passing, and shooting."

If Eric Green is incomparable on the left wing, W. M. Johnstone, Ireland's most distinguished hockey son, Ireland, the stronghold of the game, bears the same character as a right-wing forward.   Member of a well-known hockey family, whose sire is still a vigorous player at sixty, Johnstone — known to all and sundry by the sobriquet of " Johnny "—commenced his hockey career in 1896, and as a full back.   His aptitude for the game was so remarkable that he walked straight into the Dublin University team, while he was chosen, as a back, to play for Ireland against Wales in 1898.   The following year he went to outside right, and instantly proved by his brilliant play that he had found his *métier*.   From 1900 onwards he was the finest player in the Irish team, and the chief sting in the attack—easily the best right wing of the decade.   In 1900 he entered upon his famous and fruitful partnership with Douglas Dunlop, the alliance being chiefly responsible for Dublin Unversity's defeat of the well-nigh invincible Palmerston Club, and their wresting of the Irish Cup from the latter.   It was only fitting that Ireland's greatest player should have the honour of captaining his country on the occasion of their victory over England.   And Johnstone must have captained Ireland on more than a dozen occasions.   He was picked to captain Ireland fifteen times, and to play for them twenty-three times.

The following is from an Irish correspondent, R. M'William: " The strongest point of Johnstone's hockey lay in his extraordinary judgment of pace both as regards man and ball.   A most deceptive runner, his singularly smooth action often tempted backs to tackle too late, and by letting the ball apparently out of control he often lured a back to dash in, in the hopes of reaching the ball first. The back who accepted the bait was lost. No matter how good the chance appeared, Johnstone was always in time, and a left-hand lunge at the ball gave one more player reason to repent hasty conclusions. Between the Scylla of coming across too slowly, and the Charybdis of dashing for a ball seemingly within reach, most backs failed, sooner or later, to get in their tackle, and a centre right across the circle, or a sudden dash for goal, spelled disaster for Johnstone's opponents. He was a fair shot, and a tricky close dribbler, the best and most dangerous Irish forward of his or any other day."

A writer in *Fry's Magazine* of December 1905 says of him : " Endowed with a wonderful turn of speed, a compact athletic frame, and an unerring eye, Johnstone is an ideal forward of the aggressive type."

The hockey played in the Midlands is of a very decided type, aggressive and vigorous—some people might think there was a thought too much vigour in it. A player produced by the Midlands, and possessing all the virtues of the Midland style but none of its faults, was H. C. Boycott, who played over thirty times for his Territory, and was an International many times over. His début at hockey occurred in 1895 as a member of the Wolverhampton team. The following year he earned County honours, Staffordshire being the team so fortunate as to enjoy his services, which they retained for four seasons, when Boycott threw in his lot with Northants. International honours came in 1900, and many times subsequently. In the judgment of some, Boycott was on his day the first exponent of back play known to hockey. A daring and impetuous player, he was yet sound in defence and absolutely reliable, while as to his stick-work it merits the epithet " marvellous." Apart from his play, English and Midland hockey owe him a heavy debt of gratitude. He had an unerring eye for promising talent and an instinct for coaching, and two distinguished Midlands backs, who also played for England, E. V. Jones and T. C. Baillon, were the direct product of Boycott's judgment and fostering care.

There is a trite saying to the effect that small happenings often develop great issues. The saying is trite because so often proved true. One afternoon H. S. Freeman, a boating man and a stranger to hockey, was persuaded to go and watch the Staines hockey team at play. Staines chanced to be one short, and Freeman was impressed into the vacancy. In his ordinary clothes Freeman had his first game and his first experience of hockey, and he so liked it that he was henceforth a hockey enthusiast with the best. So by a mere chance England came by a player who was destined to be one of the greatest of right backs. That was in 1894. Of his education in the game Freeman says: "I learnt to play by practising at home with my three brothers once a week for several hours. Our method was to have goal-posts and circle, and then for my brothers to attack whilst I defended." Freeman commends this method as being the best possible medium for inducing fitness and making a player self-reliant, especially the defending player. "One reason for my success at hockey," he says, "was the fact that at the very outset I realised that to be first-class a back should be as fast, even faster, than the fastest of forwards. Accordingly I regularly practised sprinting." It was not for two or three seasons that Freeman discovered his true vocation. Forward and half-back positions were tried before he settled down at full back—a square peg in a square hole. And "square" is no such bad word to use of Freeman. Both his figure and his game are of the square-set, sturdy order. Describing Freeman's methods, Eric Green, his club-mate for so many years, says: "One might compare him to a cat, so watchful and quick is he. Ever on the alert, it seems a gift with him to be in the exact spot to intercept a pass, or to pounce upon the ball and pick it off the forward's stick.   The precision with which he feeds his forwards is a cause for wonder, while his pace is tremendous, as forwards who have played against him can testify.   Equally brilliant in attack and defence, he never suffers himself to be flurried, and his hitting is above reproach, the acme of cleanness and power, and never a suspicion of 'sticks' about it."   He did not develop so quickly as some, and it was not till 1903 that he came to his full powers.   That year he played for England, the first of a long series of appearances—successful appearances—for his country.   Staines, Middlesex, the South, and England he has played for and captained, while he had the honour of leading the English team to victory in the Olympic contest.   Freeman is a versatile athlete.   He is as good at ice hockey as at the field game, and was chosen to play for England in the Olympic Bandy contest, which, however, was never decided.   In conjunction with E. E. H. Green, a brother of Eric Green's, he won the Amateur Double Punting Championship of the Thames.   He has won numerous cups for rowing and sculling, and several gold medals as a motor cyclist for the London to Edinburgh run promoted by the Auto-Cycle Club.   So Freeman is a standing argument against the occasional indictment that hockey players are not of the cream of athletes.

The North of England is, and always has been, rich in hockey talent, and is fully entitled to representation in this gallery of hockey heroes.   And no better choice could be made for the honour than R. E. Knowles, closely associated with the early history and progress of Northern hockey, and largely responsible for the formation of the Northern Association in 1888.   Knowles was a right half—for many years the best in the North and the best in England. He was the most agile of players, as quick as a flash, and a merciless harasser of forwards.   Like Freeman, he was a versatile athlete, a runner and a swimmer of no mean reputation.

12

Skill is an ephemeral thing, although the aroma of it always remains. This is true in the case of great players. And it is much the same with clubs, although one is far readier to forget a bygone club than a bygone individual reputation.

Wimbledon and Surbiton, among the pioneers of English club hockey, were once names to conjure with. But where is their glory now? "Ichabod" has been written across their escutcheon. The world forgets very quickly, but the historian exists in the interests of truth, and he must breathe life into the dry bones of reputations long fallen in ruins, and win for them some recognition from the world. So let the world, forgetting the evil days which have come upon Wimbledon and Surbiton, recollect and dwell upon the former greatness of these clubs, how that they were once first in the land, the very life and soul of English hockey.

Passing to clubs whose reputation is of later date, Hampstead is perhaps the most famous. True it cannot boast of having pioneered the game in the South of England, but it can claim an antiquity shared by few Southern clubs. It is a unique club. Originally it was an off-shoot of the Hampstead Cricket Club, under whose tutelage it flourished until 1897, when it broke away from the parent club and assumed an independent existence. The dis-tinctive feature of the club has always been the strong cricketing element in its various teams. The Hampstead Club is, indeed, a striking illustration of what is now a recognised truth, namely, that hockey is essentially a game for cricketers. Most celebrated of all Hampstead's cricket-hockey players was A. E. Stoddart, who played as a wing forward, and with the self-same skill which marked his cricket, his football, or any other game to which he turned his hand. Then there were H. B. Hayman, G. Crosdale, W. Danby, S S. Pawling, cricketers all, and keen and successful hockey players. F. W. Orr and E. L. Marsden are others whose dual skill makes them useful members of both clubs. For many years Hampstead's bright particular star has been Shoveller. Without him, the club are in much the same case as Samson shorn of his locks. After Shoveller comes Logan, the great centre-forward's complement, the player who acts the part of royal pass-bearer to the king of centre forwards. Hampstead play their home matches on the Richmond Athletic Ground, on a piece of turf that is the *beau ideal* of a hockey pitch, as perfect as any in London.

And for many years Staines have been Hampstead's great rivals and vied with them for Southern supremacy. Staines are not a club of great antiquity. Their birth dates from 1892. In the early days the club's efforts did not command the remarkable success of later years. Indeed, if after an encounter with brilliant Bromley the team left the field with less than a score of double figures against them, the result was regarded as a moral victory! The year 1896 was epoch-making for Staines. A. Playford assumed the reins of leadership. He was a new broom, and he swept very clean. The old players had to go, and young ones were substituted. Playford's captaincy ushered in an era of wonderful prosperity. It did not come in full measure all at once. It was a story of steady progress, a gradual crescendo. From 1899 to 1901 the first team played regularly together every Saturday, and during that time only fifteen players served on the team. This speaks for the keenness of the players, and suggests the existence of uncommon *esprit de corps*. Then in 1902 the club entered upon the period which has made the name "Staines" one of uncommon lustre in the history of hockey. Towards the close of the season of 1901–2 Staines were defeated by Hampstead, but from that day down to December 2, 1905, they were invincible. And when they were beaten, it was by their old rivals, Hampstead. So in four seasons they lost only one match.

In 1903, Staines were one of the parties to a remarkable match. A scratch team was brought against them, consisting of no less than seven of that season's English team, two of the Irish team, and two past Internationals — a team of eleven Internationals. A grand match ended in a draw. The luck was against the club, who started one short, and suffered the additional misfortune of having the equalising goal registered against them in the last five seconds of play. From the view-point of the majority, there is a serious blemish in the play of Staines—they play four half-backs. Whether their unparalleled success has been in spite of this doubtful practice, or because of it, who shall say? But Staines' period of plenty was followed by years of—not leanness perhaps, but greatly abated success. Chief among the players who have helped to make Staines famous are H. S. Freeman, Eric Green, A. Playford, C. Pimm, and T. Pethick, while among those who have helped the club from time to time are J. N. and V. F. S. Crawford of cricket renown.

There is, or rather was,—because it disbanded in 1907, —a club who can show an even more splendid record than Staines, namely, the Irish Club, Palmerston. In five successive seasons Staines lost 2 matches out of 90 played. Palmerston, in six successive seasons, lost only 2 matches of 160 played. So on figures the palm must go to Palmerston. In one of these years Palmerston scored 102 goals, and had only 7 goals scored against them. Can Staines or any other club show such a phenomenal goal record? I trow not. And Palmerston owed its greatness to the Peterson brotherhood, a band of six brothers, whose name is a household word in hockey circles the world over. The dawn of their hockey career is dated 1896, when they commenced playing for Old Avoca on the Avoca school ground at Blackrock. In 1899 the brothers joined Palmerston, the oldest club in Ireland. The Petersons imparted new vigour and skill to the club, and carried it on their shoulders through those six happy years. The Petersons and Palmerston look askance at the seasons of 1901 and 1902. Those years laid bare their mortality,

THE PETERSONS OF PALMERSTON— N ILLUSTRIOUS HOCKEY BROTHERHOOD

Dublin University being the instruments of this exposure, defeating them on each occasion by a single goal.

Palmerston's proudest year was 1904. They supplied to the Irish team which defeated England at Dublin no fewer than nine players. Of these nine club-mates five were Petersons, and to the united fervour of the brothers' play Ireland were largely indebted for victory. The sixth brother, although not sharing directly in the kudos of that memorable triumph, had the distinction and consolation of playing twice for his country.

CHAPTER XIV

THE ART OF UMPIRING

THE umpire has so grown in importance and dignity, and has exercised such a moulding and purging influence on the game, that he and his art deserve a chapter to themselves.

Two things more than any others make for bad hockey —lax umpiring and rough grounds. These two evils, allied to ignorance of the rules, to a loose interpretation of them, and to a tacit and universal understanding that they were not to be taken at their face value, for long retarded a cleaner and more scientific type of hockey from coming into vogue. This was the state of affairs in the early days of the game. Nor was ignorance of the rules limited to the players. The umpires themselves, the arbiters of the game, their *raison d'être* the just administering of the rules, seldom had a working knowledge of the latter. But in those days the umpire was the least important item in a match. Any one would do for this unimportant and thankless office. It mattered so little to the game, which was played according to the individual preferences of twenty-two players. A team would start for an out-match minus an umpire, and if the omission were noticed, the endeavour would probably be made to collect one *en route*. But the matter would not be one for mental disquietude, as it would be nowadays. And if the umpire of those early days happened to know the rules and to enforce them, he would, in many cases, quite spoil the game, because of the constant sounding of the whistle. Unless the umpire were very determined, he would find the game completely out of hand. Round London the umpiring, as the game itself, was on a higher plane. In the provinces, however, especially in the more benighted districts, a condition of things very like anarchy reigned. A player from a good London club visiting the West of England, say, would be amazed at the licence granted by umpires. The latter would allow wholesale tackling from the left, obstruction, and a certain degree of charging; and as to keeping a player off the ball to enable another player to get in his hit, this was the commonest of practices. But that was all long ago, and, viewed in the light of modern umpiring, reads like a romance.

The improvement in umpiring synchronises with the gradual progress towards perfection of hockey itself. Possibly the former preceded the latter. Certainly nothing exerts a more beneficent influence on the game than good umpiring, and *vice versa* nothing makes good umpiring so easy or so pleasant as good hockey. Umpires were compelled to keep pace with the rules and their many revisions, and with the growing desire on the part of players that hockey should take on a more scientific character. And the acquirement of this character was largely contingent on the co-operation of umpires. So on the part of both players and umpires the latter came to be taken more and more seriously. Players recognised the fact that an umpire had it in his power to make or mar a match. Accordingly, it was natural that they should demand efficiency in umpires. There was a ready response to their demand, umpires setting to and fitting themselves for their office, while many retired players volunteered for service as umpires. And it is really remarkable how the number of efficient umpires has multiplied during the past few years. But even so those who umpire with distinction, who administer the rules according to the spirit of the law, are as rare as are distinguished persons in other spheres of activity. Indifferent umpires abound, and of bad ones there are not a few. This need not excite surprise. A good umpire is born, not made; that is to say, the mental qualifications necessary to good umpiring are native, not acquired. But before proceeding to a minute study of what an umpire must be and do, it is necessary to notice a movement and a development relative to umpires which has done much to promote good umpiring. This is the formation of divisional Umpires' Associations. Albeit but of mushroom growth — the Southern Counties Hockey Umpires' Association was formed only in 1906—these associations have gone far to fulfil the purpose for which they were instituted, namely, the betterment of umpiring and the final banishment of the club umpire who acted as a twelfth man.

As so much authority is vested in the umpire, it is highly important that he should be strictly impartial and neutral in his sympathies. And this is just the sort of umpire the Umpires' Associations make it their business to provide. Many a tale could be told of the shameless manner in which matches have been whistled away by partisan umpires. "Who are you umpiring for?" was often another way of saying, "Which team's interests are you looking after?" or "Which side are you going to favour?" The old order of umpire, thanks largely to the Umpires' Associations, has given way to the new and fair. Nor are the Associations' umpires anything but thoroughly efficient. They must satisfy a very severe test, comprising umpiring satisfactorily in four club matches, before they can qualify. Hitherto umpires have not been "fee'd"; they receive only their railway fare. But the day may come when it will be necessary to pay for their services, although many regard such a prospect with holy horror. The game is growing, and umpires are none too plentiful. Furthermore, many players play till they reach the two-score years, and then probably turn their attention to golf, instead of to umpiring, as would formerly have been the case. Golf is probably the main cause of the present paucity of umpires.

The foundation on which an umpire must build his art is an accurate and intelligent knowledge of the rules of the game. He should know the rules by heart, have them at his finger-ends, as well as the several penalties attaching to the infringement thereof. But as a supplement to his memory he will do well to carry with him a copy of the rules. This will give him a sense of confidence, and the ability to quote chapter and verse to any disputant of whom he may chance to fall foul. Or some incident may befal during the course of a game which is so unique as to catch the umpire at a loss and compel a reference to the rules. Long experience has taught, too, that nothing fades so readily from the memory as the rules of a game, and umpires who aim at thoroughness will make a practice of reading through the hockey rules at intervals. And then each year the rules undergo some change or emendation, which makes a reperusal of them necessary, at any rate at the beginning of a new season.

To his knowledge of the text of the rules the umpire must add an appreciation of their spirit. Unless he rightly apprehends the spirit of the rules, and the wide discretionary powers they give him, he cannot become a reliable arbiter of the game. A thorough knowledge of the rules, a right apprehension of their spirit, and a true conception of his discretionary powers form the basis of an umpire's proficiency in what is the most difficult and responsible office in connection with the game.

The umpire exists simply and solely in the interests of the players and the game. Let him assimilate that fact and all it covers. Let him not imagine that the game is of secondary importance to the vindication of his authority. This is the view some umpires take. They arrogate to themselves despotic powers, which are abusive of their office, galling to the players, and wholly unnecessary to the well-being of the game. They exist to flaunt their authority.

On every trivial pretext they blow the whistle, and needlessly delay the game. A noisy whistle is far worse than a silent one. And the constant application of the whistle is a sorry compliment to the players. It is the instrumental way of saying that they are playing very bad hockey. These umpires who love to parade their authority and to pipe on the whistle are small-minded men, with all the makings of tyrants about them. They are certain to be of that number who quibble eternally about the rules, and read into them what is not there. This genus of umpire is a spoil-sport on the field and a bore off it. Would that he were altogether a phantom of the imagination!

The umpire must get a mental grip of the cardinal fact that he is nothing and the game everything. Provided good clean hockey is being played, the less he advertises his presence on the field the better. Self-parade must form no part of his programme. The highest compliment he can pay to both the players and himself is a minimum use of the whistle. It is a fact that in first-class hockey the whistle is often silent for minutes at a time, which, seeing how strict the rule is regarding obstruction and how easy it is to infringe it, may be taken as an eloquent tribute to the quality of the play. The umpire whose mind gladly accepts the fact that he exists for the interests of the play and the players makes at least a good start in his career.

While warning the umpire against the extreme of over-whistling, it is also necessary to caution him against a too restrained use of the whistle. The latter is often weakness or laxity, and has an ill effect upon the game. Bad habits, even in the case of good and first-class players, grow apace when the restraining hand is removed, and slack umpiring is the most fruitful source of careless, rough, and undisciplined play. This has emphatic illustration when the Irish teams visit England. The umpiring in Ireland is far from strict; in truth, to an English way of thinking, it is decidedly lax. Consequently Irish players contract a much looser style of play, especially and chiefly in the matter of

" sticks," a fact of which they are made painfully aware
when they come under the régime of English umpires.

   If the play is of such a rough and untutored description
as to call for interference on the part of the umpire, let him
blow his whistle without hesitation.   He must be firm.
Above all things the umpire must be this, and strong and
determined.   Malpractices must be stamped out, even
though the cost be a running commentary from the whistle.
It is not pleasant this frequent blowing of the whistle and
delaying of the game, either for the umpire or the players ;
but if it is directed against bad hockey, it is on the side of
righteousness and will work for the ultimate good of the
game.   The umpire will need to steel himself against the
frowns and grumbling remarks which players will bend
upon him.   In time he will acquire a callousness proof
against all animosities.   But likely enough his decided and
militant attitude towards bad hockey will have the desired
effect before such callousness has time to flower.   A weak
umpire is an enemy to the players, to the game, and to
himself.   The umpire must make up his mind by himself.
He must not attempt to draw inspiration or help from the
faces of the players, as some umpires do.   This is the essence
of weakness.   The only safeguard for the umpire who is
tempted to this weakness is the resolve never to look at the
faces of the players.   In some few cases, of course, it will be
in the interests of strict fairness for the umpire to appeal to
the players.   For example, when a player was between him
and the ball, and he was thus prevented from seeing whether
the ball went over the goal-line off a defender or an attacker,
the umpire is wise, indeed he is bound, to inquire which
player the ball glanced off.   And hockey players being
good sportsmen, he is certain to come at the truth.   Sometimes, too, he will be uncertain about the roll-in from touch,
and it will be no confession of incompetency for him to
refer to the players.   Determined sticklers for the letter of
the law will doubtless exclaim loudly at this liberal interpretation of an umpire's discretionary powers.   But the

outcry is beside the mark if the umpire's action makes for justice. It seems impossible to nail into some people the idea of justice at all costs—*Justitia fiat, ruat cœlum.* You can never get them to go beyond the narrow limits of the rules which bind them and shape their actions. Many hockey umpires are like this. They will not venture upon independent action, if the rules do not meet or provide for the emergency. They are either apostles of red-tape, or else afraid to stray from the stereotyped path of respectability. Without making a song about it, many an umpire gives rein to his discretion in directions not suggested in the rules. If by so doing he helps the ends of justice, his action cannot be condemned.

Of course there is the abuse of discretionary powers, but not in the connection just referred to.

What makes the art of umpiring so difficult is this discretionary power with which the umpire is armed.

The novice is troubled as to when he shall blow the whistle and when refrain from doing so. The sailing is quite plain where the attacking side are concerned, but when the defending side are guilty of infringements there is the rub. Why should there be a rub? Because of this injunction in the umpire's rule: " The umpire shall refrain from putting the provision of any rule into effect in cases where he is satisfied that by enforcing it he would be giving an advantage to the offending team." It is quite obvious that the need for his observing this injunction is much more urgent when the defending side are the offenders. " Giving an advantage to the offending team " implies a disadvantage to their opponents. This is an important consideration and one that helps the umpire to a decision. Nothing in the whole of umpiring is so complex and delicate as this task of deciding whether an infringement by the defending side is to be punished or allowed to pass. And the fact of instant decision being necessary does not make the task less difficult.

Experience has taught that the only fair course is for

the umpire to pause just long enough to see what is likely to be the effect of the infringement. If it benefits the offending side, then it is only just to their opponents that a penalty should be awarded them. But if the infringement neither helps the former nor hinders the latter, then it should be suffered to go unpunished, provided the penalty were likely to be of less material value to the attacking side than the continuity of the game. A concrete instance will help to a clearer understanding.

Inside right runs down and reaches the circle. Just as he is on the point of shooting, the opposing left back tackles him on his left side, and in so doing charges him off the ball, thereby being guilty of a foul and spoiling the intended shot. Now, is the umpire to penalise this offence, or is he to refrain from doing so? If he is of opinion that inside right stands a better chance of scoring a goal by going straight on than by engaging in a penalty bully, he must keep silence. If only his action could be decided by the wishes of inside right, he would be relieved of all responsibility. And there is one way of knowing the wishes of inside right, or of any forward who chances to be thus wrongfully tackled. If that forward appeals, it may be assumed that he desires the foul to be given. Were this universally understood—that a foul of this sort is to be given only when claimed—the umpire's lot would be a happier one. Experience and careful observation help an umpire in nine cases out of ten to a right decision.

In addition to his copy of the rules and his whistle, the umpire includes in his insignia of office a ring, supplied by the Umpires' Association, or obtainable in the ordinary way. This ring is two inches in diameter, and is used for testing suspicious-looking sticks. If a stick will not pass through this ring, the umpire must forbid its owner to play with it. And it is very certain that hundreds of sticks would not survive the test. Many players delight to swathe their stick blades in some kind of surgical whipping, and as the majority of sticks are made as wide as the laws allow, it is obvious that numbers of these padded sticks would not pass through the umpire's ring. Happily for these players, few umpires carry a ring, and if they do, are very reluctant to employ it.

There are two umpires at hockey, and not one referee as in football. The game is so quick and the ball travels so fast from one end or side of the ground to the other that it is quite impossible for a single umpire to take the whole ground with any satisfaction either to himself or the players.

Under the present system each umpire takes one-half of the ground under his charge and the whole of one touch-line. When the game is being waged on the far side of the half-way line—in the half, that is, which is not under his surveillance—the umpire has nothing to do save look after his touch-line. This system is easily the best of those which have been tried. The best place for an umpire to take up his position is a few yards from the touch-line. He must avoid getting mixed up with the players or in any way hampering them or interfering with the game. The only way to do this is to keep well to the side of the ground. Some umpires run about in a fussy and excited way right in the thick of the game, much to the annoyance and balking of the players. The umpire should close in only when the game is in and near the circle. All good umpires do this, and for the obvious reason that it is then of the last importance that they should miss nothing of what goes on; so they must watch the game at close quarters. Fussiness and excitability are altogether wrong qualities for an umpire. Above all things he must be cool-headed, while the quieter he is in his demeanour the better. He needs to maintain his mind in a calm, judicial habit, allowing himself neither to be carried away by the exciting nature of the play, nor to be influenced by any appeals which the players may make. And players do appeal, despite the fact that the rules enjoin the umpire to act independently of appeals, and will continue to appeal so long as human nature bears the character it has borne for some thousands of years.

Time was when play was under appeal, when the umpire was so shackled that he could not sound his whistle unless appealed to by the players. Gross infringements of the rules might go on under his nose, and all sorts of illegal practices, which he was powerless to punish or curb unless the players appealed. Such a monstrous condition of things militated against the welfare of the game, flying as it did straight in the face of law and order. What in the wide world was the good of rules if they could be violated with impunity! But time and experience brought counsel, and for several years now the umpire has been the sole arbiter of the game. Players still appeal, and do so because they cannot forbear. Possibly they think the umpire will not be proof against their importunity. Certainly a weak umpire is more likely to blow his whistle in response to an appeal than if no such bias were levied upon him. A more sinister construction may be put upon the constant appealing of some players. Their object may well be to bluff the umpire into decisions favourable to them. But hockey is purely an amateur sport, which should mean a pure sport, and it is pleasanter to discredit the presence of such black sheep in the hockey flock.

When once the umpire has formed a decision, let him cleave to it, even though there be a contrary appeal from eleven lusty throats. The umpire may, of course, revoke his decision. To do so is more often a sign of strength than of weakness. An example of this may be quoted. From a corner the attacking side scored; the goal was sanctioned by the umpire and duly recorded. But the umpire noticed an air of discontent about the defending side, and as he had previously observed that they did not charge down the corner hit with much heartiness or unanimity, his suspicions were aroused that all was not right. These suspicions were at once confirmed by the captain of the attacking side approaching him and explaining that the defenders had not been ready for the corner, which had been taken before two of their number were the right side of the goal-line.   This explanation was backed by a request on the part of this very sporting captain that the corner hit should be taken again.   In the circumstances, and seeing that the fault was his, the umpire cancelled his decision and allowed the corner to be replayed.   As he acted in the interests of fair-play, his action must be applauded by all except a few fanatics.

The most frequent appeal by players is the appeal for " off-side."   Since the appealing player, generally speaking, has his back to part of the game, and cannot therefore know the whereabouts of players behind him, his appeal is nothing more nor less than a random shot in the dark. The umpire will ignore such appeals.   He has the whole of the game in front of him.

The question of off-side is the most difficult one the umpire must decide.   Only long practice and experience will make it easy for him.   The crux of the off-side question is the whereabouts of the player when the ball was *hit*.   If the umpire is to obviate the risk of mistakes in the matter of off-side, he must run along on a line with the forwards and keep raking this line with his eyes, noting where each of the other forwards is relative to the forward who is in possession of the ball and to the players of the defending side.   And all the time he is doing this he must also be on the watch for any of the many other illegalities with which the game abounds.   The off-side rule says that " When a player hits or rolls-in the ball, any other player of the same team who is nearer his opponent's goal-line than the striker or roller-in at the moment when the ball is hit or rolled-in is off-side, unless there be at least three of his opponents nearer to their own goal-line than he is."   That is clear and simple enough.   The great difficulty of the off-side question from the umpire's point of view is that he must keep under his observation the player with the ball, all the confrères of that player who chance to be ahead of him, as well as the defending players. His objective, in a word, is to decide whether the player to whom the ball is passed had or had not the requisite number of players between himself and the opposite goal *at the moment the ball was hit.* It simplifies an umpire's task to watch for some little time beforehand players in a suspicious position—players, that is, who are near the end of the tether allowed them by the off-side rule. The most puzzling variation of off-side is that exemplified by a player who, off-side when the ball was hit, runs back into an on-side position and plays the ball before it has been touched by any other player. To the spectators this will often look like a mistake on the umpire's part. But the latter is not concerned with the opinions of the irresponsible onlooker.

The umpire need not wait till an off-side player is within 5 yards of the ball before blowing his whistle. If a player in an off-side position " in any way interfere with any other player," he must be penalised. And if such a player by running towards the ball, even though he be a score of yards away from it, alter what would otherwise have been the tactics of his opponents, he is interfering with them, and the umpire is right in giving him off-side. Many umpires fail to understand this, not regarding any player as off-side until within 5 yards of the ball. There are times, of course, when a player in an off-side position will run towards the ball, provided he is outside the 5-yards limit, without in any way affecting the play. Another point which many umpires, and players too, miss is that which has necessitated the insertion in the off-side rule of the words, written between brackets, " subject to the 5-yards rule." To be exact, the point is this : that if a player in an off-side position gain any advantage from the fact, he must be given off-side. For example, a player is in an off-side position a yard or two from the goal-mouth, when one of his fellow-forwards shoots from, say, the middle of the circle. The goal-keeper stops the shot, but before he can clear the

13

off-side player dashes in and nets the ball.   Of course it is
no goal, although many an umpire will allow it.   The
common idea is that the mere fact of an opposing player
hitting the ball in every case converts the off-side player
into an on-side player.   Nothing of the sort !   If that were
so, the spirit and intention of the off-side rule would be
hopelessly subverted.   The umpire needs to be very much
alive to the true meaning of every phase of the off-side rule,
and equally alive to the fact of players who hang about in
off-side positions with an eye to the main chance.   These
are the pirates of the hockey-field.

Illegalities which the umpire must rigidly check are
circling on the ball, turning on the ball, blocking the ball
with the foot, and tackling wrongfully on a player's left, to
name those which are so common and so destructive of
good hockey.   It is delightful, as well as a liberal lesson in
the umpire's craft, to watch M. Baker, a famous English
umpire, officiating in this capacity, and dropping like a hot
brick upon these and all other illegalities.   No one umpire
has done so much in cleansing English hockey from all
undesirable excrescences as this " King of the Whistle," as
he has been aptly styled.   They say that ginger stands
for pluck.   So far as Baker is concerned, the assertion is
amply confirmed, because he is as plucky and as ruddy-
headed as the gods could make him.   He is very hard on
the wrong-doer, and his courage in subjugating the great
ones is of the highest British order.   Once upon a time,
when England was playing Ireland and the hard-hitting
brothers Peterson were helping the latter country at full
back, Baker had a unique opportunity of showing of what
courageous stuff he was made.   On that occasion the
brothers Peterson were holding high carnival in " sticks " in
the half of the ground remote from England's great umpire.
The lust of hitting was upon them, and higher and higher
flew their sticks, to the peril of the empyrean above them.
Seemingly blind to these celestial happenings, and with his
eyes bent upon mundane matters, the Irish umpire put no

obstacle in the way of the Petersons. The amazement of the spectators at this Irish licence mounted with the increasing elevation of the sticks. The half-time interval was busy with wonderings as to what would happen when the game was renewed. Baker knew. Nothing escaped his eagle eye, the eye that looks battle and no quarter to delinquents. No sooner was the second half entered upon than commenced the subjugation of the Petersons. Baker whistled them into a style of hitting that satisfied English ideas.

And no umpire ambitious to do honour to his office could take a better all-round model than M. Baker. You have only to look at his decisive chin and strongly marked eyebrows to know that he has a granite determination. And this is what an umpire wants. There is no fuss about Baker, and he does not delay the game for trifles. He is quick, and always in the best place for viewing the game.

It has already been stated that the less the whistle is blown the better. The umpire is under no obligation to whistle at every break or each resumption in the game. He should start the game with the whistle and end it by the same means, and use it for any infringement he sees fit to punish. It is usual, too, to sound it when a goal has been scored; but apart from these occasions he need scarcely ever blow it. The blowing of the whistle at a corner hit is very confusing, often being mistaken by the defenders as a sign that they have started to charge out too soon. The simplest and best way to start a corner hit is either by word of mouth, using the word " Play," or by a signal of the hand, or by silence, the whistle being used to stop the proceedings in the event of any irregularity. And the umpire will announce by word of mouth whether, when the ball has passed over the goal-line, it is a corner or a bye. Should a player be hurt, he will sound his whistle to stop the game, and he will sound it also when players continue playing unaware that the ball is dead, having gone over the touch- or goal-line, as the case may be.

The umpire will find his marching orders in Rule 21. Even a close study of this rule will probably leave some doubt in his mind as to one or two points. May he, for example, curtail the second half of a game if the first half has been over-long? The rule explicitly states that the time is to be "neither more nor less" than that agreed upon, and yet when the other umpire has made a mistake, through forgetfulness, to the extent possibly of ten minutes, but refuses to admit his error, it is clear that the rule is, in this respect, infringed. If the culprit acknowledges his mistake and knows exactly how much overtime has been played, the other umpire is right in abridging the second half, although his action would work most unfairly in the event of the ground sloping one way and the sun and wind favouring the slope. A strong solution of discretion on the part of the umpire is very necessary to the rules of hockey. Then he will notice that the rules do recognise the appeal, and to such an extent that they enjoin him to be guided by it. Unhappy umpire, tossed hither and thither on the waters of doubt and paradoxy! When an umpire is doubtful, he is to decide in favour of the team appealed against, so says Rule 21. This can refer only to *bona fide* appeals, made for some palpable infringement which the appealers clearly saw.

If the umpires' rule is to be taken in its strictest sense, then the umpire may not give any advice to any player between the first and the final whistle. Not even at the half-time interval may he relax this rule. And this is only just. His opportunities for forming a critical opinion of the play and players are special and unique, and it would be manifestly unfair were he to turn these opportunities to the account of one of the players or one of the teams. An umpire might offer advice or make a suggestion as to some change in the disposition of the players of one of the teams which would affect the result of the match. The umpire is frequently asked his opinion on the field. He must refuse to be drawn. Coaching, which is forbidden him, surely includes advice.

Hockey is far and away the most difficult game to umpire. The best of umpires make mistakes every match, mistakes either of omission or commission. So novices may take heart of grace, and solace themselves with the reflection that they make mistakes in good company, and that perfection is not expected of them.

CHAPTER XV

REMINISCENCES AND INCIDENTS

IT was somewhere in the eighties that I first set eyes on a hockey stick, and in the ancient city of Hereford.

I can recall the exact spot almost, scarce a stone's-throw from the Bishop's palace, where this curved and meaningless weapon met my curious gaze. I had heard of hockey. The game, or some hybrid form of it, had been played in the playground of the Cathedral school, but had either been voluntarily abandoned by the boys themselves, or else been vetoed by the Headmaster, on account of the serious bodily injuries it involved. But the ornate weapon I then saw for the first time was so unlike the crude hockey stick of my knowledge, that, unless it were some sort of boomerang, I could give no name or trade to it. And then it was carried by a very theatrical-looking person, which tended to increase the mystery. Enlightenment was speedily to come. F. R. Benson, the well-known Shakespearean actor, was playing in Hereford, and that very day the Cathedral school received a challenge to a hockey match with his company. So herein lay the solution of the mystery. The theatrical person was a member of Benson's company, and the weapon he carried a hockey stick.

Whether or no the match was played I am unable to recall; probably not, as puritanical ideas were more prevalent then than now, and "actor" stood for all sorts of ungodly qualities.

My next experience of hockey was a practical one—

actual participation in the game. This was subsequent to my Cambridge days, and in the middle nineties.

And how primitive the hockey we played in that sequestered corner of Herefordshire, on the very borders of Wales! We were absolutely self-taught, save for some smattering knowledge of the game imported by a doctor who had played for his Hospital. We played by the light of nature, and often the light had a ruddy and heathenish glow. Oh! it was a pagan proceeding when the passions ran riot, as they not infrequently did. A match that passed without the breaking of sticks or heads was voted a dull business. The timid members of the team were terrorised by the bashing tactics employed, more especially by the heavy-weights. Deliberate smashing at a stick was a common practice. Incidents of those days, which at the time seemed very much like a tragedy, take on, in retrospect, the appearance of comedy. One player, I remember, had a nasty trick of throwing his stick at the ball when he could not reach it in the legitimate manner. On one occasion he carried this trick too far. He threw his stick once, and his opponents accepted his explanation that it had slipped from his grip. He threw it a second time, but his previous explanation did not carry conviction. The game was delayed while the captains took counsel and warned the errant member. For a time this warning was observed, until in a heated moment it was forgotten, and for a third time this hurler of sticks succumbed to temptation. In a body the opposing team left the field. There was no argument, no further talking, only this silent exit of the visiting team, and the abrupt termination of the match.

But the incident did not end there. It had its sequel. It got into print, and harsh things were said of the " javelin-thrower," who was in reality nothing worse than an excitable player who lost himself in the lust of battle. He was greatly incensed by the misleading press comments, and vowed vengeance upon their author. High and low he sought him, up hill and down dale, to have his blood, but found him not. So the final scene was never written.

Nor did the ground on which we played our hockey tend to nurture or refine our game. It was an improvisation, carved out of a coarse and common meadow, and very little carving at that. On the wings the grass was so long that the ball was often hidden from view. So rough was the surface that habitual fielding with the stick was never dreamed of. As the district was one of Association football and as most of our players had been brought up on that game, fielding was usually done with the feet. Turning on the ball was rampant, and tackling from the left. It was rough-and-tumble hockey in those days, although two or three members of the club tried hard, and ultimately with no little success, to give a better tone to the play. But meanwhile we got good exercise, plenty of fun, and rather more injuries than we cared about.

One player there was who occasionally assisted us, a professional strong man, who would turn hand-springs over his stick at odd moments to diversify the proceedings, or distract his opponents, or perchance amuse the spectators. Certainly such acrobatic feats on the hockey-field had the virtue of novelty.

A most laughable incident once occurred in a match in which I was taking part. One of the players, a hard-bitten, sporting country parson, was struck a severe blow with the ball, in the mouth — scarcely a " laughable incident" for him. Up went his hand to his mouth, and into its palm he spluttered forth a mouthful of teeth—a complete artificial set. Thrusting the wreckage into his pocket, he resumed playing as though nothing unusual had happened.

The same player was due to conduct an evening service in his church, after an out-match. The match was over late, and to suit his convenience the whole team boarded the attendant brake without changing into mufti, and driving with all possible speed to the distant church, arrived there just in the nick of time.   Vaulting the churchyard wall, the curator of souls had speedily veiled his mud-plastered knees and uncleric attire in a surplice, and assumed his sacred functions.

Incidents worth recounting were of far more frequent occurrence in the earlier than in the later days of the game.

A famous cricketer, who has on several occasions figured in the Gentlemen and Players' match, was making his first hockey appearance for a prominent Southern club. During the progress of the match, an opponent dealt him, from behind, a violent and gratuitous blow across the back of his hand. " What the blazes are you playing at ? " with considerable warmth, was the very natural interrogation to escape the victim of this wanton assault.   " Well, Blank has just done the same thing to me," was the very ingenuous reply.   And, as the subject of this little incident remarked to me, " I realised that there was still a thing or two I had to learn about hockey."   Apparently, and of course erroneously, he did not think them worth learning, as he forsook hockey and took to golf, at which game he is now a scratch player.   Naturally, he thinks he has chosen the better part.

I was playing once in Wales, in Monmouthshire I think it was.   Anyhow, it was where hockey light shone with a very faltering flame.   The ground was frozen hard and the ball flew about in alarming fashion, ricochetting over the surface with lightning rapidity.   Whenever the opposing centre forward, a peppery little Welsh doctor, and my special charge, dribbled the ball near me, he would whack it straight at my shins in the hope of getting it on the rebound, and of finding me at a disadvantage after such cavalier treatment.   I resented this very unpleasant method of attack, and with pardonable asperity suggested that he should " play the game."   This heated him to another kind of attack, and in highly coloured phrases he summed up my character, and concluded by advising me to go home to my mother and play with a soft ball in the nursery. Hot tempers are not a Welsh monopoly, and had not wiser counsels prevailed we should have adjourned to the cowshed at the side of the ground which did duty for a dressing-room, and settled our differences in the good old-fashioned way. "A word in your ear," said a member of my team: "next time that little spitfire hits the ball at you, you whack him over the knees with your stick." And that was the spirit of retaliation in which much of the early hockey was played, more especially in the provinces.

It was the custom, just as it is now, for players to practise shooting at goal prior to a match. In those early days of which I am writing this custom partook of a positively criminal carelessness, which often eventuated in painful, sometimes serious, injuries. I can remember one very bad accident which occurred as the result of gross carelessness of this nature. The umpire, and quite an excellent one for the period, was standing in conversation with a player when he was violently struck in the face by the ball hit at close quarters without any warning cry having been given. He was so grievously hurt and cut about that he was obliged to leave the ground and visit a doctor. But that was not all. White and bandaged, he arrived home, and so alarming was his appearance that his wife received a shock which cost her a serious illness, and her husband a heavy doctor's bill.

It is impossible to condemn too heartily that thoughtless and often aimless slogging which precedes a match. The dangers of hockey are, albeit far less than they were, quite bad enough without players manufacturing worse ones before a match is entered upon.

When Alan Jenkins, the finest back ever produced by the West, came into Herefordshire, there came an influence which was felt throughout the county. It was remarkable the way this one player transformed the Herefordshire style of play and ideas about the game. He infused us with new principles altogether, took us in hand and taught us on and off the field, by word and by practical illustration, what a good and scientific game hockey could be.

Thanks to his influence and leadership, and his personal prowess, this humble county were soon able to make a fair show against Warwickshire, Shropshire, Worcestershire, Gloucestershire, Somersetshire. And something similar to this must be the story of many a county—ignorance, rough and untutored methods of play, and then the advent of some player or players whose superior knowledge of the game illuminates the darkness, introduces the science of hockey and a resulting period of prosperity.

I remember the first time I saw Jenkins use the reverse stroke—I thought it wonderful, and went away and talked enthusiastically about its wonder. I had never seen the stroke before, never dreamed of its existence. Such was mine and the prevailing ignorance. And now, of course, the veriest beginner essays the reverse stroke.

If it were possible to tap the memory and experiences of half a dozen of the " ancients "—those who played hockey in the seventies and early eighties—what a flow of unique and humorous incidents would be the result !

I have been fortunate in tapping the memory of one of these " ancients," to wit the Rev. A. E. Bevan. He relates how he once had the unwelcome experience of " heading " a ball out of goal. " I had run out," so goes his story, " and cleared, when our opponents' outside right, dashing up, centred hard, and whilst I was running across the mouth of the goal I received a stinging blow on the side of my head, the ball glancing over the top of the net."

A player in a fencing mask would create as much wonder at the present day on the hockey-field as would a redskin chief in full war-paint in Piccadilly. And yet Mr. Bevan met such an one in the past. " On inquiry," he says, " I learnt that, having had his nose broken some time previously, he had adopted such a means of protection rather than give up hockey. Possibly," adds Mr. Bevan, "in years to come goal-keepers may adopt the form of headgear used in single-sticks, and made of buffalo-hide. This would enable them to 'head' the ball away without fear of hurtful consequences."

To quote another of Mr. Bevan's memories : " I was playing at Aldershot against a team of soldiers. Our opponents, who were using oak sticks, suggested that at half-time we should change weapons. This was accordingly done, but with no real difference to the result ; for although we could not hit so hard, our combination did not materially suffer."

An amusing anecdote comes from Ireland in connection with the crack Irish touring club which plays under the name of "Buccaneers." Members of this club wear red stockings, and it is in connection with these stockings that the incident occurred which constitutes the anecdote referred to. In one of the Leinster *versus* Ulster matches the red stockings of W. M. Johnstone, a member of the "Buccaneers," were becoming uncomfortably prominent—that is, from an Ulster point of view. This prominence attracted a certain Ulster half-back, who proceeded to apply his stick rather freely to the shins of the too speedy Johnstone. To the subsequent remonstrances of the Ulster captain, who was also a "Buccaneer," the delinquent half-back replied that he really could not help it, as red stockings were "so darned easy to hit." Here is another "Buccaneer" incident :—

Some years ago now the "Buccaneers" were touring round London, and the never-to-be-forgotten "Mary Mitchell," who does so much for English players when they visit Dublin, was one of the team. The team, by the way, consisted of about 9 backs and 2 forwards. Mitchell, a full-back, played centre forward, the game being *v.* Surbiton. Things were going badly for the red-stockinged team, Surbiton having collected many goals. Mitchell took counsel with himself, and decided that the only thing to be done was to try the famous "Trinity Rush." This, being interpreted, means that one forward starts dribbling the ball with another forward in close attendance behind him.   When No. 1 forward is tackled, it is No. 2's duty to nip in and try and get the ball.   If successful, he then dashes off, followed closely by No. 1, and the same tactics are repeated until they achieve their desire, viz. a goal.   It is pleasant to relate that in this case " Mary Mitchell " was rewarded with their solitary goal.

Reversing the conventional order of things and keeping the ladies to the end, here is a little story which bears every mark of authenticity, but which may be accepted or rejected according to individual taste.   Were all lady hockey players, queried a friend of mine the other day, like a team he ran into in the bar parlour of a country-side inn ?   This was the scene which leapt up and hit him in the eye—a horsily dressed female, presumably the captain and leader, sitting on the table swinging her legs, and grouped around her in masculine attitudes and masculine attire the other members of the team.   Just as he entered the room he heard the horsy lady call out in strident tones, " Well, girls, what's your poison ? "

CHAPTER XVI

RULES OF THE GAME, AND NOTES THEREON

RULES OF THE GAME

1. *Teams.*—A game of hockey shall be played by two teams of eleven players. The correct constitution of a team is five forwards, three half-backs, two backs, and a goal-keeper, but this formation shall not be compulsory. The duration of the game shall be 70 minutes (unless otherwise agreed by the respective captains), half-time being called after 35 minutes' play, when the teams shall change ends.

2. *Captains.*—The captains shall (1) toss for choice of ends; (2) act as umpires, if there be no umpires, or delegate the duties of umpires to one member of their respective teams; and (3) indicate the goal-keepers for their respective teams before starting play, and after any change of goal-keeper.

3. *Ground.*—The ground shall be rectangular, 100 yards long and not more than 60 yards, nor less than 55 yards, wide. The ground shall be marked with white lines in accordance with plan given; the longer boundary lines to be called the side-lines, and the shorter boundary lines to be called the goal-lines. A flag-post shall be placed for the whole game at each corner, and at the centre of each side-line, 1 yard outside the line, and any other flag-posts must be a yard outside the ground. All flag-posts shall be at least 4 feet high.

4. *Goals, Posts, etc.*—A goal shall be in the centre of each goal-line, and shall consist of two posts 4 yards apart (inside measurement), joined together by a horizontal cross bar 7 feet from the ground. The goal-posts shall not extend upward beyond the cross bar, nor the cross bar sideways beyond the goal-posts. The posts shall be 2 inches square, and the cross bars shall have rectangular edges. Nets shall be attached to the posts, cross bars, and to the ground behind the goals.

5. *Striking Circle.*—In front of each goal shall be drawn a white line 4 yards long, parallel to, and 15 yards from, the goal-line. This line

shall be continued each way to meet the goal-line by quarter-circles, having the goal-posts as centres. The space enclosed by these lines and the goal-lines, including the lines themselves, shall be called the striking circle.

6. *Ball.*—The ball shall be a leather cricket ball, painted white, or made of white leather.

6. PENALTY.—Umpires shall forbid the use of any other ball.

7. *Sticks.*—A stick shall have a flat face on its left-hand side only, and shall have no metal or other fittings, or weights, or sharp edges, or dangerous splinters. Each stick must be of such size that it can be passed through a 2-inch ring. An indiarubber ring, 4 inches in external diameter when on the stick, may be used, but, all fittings included, the total weight must not exceed 28 oz.

7. PENALTY.—Umpires shall prohibit play with a stick which does not comply with this rule.

8. *Boots, etc.*—No player shall wear any dangerous material, such as spikes or nails, etc.

9. *Bully off.*—The game shall be started by one player of each team together bullying the ball in the centre of the ground (and after each goal and half-time). To bully the ball, each player shall strike the ground on his own side of the ball, and his opponent's stick over the ball three times alternately; after which, one of these two players must strike the ball before it is in general play. In all cases of bullying, the two players who are bullying shall stand squarely facing the side-lines. Every other player shall be nearer to his own goal-line than the ball is (except in the case of a penalty bully).

9. PENALTY.—For any breach of this rule the "bully" shall be taken again.

10. *Goal.*—A goal is scored when the whole ball has passed entirely over the goal-line under the bar, the ball, whilst within the striking circle, having been hit by or glanced off the stick of an attacker. Should the goal-posts or bar become displaced, and the ball pass at a point which, in the opinion of the umpire, is between where the posts or below where the bar should have been, he shall give a goal.

11. *Off-side.*—When a player hits or rolls-in the ball, any other player of the same team who is nearer his opponent's goal-line than the striker or roller-in at the moment *when the ball is hit or rolled-in* is off-side, unless there be at least three of his opponents nearer to their own goal-line than he is. He may not be within 5 yards of the ball, nor in any way interfere with any other player until the ball has been touched or hit by one of his opponents. No player, however, shall be off-side in his own half of the ground, nor if the ball was last touched or hit by one of his opponents (subject to the 5-yards rule), or by one of his own team who, at the time of hitting, is nearer his opponent's goal-line than himself.

11. PENALTY.—
> *Inside or outside the circles—*
> For any breach the penalty shall be a free hit by one
> of the opposing team on the spot where the breach
> occurred.

12. *General Details.*—The ball may be caught (but must be immediately released to fall perpendicularly to the ground) or stopped, but may not be picked up, carried, kicked, thrown, or knocked on or back, except with the stick. No player shall gain an advantage by the use of any part of his person or apparel except such as may accrue from stopping the ball; the foot, if used for that purpose, shall be taken away immediately. There shall be no play with the rounded back of the stick, no charging, kicking, shoving, shinning, tripping, personal handling, or hooking. Hooking sticks is allowed only when the stick hooked is within striking distance of the ball. There shall be no striking at sticks. A player may not obstruct by running in between his opponent and the ball, nor cross his opponent's left, unless he touches the ball before his opponent's person or stick, nor may he in any way interpose himself as an obstruction. The goal-keeper is allowed to kick the ball only in his own striking circle, but in the event of his taking part in a penalty bully this privilege shall not be allowed him. A ball touching an umpire or post is in play unless it goes off the ground. No player shall in any way interfere with the game unless his stick is in his hand.

12. PENALTIES.—
> (1) *Outside the circles*
> > For any breach the penalty shall be a free hit for one
> > of the opposing team on the spot where the breach
> > occurred.
> (2) *Inside the circles—*
> > (a) For any breach by the attacking team the penalty
> > shall be a free hit for the defending team.
> > (b) For any breach by the defending team the penalty
> > shall be a "penalty corner" or a "penalty bully"
> > on the spot where the breach occurred. A
> > penalty bully should only be given for a wilful
> > breach of a rule or when a goal would most
> > probably have been scored but for the occurrence
> > of the breach of the rule.
> (3) *Inside or outside the circles—*
> > In the event of two players being simultaneously at
> > fault in obstructing each other, the umpire shall
> > give a bully at the spot where the breach of rule
> > occurred.

13. *Sticks.*—When a player strikes at the ball, no part of his stick

must in any event rise above his shoulders at either the beginning or end of the stroke.

14. *Undercutting.*—No player shall intentionally undercut the ball.

> *Note.*—This rule is not intended to penalise the "scoop" stroke which raises the ball nor the hitting of the ball when in the air, except as provided for in Rule 15.

13 and 14. PENALTIES.—

(1) *Outside the circles—*

> For any breach the penalty shall be a free hit for one of the opposing team on the spot where the breach occurred.

(2) *Inside the circles—*

> (a) For any breach by the attacking team the penalty shall be a free hit for the defending team.
>
> (b) For any breach by the defending team the penalty shall be a "penalty corner" or a "penalty bully" (except in the case of "sticks," when a "penalty corner" only shall be allowed). A "penalty bully" should only be given for a wilful breach of a rule, or when a goal would most probably have been scored but for the occurrence of the breach of the rule.

15. *Free Hit.*—On the occasion of a free hit, no other player than the striker shall be within 5 yards of the spot where such hit is made, and the striker must not touch the ball again until it has been touched or hit by another player. He must fairly hit the ball, "scooping" up not being allowed. If the striker hit at but miss the ball, the stroke shall be taken again by him, provided that he has not given "sticks."

15. PENALTY.—If any player other than the striker be within 5 yards of the ball at the time of a free hit, the umpire shall order the hit to be taken again.

If the striker, after taking such hit, touches the ball again before it has been touched or hit by another player—

(1) *Inside the circles—*

> The umpire shall give a "penalty corner."

(2) *Outside the circles—*

> The umpire shall give a free hit to one of the opposite team to the offender.

If the ball is "scooped up"—

(1) *Outside the circles—*

> The umpire shall give a free hit to one of the opposite side to the offender.

(2) *Inside the circles—*

> The umpire shall give a "penalty corner."

16. *Penalty Bully.*—A penalty bully shall be played by the offender,

14

and by any player selected by the other team on the spot where the breach occurred. All other players shall be outside the striking circle in the field of play, and shall not enter the striking circle or take any further part in the game until the ball is driven outside the striking circle.

  16. PENALTY.—

     (*a*) Breach of any rule by defending team (except Rule 9)— The attacking team shall be awarded a penalty goal, which shall be of the same value as an ordinary goal.

     (*b*) Breach of any rule by attacking team (except Rule 9)— The defending team shall be allowed a free hit.

  17. *Roll-in.*—When a ball passes wholly over the side-line, it shall be rolled-in along the ground (and not bounced) into play by hand from the point where it crossed the side-line in any direction, by one of the team opposite to that of the player who last touched it. Players may cross the 5-yards line immediately the ball leaves the hand of the roller-in. The ball may be rolled-in at once, but no player shall stand (himself or his stick) within the 5-yards line ; should, however, the umpire consider that a player is standing within the 5-yards line to gain time, he shall not stop the game. The roller-in must have both feet and stick behind the side-line, and may only play the ball again after another player.

  17. PENALTIES.—

     (*a*) Breach of the rule by the player who rolls-in The roll-in shall be taken by a player of the other team.

     (*b*) Breach of the rule by any other player— The roll-in shall be taken again, except as specially provided for in this rule.

  18. *Behind.*—(*a*) If the ball is hit behind the goal-line by a player of the attacking team, or glance off the stick or person of, or be unintentionally, in the umpire's opinion, hit behind the goal-line by one of the defending team who is farther away from his own goal-line than the 25-yards line, it shall be brought out 25 yards in a direction at right angles to the goal-line from the point where it crossed the line and there "bullied."

  (*b*) If the ball glances off, or is, in the umpire's opinion, unintentionally sent behind the goal-line by any player of the defending team behind the 25-yards line, he (the umpire) shall give a corner to the attacking team.

  (*c*) If, however, the ball is intentionally, in the umpire's opinion, sent behind the goal-line by any player of the defending team, the umpire shall give a penalty corner to the attacking team.

  Provided that no player shall stand within 5 yards of the striker when a corner hit is taken, and that no goal can be scored from a corner hit by the attacking team unless the ball has been stopped motionless on the ground by one of the attacking team, or has touched the person or stick of one of the defending team before the last stroke of the attacking team. A player hitting a corner hit cannot participate in the game again until the ball has been played by another player. On hitting a corner hit, if the hitter miss the ball he shall take the hit again, provided he does not contravene Rule 13.

19. *Corner.*—A player of the attacking team shall have a hit from a point on the side- or goal-line within 3 yards of the nearest corner flag, and at the moment of such hit all the defending team (their sticks and feet) must be behind their own goal-line, and all the attacking team must be outside the circle in the field of play.

Provided that no player shall stand within 5 yards of a striker when a corner hit is taken, and that no goal can be scored from a corner hit by the attacking team unless the ball has been stopped motionless on the ground by one of the attacking team, or has touched the person or stick of one of the defending team before the last stroke of the attacking team. A player hitting a corner hit cannot participate in the game again until the ball has been played by another player. On hitting a corner hit, if the hitter miss the ball he shall take the hit again, provided he does not contravene Rule 13.

19. PENALTY.—If the striker, after taking such hit, touches the ball again before it has been touched or hit by another player, the umpire shall give a free hit to one of the opposite team to the offender.

20. *Penalty Corner.*—A player of the attacking team shall have a hit from any point on the goal-line he may choose, and at the moment of such hit all the defending team (their sticks and feet) must be behind their own goal-line, also all the attacking team must be outside the striking circle in the field of play.

Provided that no player shall stand within 5 yards of the striker when a penalty corner hit is taken, and that no penalty corner hit shall be taken at a less distance than 5 yards from the nearest goal-post, and that no goal can be scored from a corner hit by the attacking team unless the ball has been stopped motionless on the ground by one of the attacking team, or has touched the person or stick of one of the defending team before the last stroke of the attacking team. A player hitting a penalty corner hit cannot participate in the game again until the ball has been played by another player. On hitting a penalty corner hit, if the hitter miss the ball he shall take the hit again, provided he does not contravene Rule 13.

20. PENALTY.—If the striker, after taking such hit, touches the ball again before it has been touched or hit by another player, the umpire shall give a free hit to one of the opposite team to the offender.

21. *Umpires.*—Each umpire shall take half the ground for the whole game without changing ends. He shall also take one side-line and give

decisions *re* the roll-in (but not the corner hit) in both halves of the ground. If an umpire is doubtful, he shall decide in favour of the team appealed against. The umpire shall allow (the elements permitting) the full or agreed time, neither more nor less, deducting all wastage, and keep a record of the game. Until a decision is given, the ball is in play. If there be only one umpire, there should be two linesmen to give decisions as to the ball passing over the side-lines, and as to where and by which team the ball shall be rolled-in.

Umpires and linesmen are debarred from coaching or claiming during a game. The umpire shall refrain from putting the provision of any rule into effect in cases where he is satisfied that by enforcing it he would be giving an advantage to the offending team. The umpires shall give all decisions without waiting for an appeal.

22. *Rough Play and Misconduct.*—For rough play or misconduct the umpire shall have a discretionary power to warn the offending player, or to suspend him from further participation in the game.

23. *Accidents.*—When a player is temporarily incapacitated, the umpire shall suspend the game. When it is resumed, the ball shall be bullied off on a spot to be chosen by the umpire in whose half of the ground the player was hurt.

NOTE.

Official Rings for the Measurement of Sticks

Official rings can be obtained *only* from the Honorary Secretary of the Hockey Association—P. Collins, 6 Bedford Row, London, W.C.

NOTES ON THE RULES—THEIR WEAKNESSES, AND REFORMS NECESSARY, AND A COMPARISON WHERE POSSIBLE WITH THE RULES OF 1886

BY AN INTERNATIONAL

The writer will endeavour to point out any weaknesses in the rules, possible improvements, and a comparison where possible with those framed in 1886.

Rule 1 refers to the teams, and in the present-day rules mention is made of the correct constitution of a team being 5 forwards, 3 half-back, 2 backs, and a goal-keeper ; but the formation is not compulsory. From time to time there has been much discussion on teams playing 4 half-backs and no goal-keeper, and this discussion still continues ; but up to the present no suitable remedy has been suggested. Some suggest the alteration of the off-side rule to 2 instead of 3, and others that the definition of a goal-keeper be, that he may not come outside the circle; but perhaps the most satisfactory legislation would be to stipulate that, in the event of a team playing 4 halves or 3 backs, the off-side rule should read, "unless there be at least two of his opponents nearer," etc.

Rule 2. *Captains.*—No comment necessary.

Rule 3 refers to the ground, and the 1886 rule reads 100 yards long and 50 yards wide. The present rule stipulates not less than 55 yards wide nor more than 60, and nowadays in most cases the ground is 60 yards wide, and so a much more open game results.

Rule 4. *Goals, Posts, etc.*—Nowadays it is compulsory to have nets attached to the posts and ground, but no mention was made in 1886, and so one can easily realise what arguments must have arisen, as to whether the ball passed in or outside the post, and it was on this account that nets became general. Care should always be taken that the nets are fastened close to the posts and ground, so that there is no possibility of a ball passing through or under the net.

Rule 5. *Striking Circle.*—In drawing the line 15 yards from the goal-line, the distance should measure to the outside of the white line, as the rule states that the space enclosed by the lines, including the lines themselves, constitutes the striking circle.

Rule 6. *Ball.*—The rule states that the ball shall be a leather cricket ball, painted white, or made of white leather. As cricket balls vary in weight and size, we should think it advisable to add after the words "cricket ball" "of regulation match pattern and weight."

Rule 7. *Sticks.*—The original rules allowed the use of a stick any weight and 2½ inches wide, but now the weight is limited to 28 oz. all told, and must pass through a 2-inch ring. According to the strict rendering of this rule, a stick with leather tacked round the top of the handle with nails, as is very often seen, is prohibited; but there is no doubt that the rule was not intended to refer to the handle at all, but to prohibit the use of weighted heads and sticks with whalebone, etc., let in the head. Perhaps it would be as well to add the words, "below the splice" after "metal or other fittings."

Rule 8. *Boots, etc.*—This rule states that no player shall wear spikes or nails, etc. In Rules 6 and 7, with regard to "ball" and "sticks," the umpire shall forbid the use of any other ball, and prohibit play with a stick that does not comply with the rule; but no mention is made that he shall forbid the player wearing spikes or nails from taking part in the game. This should certainly be made a penalty, and the writer is aware of a case in which a player used regularly to wear boots with large hobnails, instead of bars or studs.

Rule 9. *Bully off.*—This rule is the same as originally settled in 1886, and the only penalty for any breach is that the "bully" be taken again. There is great scope for improvement in this rule, for the penalty is entirely inadequate. It is a by no means uncommon occurrence to see a player, other than the two "bullying," interfere in the "bully," before one of the two taking part in the same has hit the ball and so put it in general play, and it would make players much more careful if the penalty were a free hit or "penalty corner." The former would naturally be awarded for a breach of the rule outside the circles, and the "penalty corner" for a breach inside the circle by one of the defending team, and in the case of a breach by the attacking team, inside the circle, the defending side would be given a free hit. Of course, an "ordinary" bully inside the circle is not often seen nowadays, as it is only given in the case of two players being simultaneously at fault in obstructing each other, or when the game has been stopped for an accident in the circle.

Rule 10. *Goal.*—There is nothing in this rule that calls for any comments.

Rule 11. *Off-side.*—In comparing this rule with that of 1886, the first point that strikes one is that the old rule is to all intents the one that is now required to remedy the evils of the present one. The weakness of the existing rule is the wording, "he may not be within 5 yards of the ball," etc., and by this reading of the rule, a forward, who has dribbled down the ground, with his partner close *behind* him, can, the moment his partner takes a pass from him, be given off-side, if, at the moment of his partner accepting the pass, there are less than three of his opponents nearer their own goal-line than he is, and if he (the giver of the pass) is within 5 yards of his partner when he took the pass. As this has happened on several occasions, it is plain that the rule requires an alteration in the wording, for it is obviously most unfair to penalise a player after he has made a brilliant run and an equally brilliant pass. Now, the wording of the original rule in 1886 was as follows: "and may not touch the ball himself, nor in any way whatever prevent another player from doing so," etc. The soundest proposal put forward to remedy the existing grievance is to substitute for "he may not be within 5 yards," etc., "he may not touch the ball himself, nor in any way interfere with an opponent, or with the play, until," etc.

Rule 12. *General Details.*—The chief addition to the old rule is with regard to coming in on the left side of a player, and of course this is of paramount importance, as it entirely does away with the advantage that used to be gained by body play. The rule itself seems to be very concise and sound in principle, and it is difficult to suggest any improvement.

Rule 13. *Sticks.*—As regards the rule itself, no comment is required, but in the Penalties, (2) *Inside the circles* the penalty (*b*) reads, "For any breach by the defending team the penalty shall be a 'penalty corner' or a 'penalty bully' (except in the case of 'sticks,' when a 'penalty corner' only shall be allowed) A 'penalty bully' should only be given for a wilful breach of a rule, or when a goal would most probably have been scored but for the occurrence of the breach of the rule."

Now take the case of a goal-keeper stopping a certain goal with his stick above his shoulder or head. The rule distinctly excepts "sticks" from a "penalty bully," but yet it would come under "a goal would most probably," etc. Perhaps the following, added to the rule, would meet the case: "If, in the umpire's opinion, a wilful breach of 'sticks' is given, the umpire shall award a penalty bully."

Rule 14.—Undercutting requires no comment.

Rule 15. *Free Hit.*—The penalty enacts that if any player, other than the striker, be within 5 yards of the ball at the time of the free hit, the umpire shall order the hit to be taken again. As the rule and penalty are very clearly defined, a player has no excuse for getting within 5 yards, and as the culprit would probably be a forward, trying to poach a yard on the edge of the circle, it might be advisable to award a free hit, for a breach of this rule, to the defending team, and in the case of the defending team erring, to let the hit be taken again.

Rule 16. *Penalty Bully.*—There was no such rule framed in 1886, but the present rule has done a great deal towards checking fouling in the circle, etc., and is in every way a valuable addition.

Rule 17. *Roll-in.*—The great improvement in the roll-in, compared with the original rule, lies in the fact that the ball may now be rolled-in in any direction. Previously it had to be rolled-in at right angles to the side-line, and as a result was continually going into touch again. One often sees the ball bounced-in instead of rolled-in, and it would not only save time, but make players more careful, if a free hit were awarded, instead of the opposite side taking the roll-in, and the same penalty might be exacted for a breach of the 5-yards rule.

Rule 18. *Behind.*—This rule does not call for any comment, but it is extraordinary the number of players who think that if the ball is hit outside the 25-yards line and glance off a defender nearer his goal-line than the 25 yards, it is not a corner. It is only in the case of the defender being farther away from his goal-line than the 25-yards line that allows it to be bullied at the 25-yards line, after it has touched or been unintentionally hit by the defender.

Rule 19. *Corner.*—*Vide* Rule 20.

Rule 20. *Penalty Corner.*—The corner hit differs from the old rule, insomuch as the ball must be stopped motionless on the ground before a goal can be scored, or must have touched the person or stick of one of the defending team before the last stroke of the attacking team. The original rule allowed the flying shot to be taken from a corner hit, and it was on account of the danger of that stroke that the present rule was instituted; and even now, if a player chooses to take a flying shot, there is no penalty attached, and he has the chance of the ball hitting a defender and allowing him to get in another shot, and a goal scored from the latter would be legitimate, though not from the former. As the rule was framed to eliminate danger as much as possible, it seems incredible that there is no penalty exacted for not stopping the ball motionless. This rule (and of course the penalty corner comes under the same category) and the off-side rule are the three rules that require a much-needed reform. In the case of the corner hit, or penalty corner hit, for the ball not being stopped motionless before shooting, the penalty should be a free hit to the defending team. In Rule 20 one notices that the wording should read, " and that no goal can be scored from a penalty corner hit," etc., but in the rule the word "penalty" is omitted.

Rule 21. *Umpires.*—The only fault to be found with this rule is, that according to the wording " shall allow the full or agreed time, neither more nor less," the umpire may award a penalty bully in the last minute or so of the game, and yet would have to blow the whistle for time, perhaps, before the penalty bully had been finished, thereby causing a distinct hardship on the attacking team. Perhaps the best means of remedying this would be to add a proviso to the rule, viz., " In the event of a penalty bully being awarded, and time intervening before such penalty bully is completed, the umpire shall refrain from calling time until the penalty bully has been taken."

Rule 22. Rough play ; and

Rule 23. Accidents—call for no comment.

APPENDIX

IMPORTANT RECORDS

INTERNATIONAL RECORDS (MEN)

ENGLAND v. IRELAND

	Venue								Goals	
1895	Richmond	.	.	.	.	England	.	.	.	5	0
1896	Dublin	.	.	.	.	England	.	.	.	1	0
1897	Wimbledon					England	.	.	.	7	2
1898	Dublin	.				Drawn	.	.	.	1	1
1899	Richmond	.	.	.	.	England	.	.	.	3	
1900	Belfast	.	.	.	.	England	.	.	.	2	1
1901	Surbiton	.	.	.	.	England	.	.	.	4	2
1902	Dublin	.	.	.	.	England	.	.	.	2	0
1903	Surbiton	.	.	.	.	England	.	.	.	1	0
1904	Dublin	.	.	.	.	Ireland	.	.	.	3	2
1905	Surbiton	.	.	.	.	England	.	.	.	4	1
1906	Dublin	.	.	.	.	England	.	.	.	2	1
1907	Bromley	.	.	.	.	England	.	.	.	5	0
1908	Dublin	.	.	.	.	England	.	.	.	4	0

ENGLAND v. WALES

1898	Kersal	.	.	.	.	England	.	.	.	7	0
1899	Newport	.	.	.	.	England	.	.	.	3	0
1900	Kersal	.	.	.	.	England	.	.	.	10	0
1901	Swansea	.	.	.	.	England	.	.	.	4	0
1902	Kersal	.	.	.	.	England	.	.	.	7	0
1903	Llandudno	.	.	.	.	England	.	.	.	6	3
1904	Bath	.	.	.	.	England	.	.	.	4	1
1905	Newport	.	.	.	.	England	.	.	.	6	2
1906	Manchester					England	.	.	.	13	2
1907	Llandudno	.				England	.	.	.	6	0
1908	Bath	.	.			England	.	.	.	4	2

ENGLAND v. SCOTLAND

	Venue		Goals	
1903	Birmingham	England	5	0
1904	Glasgow	Drawn	2	2
1905	Surbiton	England	9	0
1906	Glasgow	England	3	0
1907	Birmingham	England	3	0
1908	Edinburgh	England	3	1

ENGLAND v. FRANCE

1907	Beckenham	England	14	0
1908	Paris	Drawn	2	2

IRELAND v. WALES

1895	Rhyl	Ireland	3	
1896	Rhyl	Ireland	5	
1897	Dublin	Ireland	5	
1898	Llandudno	Ireland	10	
1899	Dublin	Ireland	4	
1900	Llandudno	Ireland	5	0
1901	Dublin	Ireland	9	1
1902	Abergavenny	Ireland	7	3
1903	Limerick	Ireland	7	0
1904	Abergavenny	Ireland	4	2
1905	Cork	Ireland	8	2
1906	Cardiff	Ireland	8	0
1907	Dublin	Ireland	5	0
1908	Cardiff	Ireland	4	2

IRELAND v. SCOTLAND

1902	Belfast	Ireland	3	0
1903	Partick	Ireland	6	0
1904	Belfast	Ireland	8	1
1905	Partick	Ireland	5	0
1906	Belfast	Ireland	7	1
1907	Glasgow	Drawn	3	3
1908	Belfast	Ireland	6	0

APPENDIX

SCOTLAND v. WALES

Venue								Goals	
1903	Newport	.	.	.	.	Wales	. . .	5	1
1904	Edinburgh	.	.	.	.	Wales	. . .	5	1
1905	Llandudno	.				Drawn	. . .	2	2
1906	Edinburgh	.				Scotland	. . .	3	1
1907	Abergavenny	.	.	.		Scotland	. . .	2	
1908	Glasgow	.	.	.		Scotland	. . .	2	

INTERNATIONAL RECORDS (LADIES)

ENGLAND v. IRELAND

1895	Brighton	. . .	Drawn	. . .	0	
1896	Dublin	.	Ireland	. . .	2	
1897	Blackheath		Drawn	.	0	
1898	Dublin	. . .	England	. . .	1	
1899	Richmond	. . .	England	. . .	3	8
1900	Dublin	. . .	England	. . .	2	
1901	Richmond	. . .	England	. . .	3	
1902	Dublin	. . .	Ireland	. . .	5	
1903	Richmond	. . .	England	. . .	7	1
1904	Dublin	. . .	England	. . .	1	0
1905	Richmond	. . .	England	. . .	3	1
1906	Dublin	. . .	England	. . .	2	0
1907	Richmond	. . .	England	. . .	7	3
1908	Dublin	. . .	Ireland	. . .	4	2

ENGLAND v. SCOTLAND

1902	Glasgow	. . .	England	. . .	4	0
1903	Edinburgh	.	England	. . .	11	0
1904	Richmond	.	England	. . .	7	2
1905	Edinburgh	.	Drawn	. . .	1	1
1906	Richmond	.	England	. . .	4	
1907	Edinburgh	.	England	. . .	2	
1908	Richmond	.	England	. . .	5	

ENGLAND v. WALES

1900	Cardiff	. . .	England	.	13	0
1901	London		England	.	13	0
1902	Abergavenny	. .	England	.	15	0

Since abandoned

IRELAND *v.* WALES

Year	Venue				Winner					Goals	
1899	Llandudno .	.	.	.	Ireland	.	.	.	.	5	o
1900	Dublin	.			Ireland	.	.	.	.	9	o
1901	Llandudno .	.	.	.	Ireland	.	.	.	.	8	o
1902	Dublin	.	.	.	Ireland	.	.	.	.	7	o
1903	Wrexham .	.	.	.	Ireland	.	.	.	.	7	o
1904	Dublin	.	.	.	Ireland	.	.	.	.	10	o
1905	Swansea	.	.	.	Ireland	.	.	.	.	10	o
1906	Dublin	.	.	.	Ireland	.	.	.	.	6	1
1907	Swansea	.	.	.	Ireland	.	.	.	.	11	o
1908				No match							

IRELAND *v.* SCOTLAND

Year	Venue				Winner					Goals	
1901	Dublin	.	.	.	Ireland	.	.	.	.	2	o
1902	Edinburgh .	.	.	.	Drawn	.				o	o
1903	Dublin	.	.	.	Ireland	.	.	.	.	3	1
1904	Edinburgh .	.	.	.	Ireland	.				5	3
1905	Dublin	.	.	.	Scotland	.	.	.	.	4	3
1906	Edinburgh .	.	.	.	Scotland	.	.	.	.	7	1
1907	Rathmines .	.	.	.	Ireland	.	.	.	.	3	o
1908	Edinburgh .	.	.	.	Ireland	.	.	.	.	5	o

SCOTLAND *v.* WALES

Year	Venue				Winner					Goals
1903	Glasgow	.	.	.	Scotland	.	.	.	.	5
1904	Newport	.	.	.	Scotland	.	.	.	.	8
1905				No match						
1906	Cardiff	.	.	.	Scotland	.	.	.	.	12
1907	Glasgow	.	.	.	Scotland	.	.	.	.	12
1908				No match						

INTER-DIVISIONAL RECORDS (MEN)

SOUTH *v.* NORTH

Year	Winner	Goals		Year	Winner			Goals	
1890	South	6	o	1900	North	.	.	2	o
1891	South	5	o	1901	North			4	1
1892	South	4	2	1902	South			5	o
1893	South	4	2	1903	South			*7	o
1894	Drawn	2	2	1904	South			6	3
1895	South	3	2	1905	South			4	2
1896	South	4	2	1906	South			7	2
1897	South	1	o	1907	South			4	2
1898	South .	4	2	1908	South	.	.	4	1
1899	South .	.	3	2						

* 7—o is an error in Handbook.

SOUTH *v.* MIDLANDS

Year		Goals		Year		Goals	
1897	South	5	1	1903	South	3	2
1898	Midlands	1	0	1904	South	2	0
1899	No match			1905	South	3	2
1900	Midlands	2	0	1906	South	5	1
1901	Midlands	2	1	1907	South	2	1
1902	Drawn	2	2	1908	South	1	0

SOUTH *v.* WEST

Year				Year			
1901	West	4	2	1905	South	7	0
1902	South	4	3	1906	South	3	0
1903	South	4	1	1907	South	13	0
1904	Drawn	2	2	1908	West	4	3

NORTH *v.* MIDLANDS

Year				Year			
1895	North	5	1	1902	Midlands	4	0
1896	North	4	2	1903	North .	3	1
1897	North	1	0	1904	Midlands	2	
1898	North	3	2	1905	North .	2	
1899	North	3	2	1906	Midlands	4	
1900	North	3	2	1907	Midlands	5	1
1901	Drawn	2	2	1908	Midlands	4	3

NORTH *v.* WEST

Year				Year			
1905	North	4	2	1907	North	3	2
1906	North	2	1	1908	North	8	2

MIDLANDS *v.* WEST

Year				Year			
1895	West	1	0	1902	Midlands	7	0
1896	Midlands	4	3	1903	West .	2	1
1897	Midlands	3	2	1904	Midlands	3	2
1898	Midlands	2	1	1905	Midlands	2	0
1899	West .	4	0	1906	Midlands	9	1
1900	Midlands	3	0	1907	Midlands	6	0
1901	Midlands	4	2	1908	Midlands	3	2

INTER-TERRITORIAL RECORDS (LADIES)

SOUTH *v.* NORTH

		Goals					Goals	
1898	South	1	0	1904	South		1	0
1900	North	6	2	1905	South		11	0
1901	South	7	1	1906	South		6	1
1902	Drawn	1	1	1907	Drawn		3	3
1903	Drawn	1	1	1908	Drawn		4	4

SOUTH *v.* MIDLANDS

1900	South	4	0	1905	South		2	1
1901	Midlands	5	3	1906	South		6	4
1902	South	2	1	1907	Midlands		5	4
1903	South	2	1	1908	South		2	1
1904	South	5	0					

SOUTH *v.* WEST

1903	South	3	0	1906	South		3	0
1904	South	5	0	1907	South		6	2
1905	South	6	0	1908	West		4	1

SOUTH *v.* EAST

1907	East	10	3	1908	South	6	

NORTH *v.* MIDLANDS

1898	Drawn	0	0	1904	Midlands			7	1
1899	North	3	0	1905	Drawn .			3	3
1900	North	3	2	1906	Midlands			4	2
1901	Midlands	6	4	1907	North			3	2
1902	North	2	0	1908	North .	.	.	6	4
1903	North	7	2						

NORTH *v.* WEST

1902	North			4	0	1906	North		5	2
1903	North			4	0	1907	North		3	2
1904	North .			3	1	1908	North		4	1
1905	North .	.	.	2	1					

NORTH *v.* EAST

		Goals					Goals	
1907	North	3	2	1908	North		4	2

MIDLANDS *v.* WEST

1902	Drawn . . .	2	2	1906	Midlands	5	2
1903	West .	2	1	1907	Midlands	4	2
1904	Midlands	5	0	1908	Midlands	7	1
1905	Midlands	4	0				

MIDLANDS *v.* EAST

1907	Midlands	7	2	1908	Midlands	9

EAST *v.* WEST

1907	East	4	2	1908	East	6

INTER-UNIVERSITY RECORDS (MEN)

OXFORD *v.* CAMBRIDGE

1890	Oxford	2	0	1900	Cambridge	3	2
1891	Oxford	3	2	1901	Cambridge	4	1
1892	Drawn	2	2	1902	Oxford	3	2
1893	Oxford	3	1	1903	Oxford	3	0
1894	Drawn	1	1	1904	Oxford	1	0
1895	Drawn	3	3	1905	Oxford	3	1
1896	Cambridge .	3	1	1906	Cambridge	4	1
1897	Cambridge	4	0	1907	Cambridge	3	2
1898	Cambridge	4	0	1908	Cambridge	3	1
1899	Cambridge	5	2				

INDEX

Printed wholly in England for the MUSTON COMPANY
By LOWE & BRYDONE, PRINTERS, LTD , PARK STREET, CAMDEN TOWN, LONDON, N W.1

A FEW OF

MESSRS. METHUEN'S
PUBLICATIONS

Armstrong (Warwick W.). THE ART OF CRICKET. *Second Edition.* Illustrated. Crown 8vo, 6s. net.

Atkinson (T. D.). ENGLISH ARCHITECTURE. Illustrated. *Sixth Edition.* Fcap. 8vo, 5s. net.

Bain (F. W.)—
IN THE GREAT GOD'S HAIR (*Seventh Edition*); A DRAUGHT OF THE BLUE (*Seventh Edition*); AN INCARNATION OF THE SNOW (*Fourth Edition*); A MINE OF FAULTS (*Fifth Edition*); A DIGIT OF THE MOON (*Fourteenth Edition*); THE LIVERY OF EVE (*Third Edition*); A HEIFER OF THE DAWN (*Eleventh Edition*); AN ESSENCE OF THE DUSK (*Fifth Edition*); THE DESCENT OF THE SUN (*Ninth Edition*); THE ASHES OF A GOD (*Third Edition*); BUBBLES OF THE FOAM (*Third Edition*); A SYRUP OF THE BEES (*Second Edition*); THE SUBSTANCE OF A DREAM (*Second Edition*). Fcap. 8vo, 5s. net each. AN ECHO OF THE SPHERES. Wide Demy, 10s. 6d. net.

Baker (C. H. Collins). CROME. Illustrated. Quarto, £5 5s. net.

Bateman (H. M.).
A BOOK OF DRAWINGS. *Fifth Edition.* Royal 4to, 10s. 6d. net. SUBURBIA, Demy 4to, 6s. net. MORE DRAWINGS. *Second Edition.* Royal 4to, 10s. 6d. net.

Beckford (Peter). THOUGHTS ON HUNTING. In a series of Familiar Letters to a Friend. With an Introduction and Notes by J. OTHO PAGET. Illustrated. *Fifth Edition.* Demy 8vo, 6s. net.

Belloc (H.)—
PARIS. Illustrated. *Fourth Edition.* Crown 8vo, 8s. 6d. net. HILLS AND THE SEA. *Thirteenth Edition.* Fcap. 8vo, 6s. net. Also Fcap 8vo, 2s net. ON NOTHING. *Fourth Edition.* Fcap. 8vo, 6s. net. Also Fcap 8vo, 2s. net. ON EVERYTHING. *Fourth Edition.* Fcap. 8vo, 6s. net. Also Fcap. 8vo, 2s. net. ON SOMETHING. *Third Edition.* Fcap. 8vo, 6s. net. Also Fcap. 8vo, 2s. net. FIRST AND LAST. *Second Edition.* Fcap. 8vo, 6s. net. THIS AND THAT AND THE OTHER. *Second Edition.* Fcap. 8vo, 6s. net.

Braid (James), Open Champion, 1901, 1905, 1906, 1908, and 1910. ADVANCED GOLF. Illustrated. *Eleventh Edition.* Demy 8vo, 14s. net.

Chandler (Arthur), D.D., late Lord Bishop of Bloemfontein. ARA CŒLI; An Essay in Mystical Theology. *Eighth Edition.* 5s. net. FAITH AND EXPERIENCE. *Third Edition.* 5s. net. THE CULT OF THE PASSING MOMENT. *Fifth Edition.* 6s. net. THE ENGLISH CHURCH AND RE-UNION. 5s. net. SCALA MUNDI. 4s. 6d. net.

Chesterton (G. K.)—
THE BALLAD OF THE WHITE HORSE. *Sixth Edition.* 6s. net. ALL THINGS CONSIDERED. *Fourteenth Edition.* 6s. net; also Fcap. 8vo, 2s. net. TREMENDOUS TRIFLES. *Sixth Edition.* 6s. net; also Fcap. 8vo, 2s. net. ALARMS AND DISCURSIONS. *Second Edition.* 6s. net. A MISCELLANY OF MEN. *Third Edition.* 6s. net. THE USES OF DIVERSITY. 6s. net. WINE, WATER, AND SONG. *Twelfth Edition.* 1s. 6d. net.

Clouston (Sir T. S.). THE HYGIENE OF MIND. Illustrated. *Seventh Edition.* Demy 8vo, 10s. 6d. net.

Clutton-Brock (A.)—
THOUGHTS ON THE WAR, 1s. 6d. net; WHAT IS THE KINGDOM OF HEAVEN? 5s. net; ESSAYS ON ART, 5s. net; ESSAYS ON BOOKS, 6s. net; MORE ESSAYS ON BOOKS, 6s. net.

Conrad (Joseph). THE MIRROR OF THE SEA: MEMORIES AND IMPRESSIONS. *Fourth Edition.* Fcap. 8vo, 6s. net; also Fcap. 8vo, 2s. net.

Dickinson (G. Lowes). THE GREEK VIEW OF LIFE. *Fourteenth Edition.* Crown 8vo, 5s. net.

Dobson (J. F.). THE GREEK ORATORS. Crown 8vo, 7s. 6d. net.

Drever (James). THE PSYCHOLOGY OF EVERYDAY LIFE. *Third Edition.* Crown 8vo, 6s. net.
THE PSYCHOLOGY OF INDUSTRY. Crown 8vo, 5s. net.

Einstein (A.). RELATIVITY: THE SPECIAL AND THE GENERAL THEORY. *Seventh Edition.* Crown 8vo, 5s. net.
SIDELIGHTS ON RELATIVITY. Crown 8vo, 3s. 6d. net.
THE MEANING OF RELATIVITY. Crown 8vo, 5s. net.

Other Books on the **Einstein Theory.**

SPACE—TIME—MATTER. By HERMANN WEYL. Demy 8vo, 18s. net.
EINSTEIN THE SEARCHER: HIS WORK EXPLAINED IN DIALOGUES WITH EINSTEIN. By ALEXANDER MOSZKOWSKI. Demy 8vo, 12s. 6d. net.
AN INTRODUCTION TO THE THEORY OF RELA-TIVITY. By LYNDON BOLTON, M.A. Crown 8vo, 5s. net.
RELATIVITY AND GRAVITATION. By various Writers. Edited by J. MALCOLM BIRD. Crown 8vo, 7s. 6d. net.
RELATIVITY AND THE UNIVERSE. By HARRY SCHMIDT. *Second Edition.* Crown 8vo, 5s. net.
THE IDEAS OF EINSTEIN'S THEORY. By J. H. THIRRING, Ph.D. *Second Edition* Crown 8vo, 5s. net.

Evans (Lady). LUSTRE POTTERY. With 24 Plates. Royal Quarto, £2 12s. 6d. net.

Fyleman (Rose). FAIRIES AND CHIMNEYS. *Fourteenth Edition.* Fcap. 8vo, 3s. 6d. net.
THE FAIRY GREEN. *Seventh Edition.* Fcap. 8vo, 3s. 6d. net.
THE FAIRY FLUTE. *Third Edition.* Fcap. 8vo, 3s. 6d. net
THE RAINBOW CAT AND OTHER STORIES. Fcap. 8vo, 3s. 6d. net.

Gibbins (H. de B.). THE INDUSTRIAL HISTORY OF ENGLAND. With 5 Maps and a Plan. *Twenty-seventh Edition.* Crown 8vo, 5s.

Gibbon (Edward). THE DECLINE AND FALL OF THE ROMAN EMPIRE. Edited, with Notes, Appendices, and Maps, by J. B. BURY. Illustrated. Seven Volumes. Demy 8vo, each 12s. 6d. net. Also Seven Volumes. Unillustrated. Crown 8vo, each 7s. 6d. net.

Glover (T. R.). THE CONFLICT OF RELIGIONS IN THE EARLY ROMAN EMPIRE. *Ninth Edition.* Demy 8vo, 10s. 6d. net.

THE CHRISTIAN TRADITION AND ITS VERIFICATION. *Second Edition.* Crown 8vo, 6s. net.

POETS AND PURITANS. *Second Edition.* Demy 8vo, 10s. 6d. net.

VIRGIL. *Fourth Edition.* Demy 8vo, 10s. 6d. net.

FROM PERICLES TO PHILIP. *Third Edition.* Demy 8vo, 10s. 6d. net.

Grahame (Kenneth), Author of "The Golden Age." THE WIND IN THE WILLOWS. With a Frontispiece by GRAHAM ROBERTSON. *Twelfth Edition.* Crown 8vo, 7s. 6d. net.
Illustrated Edition. With drawings in colour and line, by NANCY BARNHART. Small 4to, 10s. 6d. net.

Hall (H. R.). THE ANCIENT HISTORY OF THE NEAR EAST FROM THE EARLIEST TIMES TO THE BATTLE OF SALAMIS. Illustrated. *Fifth Edition.* Demy 8vo, £1 1s. net.

Herbert (A. P.). THE WHEREFORE AND THE WHY. NEW RHYMES FOR OLD CHILDREN. Illustrated by GEORGE MORROW. Fcap. 4to, 3s. 6d. net.

"TINKER, TAILOR . . ." A Child's Guide to the Professions. Illustrated by GEORGE MORROW. Fcap. 4to, 3s. 6d. net.

LIGHT ARTICLES ONLY. Illustrated by GEORGE MORROW. *Second Edition.* Crown 8vo, 6s. net.

Holdsworth (W. S.). A HISTORY OF ENGLISH LAW. Vols. I., II., III. Each *Second Edition.* Demy 8vo, each £1 5s. net.

Hutton (Edward)—
THE CITIES OF UMBRIA (*Fifth Edition*); THE CITIES OF LOMBARDY; THE CITIES OF ROMAGNA AND THE MARCHES; FLORENCE AND NORTHERN TUSCANY, WITH GENOA (*Third Edition*); SIENA AND SOUTHERN TUSCANY (*Second Edition*); VENICE AND VENETIA; THE CITIES OF SPAIN (*Fifth Edition*); NAPLES AND SOUTHERN ITALY. Illustrated. Crown 8vo. Each 8s. 6d. net. ROME (*Fourth Edition*), 6s. net.

Inge (W. R.). CHRISTIAN MYSTICISM. (The Bampton Lectures for 1899). *Fifth Edition.* Crown 8vo, 7s. 6d. net.

Jenks (E.). A SHORT HISTORY OF ENGLISH LAW. *Second Edition.* Demy 8vo, 12s. 6d. net.

Julian (Lady), Anchoress at Norwich, A.D., 1373. REVELATIONS OF DIVINE LOVE. A Version from the MS. in the British Museum. Edited by GRACE WARRACK. *Seventh Edition.* Crown 8vo, 5s. net.

Kidd (Benjamin). THE SCIENCE OF POWER. *Ninth Edition.* Crown 8vo, 7s. 6d. net.

SOCIAL EVOLUTION. A New Ed. Demy 8vo, 8s. 6d. net.

A PHILOSOPHER WITH NATURE. *Second Edition.* Crown 8vo. 6s. net.

Kipling (Rudyard). BARRACK-ROOM BALLADS. *228th Thousand. Fifty-fifth Edition.* Crown 8vo, 7s. 6d. net. Also Fcap. 8vo, 6s. net ; leather 7s. 6d. net. Also a Service Edition. Two Volumes, Square Fcap. 8vo. Each 3s. net.

THE SEVEN SEAS. 161st *Thousand*. *Thirty-fourth
Edition.* Crown 8vo, 7s. 6d. net. Also Fcap. 8vo. 6s. net; leather,
7s. 6d. net. Also a Service Edition. Two Volumes. Square Fcap.
8vo. Each 3s. net.

THE FIVE NATIONS. 129th *Thousand*. *Twenty-
third Edition.* Crown 8vo, 7s. 6d. net. Also Fcap. 8vo, 6s. net;
leather, 7s. 6d. net. Also a Service Edition. Two volumes. Square
Fcap. 8vo. Each 3s. net.

DEPARTMENTAL DITTIES. 102nd *Thousand*. *Thirty-
fourth Edition.* Crown 8vo, 7s. 6d. net. Also Fcap. 8vo, 6s. net.;
leather, 7s. 6d. net. Also a Service Edition. Two Volumes
Square Fcap. 8vo. Each 3s. net.

THE YEARS BETWEEN. 95th *Thousand*. Crown
8vo, 7s. 6d. net. Also Fcap. 8vo, 6s. net; leather, 7s. 6d. net. Also
a Service Edition. Two Volumes. Square Fcap. 8vo. Each 3s.
net.

TWENTY POEMS FROM RUDYARD KIPLING.
Fcap. 8vo, 1s. net.

A KIPLING ANTHOLOGY—VERSE: Selected from
the Poetry of RUDYARD KIPLING. *Third Edition.* Fcap. 8vo, 6s.
net. Leather, 7s. 6d. net.

Lamb (Charles and Mary). THE COMPLETE WORKS.
Edited by E. V. LUCAS. A New and Revised Edition in Six Volumes.
With Frontispiece. Fcap. 8vo. Each 6s. net.
The Volumes are :—
I. MISCELLANEOUS PROSE. II. ELIA AND THE LAST ESSAYS
OF ELIA. III. BOOKS FOR CHILDREN. IV. PLAYS AND POEMS.
V. and VI. LETTERS.

**Lankester (Sir Ray). SCIENCE FROM AN EASY
CHAIR.** First Series. Illustrated. *Fifteenth Edition.* Crown
8vo, 7s. 6d. net. Also Fcap. 8vo, 2s. net.

SCIENCE FROM AN EASY CHAIR. Second Series.
Illustrated. *Third Edition.* Crown 8vo, 7s. 6d. net. Also as MORE
SCIENCE FROM AN EASY CHAIR. Fcap. 8vo, 2s. net.

DIVERSIONS OF A NATURALIST. Illustrated.
Third Edition. Crown 8vo, 7s. 6d. net.

SECRETS OF EARTH AND SEA. Illustrated. Crown
8vo, 8s. 6d. net.

Lescarboura (A. C.). RADIO FOR EVERYBODY.
Edited by R. L. SMITH-ROSE, M.Sc. Illustrated. Crown 8vo,
7s. 6d. net.

Lodge (Sir Oliver)—
MAN AND THE UNIVERSE, Crown 8vo, 7s. 6d. net; also Fcap. 8vo,
2s. net; THE SURVIVAL OF MAN; A Study in Unrecognised Human
Faculty, Crown 8vo, 7s. 6d. net; also Fcap. 8vo, 2s. net; REASON
AND BELIEF, 2s. net; THE SUBSTANCE OF FAITH, 2s. net: RAYMOND
REVISED, 6s. net.

Lucas (E. V.)—
THE LIFE OF CHARLES LAMB, two volumes, Fcap. 8vo, 21s. net; EDWIN AUSTIN ABBEY, R.A., 2 vols., £6 6s. net: VERMEER OF DELFT, Fcap. 4to, 10s. 6d. net. A WANDERER IN HOLLAND, 10s. 6d. net; A WANDERER IN LONDON, 10s. 6d. net; LONDON REVISITED, 10s. 6d. net; A WANDERER IN PARIS, Crown 8vo, 10s. 6d. net; also Fcap. 8vo, 6s. net; A WANDERER IN FLORENCE, 10s. 6d. net; A WANDERER IN VENICE, 10s. 6d. net; THE OPEN ROAD: A Little Book for Wayfarers, Fcap. 8vo, 6s. 6d. net; THE FRIENDLY TOWN: A Little Book for the Urbane, 6s. net; FIRESIDE AND SUNSHINE, 6s. net; CHARACTER AND COMEDY, 6s. net; THE GENTLEST ART: A Choice of Letters by Entertaining Hands, 6s. 6d. net; THE SECOND POST, 6s. net; HER INFINITE VARIETY: A Feminine Portrait Gallery, 6s. net; GOOD COMPANY: A Rally of Men, 6s. net; ONE DAY AND ANOTHER, 6s. net; OLD LAMPS FOR NEW, 6s. net; LOITERER'S HARVEST, 6s. net; CLOUD AND SILVER, 6s. net; A BOSWELL OF BAGHDAD AND OTHER ESSAYS, 6s. net; 'TWIXT EAGLE AND DOVE, 6s. net; THE PHANTOM JOURNAL, AND OTHER ESSAYS AND DIVERSIONS, 6s. net; GIVING AND RECEIVING, 6s. net; SPECIALLY SELECTED: A Choice of Essays, illustrated by G. L. STAMPA, 7s. 6d. net; URBANITIES, illustrated by G. L. STAMPA, 7s. 6d. net; YOU KNOW WHAT PEOPLE ARE, illustrated by GEORGE MORROW, 5s. net; THE BRITISH SCHOOL: An Anecdotal Guide to the British Painters and Paintings in the National Gallery, 6s. net: ROVING EAST AND ROVING WEST: Notes gathered in India, Japan, and America, 5s. net.

McDougall (William). AN INTRODUCTION TO SOCIAL PSYCHOLOGY. Seventeenth Edition. Cr. 8vo, 8s. 6d. net.

BODY AND MIND: A HISTORY AND A DEFENCE OF ANIMISM. With Diagrams. Fifth Edition. Demy 8vo, 12s. 6d. net.

Maeterlinck (Maurice)
THE BLUE BIRD: A Fairy Play in Six Acts, 6s. net and 2s. net. THE BETROTHAL, Fcap, 6s. net, paper 3s. 6d. net; MARY MAGDALENE, 5s. net and 2s. net; DEATH, 3s. 6d. net; OUR ETERNITY, 6s. net; THE UNKNOWN GUEST, 6s. net; THE WRACK OF THE STORM, 6s. net; THE MIRACLE OF SAINT ANTHONY: A Play in One Act, 3s. 6d. net; THE BURGOMASTER OF STILEMONDE: A Play in Three Acts, 5s. net; MOUNTAIN PATHS, 6s. net; TYLTYL, Told for Children (illustrated), 21s. net. (The above books are Translated by A TEIXEIRA DE MATTOS) POEMS, 5s. net. (Done into English by BERNARD MIALL).

THE GREAT SECRET. (Translated by BERNARD MIALL), 7s. 6d. net.

Methuen (A.). AN ANTHOLOGY OF MODERN VERSE. With Introduction by ROBERT LYND. Eleventh Edition. Fcap. 8vo, 6s. net. Thin paper, leather, 7s. 6d. net.

SHAKESPEARE TO HARDY: AN ANTHOLOGY OF ENGLISH LYRICS. Fcap. 8vo, 6s. net. Leather, 7s. 6d. net.

Milne (A. A.). NOT THAT IT MATTERS. Third Edition. Fcap. 8vo, 6s. net.

IF I MAY. Third Edition. Fcap. 8vo, 6s. net.

THE SUNNY SIDE. Crown 8vo, 6s. net.

Norwood (Gilbert). GREEK TRAGEDY. Demy 8vo, 12s. 6d. net.

Oxenham (John). Nine Volumes of Poems. Small pott 8vo, 1s. 3d net each volume.
BEES IN AMBER. 2s. net. ALL'S WELL; THE KING'S HIGH WAY; THE VISION SPLENDID; THE FIERY CROSS; HEARTS COURAGEOUS; HIGH ALTARS; ALL CLEAR! GENTLEMEN—THE KING! 2s. net.

Petrie (W. M. Flinders). A HISTORY OF EGYPT. Illustrated. Six Volumes. Crown 8vo, each 9s. net.
I. FROM THE IST TO XVIITH DYNASTY. *Ninth Edition.* (12s. net). II. THE XVIITH AND XVIIITH DYNASTIES. *Sixth Edition.* III. XIXTH TO XXXTH DYNASTIES. *Second Edition.* IV. EGYPT UNDER THE PTOLEMAIC DYNASTY. J. P. MAHAFFY. *Second Edition.* V. EGYPT UNDER ROMAN RULE. J. G. MILNE. *Second Edition.* VI. EGYPT IN THE MIDDLE AGES. STANLEY LANE-POOLE. *Second Edition.*

Pollard (A. F.). A SHORT HISTORY OF THE GREAT WAR. With 19 Maps. *Second Edition.* Crown 8vo, 10s. 6d. net.

Pollitt (Arthur W.). THE ENJOYMENT OF MUSIC. Crown 8vo, 5s. net.

Rees (J. F.). A SOCIAL AND INDUSTRIAL HISTORY OF ENGLAND. 1815-1918. Crown 8vo, 5s. net.

Smith (S. C. Kaines). LOOKING AT PICTURES. Illustrated. Fcap. 8vo, 6s. net.

Stancliffe. GOLF DO'S AND DON'TS. Being a very little about a good deal; together with some new saws for old wood—and knots in the golfer's line which may hei a good memory for forgetting. *Ninth Edition.* Fcap. 8vo, 2s. 6d net.

QUICK CUTS TO GOOD GOLF. *Second Edition.* Fcap. 8vo, 2s. 6d. net.

Stevenson (R. L.). THE LETTERS OF ROBERT LOUIS STEVENSON TO HIS FAMILY AND FRIENDS. Selected and Edited by SIR SIDNEY COLVIN. Four Volumes. *Fifth Edition.* Fcap. 8vo, 6s. net each.

Tilden (W. T.). THE ART OF LAWN TENNIS. Illustrated. *Fourth Edition.* Crown 8vo, 6s. net.

LAWN TENNIS FOR YOUNG PLAYERS: LAWN TENNIS FOR CLUB PLAYERS: LAWN TENNIS FOR MATCH PLAYERS. Each Fcap. 8vo, 2s. 6d. net.

Tileston (Mary W.). DAILY STRENGTH FOR DAILY NEEDS. *Twenty-seventh Edition.* Medium 16mo, 3s. 6d. net.

Turner (W. J.). MUSIC AND LIFE. Crown 8vo, 7s. 6d. net.

Underhill (Evelyn). MYSTICISM. A Study in the Nature and Development of Man's Spiritual Consciousness. *Eighth Edition.* Demy 8vo, 15s. net.

THE LIFE OF THE SPIRIT AND THE LIFE OF TO-DAY. *Third Edition.* Crown 8vo, 7s. 6d. net.

Vardon (Harry). HOW TO PLAY GOLF. Illustrated. *Fifteenth Edition.* Crown 8vo, 5s. 6d. net.

Waterhouse (Elizabeth). A LITTLE BOOK OF LIFE AND DEATH. Selected and Arranged. *Twenty-first Edition.* Small Pott 8vo, cloth, 2s. 6d. net; paper, 1s. 6d.

Wilde (Oscar). THE WORKS OF OSCAR WILDE. Fifteen Volumes. Fcap. 8vo, each 6s. 6d. net. Some also Fcap. 8vo, 2s. net.
I. LORD ARTHUR SAVILE'S CRIME AND THE PORTRAIT OF MR. W. H. II. THE DUCHESS OF PADUA. III. POEMS. IV. LADY WINDERMERE'S FAN. V. A WOMAN OF NO IMPORTANCE. VI. AN IDEAL HUSBAND. VII. THE IMPORTANCE OF BEING EARNEST. VIII. A HOUSE OF POMEGRANATES. IX. INTENTIONS. X. DE PROFUNDIS AND PRISON LETTERS. XI. ESSAYS. XII. SALOME, A FLORENTINE TRAGEDY, AND LA SAINTE COURTISANE. XIII. A CRITIC IN PALL MALL. XIV. SELECTED PROSE OF OSCAR WILDE. XV. ART AND DECORATION.

A HOUSE OF POMEGRANATES. Illustrated. Crown 4to, 21s. net.

FOR LOVE OF THE KING: A Burmese Masque. Demy 8vo, 8s. 6d. net.

Wilding (Anthony F.), Lawn-Tennis Champion 1910-1911. ON THE COURT AND OFF. Illustrated. *Eighth Edition.* Crown 8vo, 7s. 6d. net.

Young (G. Winthrop). MOUNTAIN CRAFT. Illustrated. Demy 8vo, £1 5s. net

The Antiquary's Books

Illustrated. Demy 8vo, 10s. 6d. net each volume

ANCIENT PAINTED GLASS IN ENGLAND ; ARCHÆOLOGY AND FALSE ANTIQUITIES ; THE BELLS OF ENGLAND ; THE BRASSES OF ENGLAND ; CELTIC ART IN PAGAN AND CHRISTIAN TIMES ; CHURCHWARDENS' ACCOUNTS ; THE DOMESDAY INQUEST ; THE CASTLES AND WALLED TOWNS OF ENGLAND ; ENGLISH CHURCH FURNITURE ; ENGLISH COSTUME, from Prehistoric Times to the End of the Eighteenth Century ; ENGLISH MONASTIC LIFE ; ENGLISH SEALS ; FOLK-LORE AS AN HISTORICAL SCIENCE ; THE GILDS AND COMPANIES OF LONDON ; THE HERMITS AND ANCHORITES OF ENGLAND ; THE MANOR AND MANORIAL RECORDS ; THE MEDIÆVAL HOSPITALS OF ENGLAND ; OLD ENGLISH INSTRUMENTS OF MUSIC ; OLD ENGLISH LIBRARIES ; OLD SERVICE BOOKS OF THE ENGLISH CHURCH ; PARISH LIFE IN MEDIÆVAL ENGLAND ; THE PARISH REGISTERS OF ENGLAND ; REMAINS OF THE PREHISTORIC AGE IN ENGLAND ; THE ROMAN ERA IN BRITAIN ; ROMANO-BRITISH BUILDINGS AND EARTHWORKS ; THE ROYAL FORESTS OF ENGLAND ; THE SCHOOLS OF MEDIÆVAL ENGLAND ; SHRINES OF BRITISH SAINTS.

The Arden Shakespeare

Demy 8vo, 6s. net each volume

An edition of Shakespeare in Single Plays. Edited with a full Introduction, Textual Notes, and a Commentary at the foot of the page. *Thirty-seven Volumes are now ready.*

Classics of Art

Edited by Dr. J. H. W. LAING

Illustrated. Wide Royal 8vo, from 15s. net to £3 3s. net.

THE ART OF THE GREEKS ; THE ART OF THE ROMANS ; CHARDIN ; DONATELLO ; GEORGE ROMNEY ; GHIRLANDAIO ; LAWRENCE ; MICHELANGELO ; RAPHAEL ; REMBRANDT'S ETCHINGS ; REMBRANDT'S PAINTINGS ; TINTORETTO ; TITIAN ; TURNER'S SKETCHES AND DRAWINGS ; VELAZQUEZ.

The " Complete " Series

Illustrated. Demy 8vo, from 5s. net to 18s. net

The Complete Airman; The Complete Amateur Boxer; The Complete Association Footballer; The Complete Athletic Trainer; The Complete Billiard Player: The Complete Cook; The Complete Foxhunter; The Complete Golfer; The Complete Hockey Player; The Complete Horseman; The Complete Jujitsuan (Crown 8vo); The Complete Lawn Tennis Player; The Complete Motorist; The Complete Mountaineer; The Complete Oarsman; The Complete Photographer; The Complete Rugby Footballer, on the New Zealand System; The Complete Shot; The Complete Swimmer; The Complete Yachtsman.

The Connoisseur's Library

Illustrated. Wide Royal 8vo, 31s. 6d. net

English Coloured Books; Etchings; European Enamels; Fine Books; Glass; Goldsmiths' and Silversmiths' Work; Illuminated Manuscripts; Ivories; Jewellery; Mezzotints Miniatures; Porcelain; Seals; Wood Sculpture.

Eight Books by R. S. Surtees

With the original Illustrations in Colour by J. LEECH and others.

Fcap. 8vo, 6s. net and 7s. 6d. net.

Ask Mamma; Handley Cross; Hawbuck Grange; Hillingdon Hall; Jorrocks's Jaunts and Jollities; Mr. Sponge's Sporting Tour, Mr. Facey Romford's Hounds; Plain or Ringlets?

Plays

Fcap. 8vo, 3s. 6d. net

Kismet; Milestones; Typhoon; An Ideal Husband; The Ware Case; General Post; The Great Adventure; The Honey-moon; Across the Border. (Crown 8vo.)

Fiction

Novels by Richard Bagot, H. C. Bailey, Arnold Bennett, G. A. Birmingham, Marjorie Bowen, Edgar Rice Burroughs, G. K. Chesterton, Joseph Conrad, Dorothy Conyers, Marie Corelli, Beatrice Harraden, R. S. Hichens, Anthony Hope, W. W. Jacobs, E. V. Lucas, Stephen McKenna, Lucas Malet, A. E. W. Mason, W. B. Maxwell, Arthur Morrison, John Oxenham, Sir Gilbert Parker, Alice Perrin, Eden Phillpotts, Richard Pryce, " Q," W. Pett Ridge, H. G. Wells, and C. N. and A. M. Williamson.

A Complete List can be had on application.

Methuen's Two Shilling Series

This is a series of copyright books—fiction and general literature—which has been such a popular success. If you will obtain a list of the series you will see that it contains more books by distinguished writers than any other series of the same kind. You will find the volumes at all booksellers and on all railway bookstalls.

CPSIA information can be obtained at www.ICGtesting.com
Printed in the USA
LVOW07s1118120216

474851LV00019B/190/P